Rodney R. Hutton

D1423948

Charisma and Authority in Israelite Society

Fortress Press
Minneapolis

CHARISMA AND AUTHORITY IN ISRAELITE SOCIETY

Scripture quotations, unless otherwise noted, are from the New Revised Standard Version of the Bible, copyright © 1989 by the Division of Christian Education of the National Council of Churches of Christ in the United States of America.

Interior design and typesetting: The HK Scriptorium, Inc.
Cover art: "Aaron's Breastplate" by Sandra Bowden
Cover design: Ann Elliott Artz Hadland

Library of Congress Cataloging-in-Publication Data

Hutton, Rodney R., 1948–
    Charisma and authority in Israelite society / Rodney R. Hutton.
      p.   cm.
    Includes bibliographical references and index.
    ISBN 0-8006-2832-2
    1. Leadership—Biblical teaching. 2. Authority—Biblical
teaching. 3. Sociology, Biblical. 4. Bible. O.T.—Criticism,
interpretation, etc. 5. Jews—Politics and government—To 70 A.D.
I. Title.
BS1199.L4H88 1994
296′.8′0901—dc20   93-43576
                                              CIP

The paper used in this publication meets the minimum requirements of American National Standard for Information Sciences—Permanence of Paper for Printed Library Materials, ANSI Z329.48–1984.   ∞

Manufactured in the U.S.A.   AF 1-2832
98   97   96   95   94   1   2   3   4   5   6   7   8   9   10

Contents

PREFACE   v

ABBREVIATIONS   ix

CHAPTER

1   Charisma, Office, and Theological Method   1

2   Mosaic Authority: The Intimate Outsider   17

3   The Judges: Charisma and Qualification   43

4   The Kings and Charisma:
     Foundations of Royal Authority   71

5   The Prophetic Word:
     Stretching the Mythic Consciousness   105

6   The Priest: Charisma by the Book   138

7   Wisdom: The Charisma of Order   172

CONCLUSION: CHARISMA AND LEADERSHIP   206

BIBLIOGRAPHY   211

INDEX   220

Preface

THIS BOOK is about power—more precisely, about how power is perceived and how it is exercised in human societies. The terms "charisma" and "institution" have come to designate indices of power that are thought to stand in polar opposition to each other, with the charismatic representing one who is unencumbered by formal paradigms and free to shatter expectations. The charismatic leads by divine appointment, whereas the institution usurps authority for itself and selects its own leaders in an exercise of ideological self-justification or self-perpetuation.

There is a ring of truth to this observation sufficient to make it seem almost a truism. The purpose of this study, however, is to suggest that the distance between "charisma" and "institution" is not as great as is often supposed. This study is concerned to challenge some long-held assumptions and to place conversation about any specific forms of empowered leadership within the broader framework of the interplay of charisma and institution. The thesis of this book is that charisma is itself a social phenomenon. It is not essentially anti-institutional but in fact is given firm social and cultural definition within an institutional framework. This thesis is the platform from which the broad horizon of Israel's social institutions will be surveyed in order to revisit some of the common assumptions made during this century regarding the emergence of Israel's central institutions.

In many ways this study grows out of my long-standing interest in the exercise of authority in Israelite institutions. My doctoral dissertation, which focused on the use of the "declaratory formula," concentrated on form-critical questions but gave a strong nod to sociological issues. Many of my earlier instincts have found more vigorous application in the present work, which is both broader in scope and more intentionally in dialogue with sociological questions than was the earlier work. The methods employed, however, are eclectic, being shaped most importantly by tradition-historical and theological concerns, but also applying rhetorical-critical insights.

The task of providing an analysis of "how authority works" is of considerable importance, particularly among those who seek to understand the exercise of empowerment within the institutionalized forms of ordination and ministry within the church. The question of how the Bible understands "power" can easily be bypassed, dismissed, or subverted by arguing that true power is ultimately the divestment of all power. The message of the gospel, after all, is that power is exercised in absolute powerlessness. While theologically sublime, this definition does little to help those within the church sort out the very practical and complex problems associated with the abuse of power, for power *will* be asserted by any social group in one form or another, the church included. To deny the existence or exercise of power, or to hope to co-opt it by inverting "power" and "powerlessness," will not be helpful as churches today struggle with the significance of the exercise of ministry and as congregations continue to define themselves in relationship to the bishops, pastors, and ministers who serve them.

This study is not an attempt to provide a biblical model for ministry, nor is it interested in repristinating any biblical forms of ministry within the church even if they might be detected. This study has two primary methodological concerns: first, to introduce the Old Testament into the discussion of a "biblical" view of empowerment, a discussion from which it has unfortunately been excluded or dismissed as having no particular competency; and, second, to provide a broader framework within which the church might subsequently find it helpful to consider other issues such as ordination. By discussing how the empowering character of both charisma and institution relate to each other in such figures as Moses, the judge, the prophet, the king, the priest, and the sage, it is hoped that a new perspective from which to understand the issue of social empowerment might in some sense be given shape, and a foundation laid for further studies.

Many fruitful conversations have helped frame the question addressed in this book and have provided refreshing insights. Most especially I am grateful to my biblical colleagues at Trinity Lutheran Seminary for having taken time to read various chapters, but also to Walter Brueggemann, who, though not in total agreement with some perspectives, kindly served as a "debate partner" on a number of significant issues during a series of visits. I am also indebted to the generosity of colleagues and friends at the University of Tübingen, especially Prof. Hans-Jürgen Hermisson, Jörg Barthel, and Matthias Morgenstern, as well as to the staff of the Theologicum, for their hospitality while I was there on sabbatical leave. Generous financial assistance was provided by grants from the Association of Theological Schools as well as by the Lutheran Brotherhood and the Aid Association for Lutherans. Above all, however, is the support offered by my wife, Kathy, and my sons, Jeremy and Eric, who have in many ways been witnesses to me of devotion and perseverance. It is to my sons that I dedicate this book, in hopes that their lives might seek the balance envisioned here.

Abbreviations

AJS   *American Journal of Sociology*
ANET   James B. Pritchard, ed., *Ancient Near Eastern Texts Relating to the Old Testament* (3rd ed.; Princeton: Princeton University Press, 1969)
ArOr   *Archiv orientální*
ArRel   *Archiv für Religionspsychologie*
ASR   *Americal Sociological Review*
BARev   *Biblical Archaeology Review*
BDB   F. Brown, S. R. Driver, and C. A. Briggs, *Hebrew and English Lexicon of the Old Testament* (Oxford: Oxford University Press, 1952)
BHS   *Biblia hebraica stuttgartensia* (Stuttgart: Deutsche Bibelstiftung, 1977)
Bib   *Biblica*
BTB   *Biblical Theology Bulletin*
BZ   *Biblische Zeitschrift*
CBQ   *Catholic Biblical Quarterly*
CurTM   *Currents in Theology and Mission*
EgT   *Eglise et Théologie*
EvT   *Evangelische Theologie*
ExpTim *Expository Times*
HAR   *Hebrew Annual Review*
HBT   *Horizons in Biblical Theology*
HR   *History of Religions*
HTR   *Harvard Theological Review*

HUCA	*Hebrew Union College Annual*
Int	*Interpretation*
JAAR	*Journal of the American Academy of Religion*
JBL	*Journal of Biblical Literature*
JSOT	*Journal for the Study of the Old Testament*
JTS	*Journal of Theological Studies*
KD	*Kerygma und Dogma*
LavTP	*Laval théologique et philosophique*
LXX	Septuagint
MT	Masoretic Text
OTS	*Oudtestamentische Studiën*
RB	*Revue Biblique*
RevExp	*Review and Expositor*
RelSRev	*Religious Studies Review*
RSV	Revised Standard Version
SJOT	*Scandinavian Journal of the Old Testament*
SJT	*Scottish Journal of Theology*
TBT	*The Bible Today*
TGl	*Theologie und Glaube*
TLZ	*Theologische Literaturzeitung*
TS	*Theological Studies*
TTod	*Theology Today*
VT	*Vetus Testamentum*
VTSup	Vetus Testamentum Supplement
W & W	*Word and World*
ZAW	*Zeitschrift für die alttestamentliche Wissenschaft*
ZRG	*Zeitschrift für Religions- und Geistesgeschichte*
ZTK	*Zeitschrift für Theologie und Kirche*

1

Charisma, Office, and Theological Method

THE QUESTION of how leadership is defined and exercised within the context of Israel's social institutions forms the background for this study. The question of how power is legitimated and exercised has perplexed scholars for centuries. It is an issue that impinges directly on all aspects of life in society, and not least on communities of faith as they attempt to forge new patterns of leadership or to renew existing ones. Many denominations are divided, sometimes bitterly, over the issue of the proper exercise of power and authority. The present study attempts to marshal an often-neglected resource, the Old Testament, in order to provide more information on the issue of authority in its biblical context.

The focus of chapter 1 will be on two methodological questions. First, what are some contemporary issues relating to the definition of authority in its "charismatic" and "institutional" forms? Second, what are the hermeneutical issues that must be addressed in a study that seeks intentionally to bridge sociological and theological questions?

Charisma and Office:
The Influence of Max Weber

"By what authority are you doing these things?" The question addressed by the Jewish chief priests and elders to Jesus in Matt 21:23 has been asked in every society of every leader throughout human

1

history. The source of Jesus' authority has proved to be elusive and impossible to define. Did it derive from the power of his teaching? From his charismatic presence? From his eschatological fervor?[1] Likewise, from what source does authority within faith communities in general derive?

The debate concerning the locus of authority in the church has centered on the question of its institutional versus charismatic origins. The debates between Rudolph Sohm and Adolf von Harnack over whether leadership in the emerging church was primarily due to anti-institutional charismatic impulses (Sohm) or to a coalescence of forms, including those long institutionalized (von Harnack), is well rehearsed and need not detain us here.[2] Many historians of the early church have finally wearied of attempts to pit charismatic and institutionalized impulses over against one another or even to distinguish too clearly between them, arguing instead as Ulrich Wilckens does when he speaks of "the Office of the Spirit and the Spirit of the Office."[3]

---

[1] For an excellent discussion of the issue, see Martin Hengel, *The Charismatic Leader and His Followers* (Edinburgh: T. & T. Clark, 1981). Hengel's primary concern is to contend against those who would domesticate Jesus' authority by locating it in his teaching ministry.

[2] Rudolph Sohm, *Wesen und Ursprung des Katholizismus* (Leipzig, 1909). Adolf von Harnack, *Entstehung und Entwicklung der Kirchenverfassung und des Kirchenrechts in den zwei ersten Jahrhunderten* (Leipzig, 1910). The position of Sohm is still popular, particularly among those who for varied reasons seek to repristinate a form of church governance free of hierarchy or power. Letty Russell, for instance, idealizes the early "egalitarian house church," which eventually succumbed to the old patriarchal patterns, as evidenced in the later writings of the New Testament (*Household of Freedom: Authority in Feminist Theology* [Philadelphia: Westminster, 1987] 39–40). Leonardo Boff holds up as a model the "church of the Acts of the Apostles," in which membership was based on sharing in all things, including authority, an ideal situation into which hierarchy only later intruded (*Church: Charism and Power. Liberation Theology and the Institutional Church* [New York: Crossroad, 1985] 120–28). Even the more comprehensive and critical work of Bernard Cooke, judicious in most respects, fails to avoid the Sohmian temptation. Cooke argues that the adoption of "priestly" terminology by the church represents the "creeping back in" of Old Testament categories and a concomitant betrayal of the radical rejection of Jewish structures by the early Christian community (*Ministry to Word and Sacraments: History and Theology* [Philadelphia: Fortress, 1976] 541–42).

[3] Ulrich Wilckens, "Das Amt des Geistes und der Geist des Amtes: Neutestamentliche Einsichten und kirchliche Erfahrungen," in *Charisma und Institution* (ed. Trutz Rendtorff; Gütersloh: Gerd Mohn, 1985) 28. Cf. Ferdinand Hahn, who calls for the development of a doctrine of "geistlichen Amt" ("Charisma und Amt: Die

The popular portrayal of Israel's central institutions, however, is still largely infused with the notion that they developed principally as a result of institutionalized forces coming into heated conflict with supercharged charismatic impulses. One primary reason for the popular notion that positions charismatic and institutionalized forces against each other when discussing Israel's central institutions is the work of Max Weber, whose theoretical work in sociology bore direct fruit when he turned to consider the sociology of religion in general and of Israel in particular.[4] Weber, whose major works were produced shortly before and after his death in 1920, distinguished between three ideal forms of authority: rational authority, which rests on legal process and bureaucratic order; traditional authority, which rests on the regularized belief in the sanctity of eternally valid traditions which themselves impart authority; and charismatic authority, which rests on the "extra-ordinary" (*ausseralltäglich*) appeal to the holiness or the heroic or exemplary qualities of a person.[5]

Weber developed his notions of social organization on the basis of the distinction that Ferdinand Tönnies had earlier made between

Diskussion über das kirchliche Amt im Lichte der neutestamentlichen Charismenlehre," *ZTK* 76 [1979] 419–49). Also Eduard Schweizer, who suggests that charisma and office are not opposites but rather "office" in the New Testament is simply a particular type of charisma ("Konzeptionen von Charisma und Amt im Neuen Testament," in *Charisma und Institution* [above], 317–23).

[4] Max Weber, *The Sociology of Religion* (Boston: Beacon Press, 1963), first published in 1922 as "Religionssoziologie" in *Wirtschaft und Gesellschaft*. For an English translation of the German 4th edition, see *Economy and Society: An Outline of Interpretive Sociology* (New York: Bedminster Press, 1968). For the German 5th edition, see *Wirtschaft und Gesellschaft: Grundriss der verstehenden Soziologie* (Tübingen: J. C. B. Mohr, 1972). Also, Max Weber, *Ancient Judaism* (Glencoe, IL: Free Press, 1952), originally published as essays from 1917 to 1919 and, posthumously, in 1921 as *Das antike Judentum*, vol. 3 of his *Gesammelte Aufsätze zur Religionssoziologie* (Tübingen).

[5] Max Weber, *Wirtschaft und Gesellschaft*, 1:122–76. Concerning leadership in the early church, Weber's influence can be detected, for example, in the work of Hans von Campenhausen, who argued that leadership in the early church resulted from the coalescence of the presbyteral leadership of the Jewish elders (corresponding to Weber's "traditional" authority), the spirit-empowered free exercise of authority in the Pauline congregations (corresponding to Weber's "charismatic" authority), and the "routinization" of this charisma under the impact of the bureaucratic structures of Hellenism (corresponding to Weber's "legal/rational" authority) (Hans Freiherr von Campenhausen, *Ecclesiastical Authority and Spiritual Power in the Church of the First Three Centuries* [London: Adam & Charles Black, 1969] esp. 56-85).

a "community" (*Gemeinschaft*) and a "society" (*Gesellschaft*).[6] For Weber the characteristics of a "community" were its relatively small size, its social cohesiveness based on a "subjective feeling of belonging" expressed in "face-to-face" relationships, and its being bound by such mechanisms as love, thanks, faith, honor, trust, duty, and hope. Obviously one can associate Weber's second type of leadership—the "traditional"—with this "communal" form of social organization. By "society" Weber envisioned a highly complex social structure resting on rationally motivated common interests and agreements, governed not by a system of personal and emotional obligations but rather by the marketplace and a complex system of exchange. Weber's first form of leadership—the "legal/rational"—aligns with Tönnies's "society."

Given the fact that Weber was operating with two forms of social organization but with three forms of leadership, and given that there was an almost predetermined correlation of "rational" authority with "society" and "traditional" authority with "community," the result is that Weber's third type of leadership—"charismatic"—was an anomaly from the very beginning. It had no basic social structure into which it could be fit, and therefore Weber was forced to define it in anti-social terms. Charisma was the term given to those who, wanting to create *new* structures, neither can nor want to base their authority on recognized social bases of authority. At best Weber could speak of "charisma of office" and of the "routinization of charisma," by which he meant that charisma becomes accommodated to legal/rational social processes and is eventually institutionalized. But the need for recourse to a concept such as that of "routinization" points out all the more the anomalous nature of "charisma" in Weber's system.

In essence, then, "charisma" was fated by the very nature of Weber's system to be held in the strictest opposition to other forms of authority, particularly the legal/rational. Weber's social analysis, as penetrating as it was, has come under critical scrutiny from a number of sides, both with regard to his "idealism" (i.e., the notion that "ideas" rather than "material" provide the driving force for society and

---

[6] Ferdinand Tönnies, *Gemeinschaft und Gesellschaft: Grundbegriffe der reinen Soziologie* (1887; Darmstadt: Wissenschaftliche Buchgesellschaft, 1970).

history)[7] as well as the positivism, reductionism, relativism, and determinism toward which his social analysis tends.[8] Our concern here focuses on the fact that Weber's notion of charisma was itself an anomaly within his own system, without a social setting, and therefore was bound to be misconstrued and misused in the ensuing conversation.[9]

It was noted above, however, that there is an attempt to move away from the crude wrenching apart of "charisma" and "authority" in considering the issue of the emergence of leadership in the early Christian community. In their study of the issue, A. H. J. Gunneweg and W. Schmithals attempted to avoid the difficulty by distinguishing not between "charismatic" and "institutional" authority but rather between *potestas*—the power of the office—and *auctoritas*—informal authority and dignity earned apart from that gained by rank and position alone. In their definition *auctoritas* is measured by such personal attributes as experience, age, wisdom, talent, charisma, ability, equanimity, and selflessness.[10]

Such a definition has the advantage of suggesting that charisma is not a unique form of authority that stands over against other more "regularized" forms. In such a scheme "charisma" is only one type of *auctoritas* producing behavior, alongside many others. The difficulty with the proposal of Gunneweg and Schmithals is that "charisma" is reduced to the point where it means simply "force of personality," a long distance from the definition given the term by Weber. Furthermore, when the authors say that authority cannot be bestowed or produced but must emerge from the individual,[11] the focus is limited exclusively to the individual rather than taking into consideration the larger group which evaluates specific modes

---

[7] See the rather trenchant and unbalanced critique of Itumeleng J. Mosala, "Social Scientific Approaches to the Bible: One Step Forward, Two Steps Backward," *Journal of Theology for Southern Africa* 55 (1986) 15–30. Mosala labors under a heavy-handed materialist methodology.

[8] Especially Gary A. Herion, "The Impact of Modern and Social Science Assumptions on the Reconstruction of Israelite History," *JSOT* 34 (1986) 3–33.

[9] One example of the misuse of Weber's notion of charisma is illustrated by Jay Holstein, "Max Weber and Biblical Scholarship," *HUCA* 46 (1975) 159–79.

[10] Antonius H. J. Gunneweg and Walter Schmithals, *Authority* (Nashville: Abingdon, 1982) 17.

[11] Ibid.

of behavior and which, by its consent or denial, does indeed grant such authority.

One of the most sophisticated treatments of the subject has been Bengt Holmberg's study *Paul and Power*, in which he attempts to discuss Paul's authority vis-à-vis the Jerusalem church by means of a more careful social analysis.[12] Holmberg seeks to shift the question of authority away from the individual, in this case Paul, to a consideration of the larger group dynamics at work in the broader church. By focusing on the group, Holmberg suggests, we understand how charismatic authority rests not on the extraordinary personal qualities of the "charismatic" individual but rather on the group's own shared belief that it is legitimate for this particular "charismatic" person to impose his or her will on it. Charismatic leadership is built on the *group's* conviction that the leader stands in an exceptionally close relationship to the normative center of society's symbolic universe.[13] In other words, the "charisma" exhibited by the leader is defined as such primarily insofar as it accords with two issues: first, the group's own conceptions of what constitutes charismatic leadership; and, second, whether the leader's direction is harmonious with the group's own self-perceived "symbolic universe." Whether Holmberg is correct or not in his contention that "Paul is neither willing nor able to deny the fact of [his] dependence" on the Jerusalem church,[14] he at least has moved the question of "charisma" as it relates to institutionalized forms of authority a considerable distance. Similarly, both Burke Long and Thomas Overholt have insisted that the focus of charisma must be less on the personal qualities of the individual and more on the nature of the relationship between such individuals and various groups within their societies at large.[15]

---

[12] Bengt Holmberg, *Paul and Power: The Structure of Authority in the Primitive Church as Reflected in the Pauline Epistles* (Lund: Gleerup, 1978).

[13] Ibid., 141–46.

[14] Ibid., 57.

[15] Burke O. Long, "Prophetic Authority as Social Reality," in *Canon and Authority: Essays in Old Testament Religion and Theology* (ed. G. W. Coats and B. O. Long; Philadelphia: Fortress, 1977) 3–4; Thomas Overholt, "Thoughts on the Use of 'Charisma' in Old Testament Studies," in *In the Shelter of Elyon* (ed. W. B. Barrick and J. R. Spencer; Sheffield: JSOT Press, 1984) 299.

In a similar fashion, M. Hennen and W.-U. Prigge have also attempted to blunt or deflect the impact of Weber's analysis of leadership by insisting that the individual quality of "authority" is not conceivable outside of social relationships, that is, outside of formalized "rule" (*Herrschaft*). Personal authority is simply the momentary manifestation of complex social processes, and it is this complex function of social interaction that they define as "rule."[16] They distinguish five different forms of "rule": leadership, authoritarianism, competence, informal influence, and manipulation/power. Each type is typical of certain social structures. "Leadership" is characteristic of "segmentary societies" (Tönnies's "community"); "authoritarianism" is characteristic of the family, hospitals, prisons, and similar social units; "competence" is typically found in bureaucratic organizations (Tönnies's "society"); "informal influence" functions alongside formal competence in such bureaucratic societies; and "manipulation and power" are characteristic of "authority cartels," by which they mean the "power brokers" of a community, such as the banker, judge, mayor, and clergy of a small town, taken together as a group.[17]

Hennen and Prigge make no reference at all to "charismatic authority" as a separate type of "rule," preferring instead to speak simply of the power of "suggestion" and of its reception as "enthusiasm."[18] Their analysis also makes it clear that authority is in fact derived from a mixture of such systems, and that one and the same person can and must evidence different forms of authority even though each is related to a different principle of "rule."[19] It is therefore incumbent upon those analyzing such authority to be aware of the complex social interaction that is occurring at a number of different levels, and not to assume that one particular form of authority is at work when in fact it may be quite another.

This marked shift in the way "charisma" is understood as an index of authority makes it all the more surprising that analyses of the exercise of power and authority within Israelite institutions are still dominated by an uncritical acceptance of Weber's theory of the three

---

[16] Manfred Hennen and Wolfgang-Ulrich Prigge, *Authorität und Herrschaft* (Darmstadt: Wissenschaftliche Buchgesellschaft, 1977) 10–14.

[17] Ibid., 85–125.

[18] Ibid., 30.

[19] Ibid., 17–18, 103, 114.

ideal types of leadership. A warning was sounded already in 1963
when the sociologist Peter Berger suggested that the relationship of
charisma and institution is much more complicated than is generally presumed. Berger wrote:

> Charismatic innovation need not necessarily originate in social mar-
> ginality. It may also originate within the traditionally established
> institutions—and, even there, be sufficiently powerful to effectively change
> these institutions. . . . [Charisma] may also be a trait of individuals located
> at the center of the institutional fabric in question, a power of "radicali-
> zation" from within rather than of challenge from without.[20]

Berger's invitation to reconsider the matter percolated in the minds
of his audience until fairly recently. There are now isolated pockets
of movement, particularly in the discussion of the question relating
to "prophetic authority," as we shall see below in chapter 5. Many
scholars are calling for a serious rethinking of the issue of how
authority was exercised in Israelite society. Nevertheless, it is still
highly popular to conceive of some monumental chasm inserted
between charismatic and institutionalized forms of Israelite social
structures. The judges were bearers of pure charisma, charged by
the divine spirit with their appointed tasks, whereas the kings were
supported by the sheer oppressive bureaucratic weight of their thrones
and lacked any pretense to charismatic appointment, at least after
Saul and at least in Judah. The prophets provided the charismatic
counterweight to the monarchy, whereas the priests were bound and
gagged by their official constraints and ideological blinders.

The succeeding chapters will consider a number of Israel's primary
social institutions in order to map out the nature of authority as
it relates to the interplay of charisma and institution. Charisma will
be understood not primarily as a personal trait exhibited by a
"charismatic" individual independent of social context but rather as
an essentially social phenomenon that is a function of broader group
dynamics and fixed social relationships. These relationships are
generally definable as "roles," and the bearer of charisma is thus
understood to be one who meets certain social role expectations
and whose social function is evaluated on the basis of those expec-

---

[20] Peter Berger, "Charisma and Religious Innovation: The Social Location of Israelite
Prophecy," *ASR* 28 (1963) 950.

tations. From this social analysis the study will proceed to theological application in order to draw out some of the implications for leadership among God's people in our present climate.

Social Reconstruction and Theological Reflection _____

A study with the goals of this one faces two methodological questions that demand attention. First, what is the legitimation of applying social-scientific principles to biblical texts and to what extent are such texts amenable to sociological investigation? Second, even assuming that sociological analysis is a possibility, what is the relationship between the results of such analysis and any ensuing theological discussion?

Looking at texts from a sociological perspective is hardly a new enterprise. The social-scientific analysis of biblical texts arose alongside the very development of those methods themselves. One of the early, great syntheses of anthropological, sociological, and folkloristic insights as applied to a study of "Semitic religion as a whole in its common features and general type" was that of William Robertson Smith, *Lectures on the Religion of the Semites,* originally presented as a series of addresses from 1888 to 1891.[21] The significant social-scientific studies of Max Weber, published between 1911 and 1920, as well as those of Émile Durkheim and Lucien Levy-Bruhl formed the basis for considerable sociological reflection on biblical texts throughout this century.[22] Weber himself offered what has been perhaps the most influential study in his work on the relationship of socioeconomic and religious factors in ancient Judaism and their impact on modern capitalism.[23] The work of the Old Testament

[21] William Robertson Smith, *Lectures on the Religion of the Semites: The Fundamental Institutions* (3rd ed.; London: A. & C. Black, 1927).

[22] Max Weber, *Economy and Society: An Outline of Interpretive Sociology* (ed. Günther Roth and Claus Wittich; New York: Bedminster, 1968 [from the German 4th edition]); Émile Durkheim, *De la division du travail social* (Paris: Alcan, 1893); idem, *The elementary forms of the religious life: A study in religious sociology* (Glencoe, IL: Free Press, 1947); Lucien Levy-Bruhl, *Die Geistige Welt der Primitiven* (Darmstadt: Wissenschaftliche Buchgesellschaft, 1966); originally published as *La mentalité primitive,* 1925).

[23] Weber, *Ancient Judaism.*

social historian Antonin Causse was largely dependent on the work of Durkheim and Levy-Bruhl, particularly in focusing on the latter's distinction between pre-logical primitive mentality and empirical-logical and logical forms of human thought.[24] This new interest in the relationship of religion to anthropological and social structures also gave rise to the study by Adolphe Lods of "primitive nomadism" and its impact on the sociocultural history of Israel as well as the monumental work of Johannes Pedersen on Israel's culture.[25] The most well known recent summation of such efforts, and still highly regarded, is the work by Roland de Vaux on Israel's social and religious institutions.[26]

Two of the most common points of resistance to bringing the laws of social theory to bear on biblical studies concern, first, the problem of the paucity and uncontrollability of the data and, second, the misbegotten nature of the method itself. The general complaint is that past communities are simply not amenable to social-scientific examination because such examination requires experiment, participant observation, and testing, none of which is possible with historical sociology.[27] A second problem, quite apart from the "frozen" nature of the evidence, is the criticism that biblical texts cannot be used as evidentiary for the reconstruction of a historical enterprise, including social reconstruction, until they have been evaluated as literature.[28]

Against the charge that history is not amenable to social-scientific investigation, Bruce Malina responds that it would indeed be invalid

[24] Antonin Causse, *Du groupe ethnique à la communauté religieuse: Le problem sociologique de la religion d'Israël* (Paris: Alcan, 1937). On the relationship of the work of Causse to both Durkheim and Levy-Bruhl, see S. T. Kimbrough, Jr., *Israelite Religion in Sociological Perspective: The Work of Antonin Causse* (Wiesbaden: Otto Harrassowitz, 1978).

[25] Adolphe Lods, *Israel from its Beginnings to the Middle of the Eighth Century* (London: Routledge & Kegan Paul, 1948); Johannes Pedersen, *Israel, Its Life and Culture* (4 vols.; London: Oxford University Press, 1926, 1940; originally published in 1920 and 1934).

[26] Roland de Vaux, *Ancient Israel* (2 vols.; New York: McGraw-Hill, 1965; originally published as *Les institutions de l'ancien testament* in 1958 and 1960).

[27] Cyril Rodd, "On Applying a Sociological Theory to Biblical Studies," *JSOT* 19 (1981) 95–106.

[28] Dennis Jobling, "Sociological and Literary Approaches to the Bible: How Shall the Twain Meet?" *JSOT* 38 (1987) 85–93.

to use social-scientific methodology for predictive purposes, to develop a model of "final causality." However, when applied to biblical texts, it is not for prediction, since "we have some idea about how the story turned out." Rather, it is for the purposes of retrodiction, that is, to develop a model of "efficient causality."[29]

The charge that texts are first of all "literary creations" and only secondarily "historical evidence" is much more serious and raises the question of how a history can ever be written, whether social or otherwise.[30] The question is how one moves from literary sources to historical reconstruction; but here is precisely where many who are interested in social reconstruction agree. Texts are insufficient. Keith Whitelam is obviously correct when he states that the study of literary remains often reveals only the self-perceptions of an intellectual elite rather than the wide diversity of social reality. He argues that historians must explore the complex forces of social change by being freed from the constraint of the written text, and must engage in an interdisciplinary search involving history, archaeology, and the social sciences.[31]

Perhaps the most serious charge is that the entire program of social-scientific investigation of biblical texts is predicated on presuppositions that, in themselves, are seriously misbegotten. Itumeleng J. Mosala, for example, has challenged the underlying presuppositions of most such sociological investigation. He charges that it rests on the principles of idealistic Durkheimian structural-functionalism that, Mosala insists, is the guiding principle of bourgeois society.[32] In addition, Gary Herion has criticized sociological-anthropological models as being themselves the product of certain modern urban social configurations that have illegitimately imposed an urban scheme of positivism, reductionism, relativism, and determinism on ancient nonurban civilizations.[33]

[29] Bruce J. Malina, "The Social Sciences and Biblical Interpretation," in *The Bible and Liberation: Political and Social Hermeneutics* (ed. N. K. Gottwald; Maryknoll, NY: Orbis, 1983) 19–20.

[30] Rodd, too, acknowledges that his concerns would, if taken to their extreme, vitiate any efforts to reconstruct Israel's history ("On Applying a Sociological Theory to Biblical Studies," 105).

[31] Keith W. Whitelam, "Recreating the History of Israel," *JSOT* 35 (1986) 54–62.

[32] Mosala, "Social Scientific Approaches to the Bible," 29.

[33] Herion, "Impact of Modern and Social Science Assumptions," 4–8.

Mosala's criticism that the entire enterprise rests on the principles of "structural-functionalism" and is a product of Western bourgeois capitalism is possibly correct, though the problem has less to do with how one views capitalism than with how one views human nature. A structural-functionalist view regards society as a cohesive organism that is integrated by its core values and is in a greater or lesser state of social equilibrium. Change results from a gradual process of adaptation, and the emphasis is on order, stasis, rational utility, and the parts "pulling together" for the benefit of the whole. Whether such a view of social interaction is "bourgeois" or not, at least it does not come to terms adequately with what in Christian tradition would be referred to as the "brokenness" of human existence, our individual and collective propensity toward jealous and even violent self-interest. The other possibility would be to adopt a "conflict" model, which would stress the "dog-eat-dog" nature of social interaction. According to the conflict model, society is less like a healthy organism striving for equilibrium than like a brawl at a hockey game. What keeps it going is not cohesion but coercion, not rational utility but narrow self-interest kept in check by strength of force. Society is viewed not as a team pulling together but rather as a tug-of-war in which groups are forced to make common cause with one another for the sake of their own goals, not for any broader social program. The focus here is on change driven by conflict and on forced constraint, which is required to achieve a viable social system.

Both models account for only a partial truth, and to that extent Mosala is correct in his critique of structural-functionalism. Recognizing this problem, Malina suggests a "symbolic interactionist" model, which would view social systems in terms of the conceptual symbols around which human behavior is organized. Societies embody a complex of symbolic patterns which temporarily at least maintain social equilibrium (stasis) but which also require continual readjustments in new and shifting situations (change). Human interactions are symbolic interactions in which people are always "wrapped in social roles." These roles correlate to sets of social rights and obligations relative to each other and provide the individual with definition and status. Thus, the social system is a patterned arrangement of "role sets, status sets, and status sequences" consciously recognized and regularly at work, providing both cohesion and constraint.[34] Such a model is cognizant of the variability by which humans understand their environment and social organization, and has the advantage of holding cohesion and constraint as well as stasis and change in equal relationship to one another.

As concerns Herion's criticism that the application of social-scientific methodology is itself a foreign imposition on Israelite culture, it seems quite clear that any "reading" of a culture unknown to the "reader" is going to involve the imposition of some particular domain of reference. Here again Malina's argument is prudent: the best that biblical scholars could offer the public is a "set of domains of reference deriving from and appropriate to the social world from which the texts derive and thus facilitate biblical understanding."[35]

Given the seriousness of these issues, one ought never be overly confident of one's conclusions. Nevertheless, if the biblical text is a historically and culturally conditioned document, which very few would dispute, it seems imperative to take the risks involved in order to clarify the various social forces that are reflected in its pages. Having said this, however, we have introduced what has perhaps been the point of fiercest debate on the subject—namely, how one moves from cultural-historical context to theological meaning.

The primary question is this: Are religious views, once extrapolated from their social context, to be regarded as anything other than ideology that articulates the vested interests and social arrangements of particular groups? Do such views carry any normative freight, and can they be used in any way as absolute paradigms? Are they transferable from one social context to another?

The debate between George Mendenhall and Norman Gottwald concerning the role played by "Yahwism" in Israel's formative stages is illustrative of this problem. Mendenhall viewed Yahwism as the major force that defined Israel's destiny and gave shape to its social character, whereas Gottwald suggested that Yahwism was to some extent a projection of the economic and political interests of Israel's social organization. In other words, Mendenhall has argued that Yahwism gave rise to Israelite society, whereas Gottwald has argued

[34] Malina, "Social Sciences and Biblical Interpretation," 18.
[35] Ibid., 14.

that Israelite society gave rise to Yahwism.[36] The question becomes, Is theology a function of culture, or is culture a function of theology?

Actually, Gottwald's position is a lot less clear on the matter than is usually suggested. Gottwald does *not* view Yahwism as a simple reflex of social arrangements. In fact, Gottwald has fairly consistently stated that theology and social system are in some vague state of mutual interdependence. In his *Tribes of Yahweh* he suggested that the two are interdependently or reciprocally related as functions one of the other.[37] Yahwism does not function simply as the "legitimator" of the Israelite social order but also as a "facilitator" of the egalitarian movement.[38] Gottwald stresses that Yahwism "arose co-terminously with their social and political struggle and was both the ideological propulsion for and the most distinctive cultural expression of their movement."[39] He argues that theological themes, such as "Yahweh's jealousy," *correspond to* and are *consistent with* social factors, such as the commitment to the "singularity and excessive passion of the Israelite social revolutionary movement."[40] The use of such phrases as "correspond to" and "consistent with" allows Gottwald to maintain a certain ambiguity, so as to suggest that there is a general symmetry and symbiosis between Yahwism and Israel's social structures, with neither being reduced to serving as the simple "function" or "reflex" of the other. Gottwald does not "simply" reduce religion to being an ideological function of social conventions. Gottwald is consistently able to maintain this even-handedness until he is pressed to decide the issue. When forced to go one way or the other, he admits that it is "necessary to take our cue from the methodological insight that religion is the function of social relations rooted in cultural-material conditions of life."[41]

[36] See, e.g., Herion's synopsis in "Impact of Modern Social Science Assumptions," 14–16.

[37] Norman K. Gottwald, *The Tribes of Yahweh: A Sociology of the Religion of Liberated Israel, 1250–1050 B.C.E.* (Maryknoll, NY: Orbis, 1979) 618.

[38] Ibid., 642.

[39] Norman K. Gottwald, "Social Matrix and Canonical Shape," *T Tod* 42 (1985–86) 309. Compare similar earlier remarks in "The Theological Task after *The Tribes of Yahweh*," in *The Bible and Liberation: Political and Social Hermeneutics* (ed. N. K. Gottwald; Maryknoll, NY: Orbis, 1983) 194.

[40] Gottwald, "Theological Task."

[41] Ibid., 195.

One can sense in all this Gottwald's deep ambivalence, and his position ought not be caricatured as is often done by those who suggest that he *simply* sees religion as a reflex of social arrangements. There is nothing simple about it! What Gottwald is most deeply interested in saying is that although religion, in this case Yahwism, was a "mover" of Israelite society it was not an "unmoved mover."[42] Many, however, have sought to "resurrect" theology from the death they imagine it suffers at the hands of such reductionist readings, to extract theology from the death grip of the social conventions that threaten to devour it. Herion has insisted that Gottwald's theory is based on nineteenth-century presuppositions which themselves are eroding as there is a shift today away from "materialism" back to "idealism"–that is, the notion that values and beliefs are the chief driving forces in society.[43] A. D. H. Mayes likewise criticizes materialistic readings of Old Testament texts. Following A. Giddens's *Social Theory and Modern Sociology,* Mayes makes a case for the reemergence of the human individual as a free and purposeful actor who creatively responds to situations. The human actor once again becomes a "real cause in history."[44]

What neither Herion nor Mayes is able to do, however, is to address the real *crisis point* of the issue. Even if Herion is correct that "ideas" drive history and society rather than society driving ideas, and even if Mayes is correct that the individual is not simply acted on by his or her social environment but is also a free and creative actor who shapes the environment, the issue of normative theological meaning is still unresolved. In other words, even if "Yahwism" was not simply a reflex of social arrangements but was a force that shaped Israel's existence, how does that make it speak to our time? Even if Yahwism was the "truth" for a freely acting individual in ancient Israel, how does it become "our truth"?

Here is the issue that produces the *real* lump in the throat. Trying

---

[42] Norman K. Gottwald, "Sociological Method in the Study of Ancient Israel," in *The Bible and Liberation: Political and Social Hermeneutics* (ed. N. K. Gottwald; Maryknoll, NY: Orbis, 1983) 35.

[43] Herion, "Impact of Modern and Social Science Assumptions," 19–20.

[44] A. D. H. Mayes, "Sociology and the Study of the Old Testament," *Irish Biblical Studies* 10 (1988) 184–85; Anthony Giddens, *Social Theory and Modern Sociology* (Cambridge, MA: Blackwell, 1987).

to extract theology from its social garb, whether by recourse to idealism or to human freedom, is impossible, and that is the dilemma of which Gottwald has been aware. To use a terribly trite illustration, it is like trying to extract the heavenly God from the earthly Jesus, an enterprise with which the church never felt comfortable. The church could have chosen to lament the impossibility of extracting deity from humanity. Instead it chose to celebrate the matter. It chose to rejoice in the fact that God gets inevitably, irrevocably, and *inextricably* tangled up with human existence. It was a dangerous notion, because it meant that divine transcendence was being focused with all its intensity in human particularity. And why *that* particular human? Why not other humans or "humanity in general"? Nonetheless, the consequences to be suffered from any other conclusion seemed worse than the consequences of admitting to such "radical incarnation."

From a theological perspective, this seems to be where the question rests with regard to the relationship of theology and society. One might be able to extract one out of the other, but at what consequence and cost? Only when we acknowledge that same dangerous and radical incarnation, only when we accept the fact that God gets inevitably, irrevocably, and *inextricably* tangled up with human society, can we surmount the impasse and celebrate our fortune rather than lament our plight. It is a dangerous notion, because it brings with it once again the question, "Why *that* particular society?" Why not other human societies or "society in general"? It is dangerous to assume that God somehow got so totally immersed in the particular and historically contingent social configuration of ancient Israel that the divine presence would not be totally consumed by it. From a theological perspective that is precisely the "risk of faith" which we take as a community gathered around God's incarnate presence among us. It is this theological commitment which provides the driving force for the investigation that lies before us.

2

####

Mosaic Authority:
The Intimate Outsider

Moses' Canonical Function _____

IN ONE SENSE, Israelite history has its genesis with Moses and he is the first of Israel's authority figures. However, it is for quite the opposite reason that we begin our study with him. He is, in effect, the *last* of its authority figures. He comes at the conclusion of the canonical process. Further, the person who has the "last" say is in a position to serve as the "canon" or measure of authority over all that has preceded. In just this way Moses serves symbolically as the canon of Israel's religious self-consciousness.

In suggesting that Moses comes at the conclusion of the process we are simply alluding to what has been called the "scribalization" of Israel's religious traditions. The tensions within Israel's developing religious traditions, the conflicting claims to authority, were eventually subjected to a normalizing scribalization process. This process resulted in the eventual incorporation of competing and conflicting claims into a coherent and authoritatively fixed institutional grid, as when the potentially disruptive prophetic tradition was "normalized" by bringing it into alignment with Israel's Torah tradition. This normalization process is already identifiably at work in the Deuteronomistic (dtr) History, as Moses comes to serve as the mouthpiece for a particular historical and theological perspective.[1] It was

---

[1] See especially Robert Polzin, *Moses and the Deuteronomist: A Literary Study of the Deuteronomic History, Part One* (New York: Seabury, 1980). Polzin overstates the case when insisting that Moses decreases so that the dtr historian might increase,

17

particularly in the Priestly tradition that such disparate voices were
assimilated to the institutional grid of the priesthood, and the ascription of the Pentateuch to Moses was the logical outcome of this need
for legitimation. Everything essential for life was thought to have
been revealed at Sinai, including not only the Prophets and the
Writings but also the Mishna and Gemara of later rabbinic tradition.[2]

As a result of this scribalization process the normative canonical
tradition had the last say *in the name of Moses.* This scribalization
process, by which potentially disparate and conflicting voices were
normalized under the auspices of the Torah tradition, represents the
primary authoritative function of the figure of Moses and shapes
the nature of our investigation.

Mosaic Authority: Charismatic or Institutional? _____

A second reason for beginning with Moses, however, is that he
presents an excellent case study of the problem of "charisma" in relationship to "institution." To the extent that Moses serves to symbolize the canonical scribalization process he might be said to
symbolize the final "institutional grid" upon which Israel's religious
traditions were ultimately charted. Can it be said, however, that the
word "Moses" always carried this exact social function?

The history of scholarship has equivocated considerably on the
question of whether Moses represents primarily a form of "charismatic" leadership or "institutional" authority. Biblical scholarship
of the last century tended to stress the significance of the individual
and the power of personality along with the notion of development
and a search for historical origins. This focus on personality and
origins combined to produce a view of Moses that stressed his
charismatic nature and his foundational importance for Israelite

---

and especially in arguing that the dtr historian overcomes the authoritarian dogmatism
and religious tyranny of the Mosaic tradition. Polzin is too obviously led by his
commitments to Gadamerian hermeneutics and, therefore, not surprisingly, finds
in Deuteronomy 18 divine sanction and mandate for the interpretative process.

    [2] See especially Joseph Blenkinsopp, *Prophecy and Canon: A Contribution to the
Study of Jewish Origins* (South Bend, IN: University of Notre Dame Press, 1977).

religion, often leading to the conviction that Moses was the "founder" of (primitive) Yahwism, endowed with charismatic zeal to lead Israel to a fundamentally new relationship with God and correspondingly to a distinctively new social arrangement and identity.[3] So, for example, Hugo Gressmann understood Moses to be the very one who led Israel from polytheism to monotheism, though monotheism of a particular sort.[4] Similarly, Adolphe Lods characteristically considered Moses to be the source of Israel's "lofty moral inspiration,"[5] a prominent theme since the work of Wellhausen.

The focus on the historical Moses has continued to correlate with an emphasis on Moses' "charismatic" quality. So, for example, W. F. Albright combined the two in his overly optimistic assessment that Moses was "the first great individual in history whose life and personality we can sketch with any degree of clarity. To Moses we owe the emergence of higher religious life and moral culture in Western civilization."[6] Though less boldly overstated, a similar correlation of Moses' "historicity" and the "charismatic endowment" of the founder of Yahwism is also to be found in the works of Elias Auerbach, Siegfried Herrmann, Walther Eichrodt, Edward Campbell, Dewey Beegle, and Eva Osswald, among others.[7]

---

[3] An overview of the work of Wellhausen, Ewald, Söderblom, Vriezen, Reuss, Stade, Budde, and others is provided by Rudolf Smend, *Das Mosebild von Heinrich Ewald bis Martin Noth* (Tübingen: J. C. B. Mohr, 1959) 29–41.

[4] Hugo Gressmann, *Mose und seine Zeit: Ein Kommentar zu den Mose-Sagen* (Göttingen: Vandenhoeck & Ruprecht, 1913) 435–47. The chief difficulty with Gressmann's thesis, however, is that it is self-contradictory. Although Moses is regarded as the *Stifter* of Yahwism, Gressmann acknowledges that the people really learned it from the Midianites (Moses simply being a *Priesterlehrling* of Jethro). Further, Moses and the people experienced the greatness of Yahweh *at the same time* in the events at the Reed Sea, and it was *this* that led to the assumption of Yahwism. One wonders, then, whether by Gressmann's own thesis the person of Moses is required at all to account for the origins of Yahwism in Israelite religion.

[5] Adolphe Lods, *Israel from its Beginnings to the Middle of the Eighth Century* (London: Routledge & Kegan Paul, 1948) 311–12.

[6] William F. Albright, "Moses in Historical and Theological Perspective," in *Magnalia Dei: The Mighty Acts of God. Essays on the Bible and Archaeology in Memory of G. Ernest Wright* (ed. F. M. Cross et al.; Garden City, NY: Doubleday, 1976) 131.

[7] Elias Auerbach locates Moses' genius in the ascription to him of the ethical decalogue, which formed the heart and soul of Moses' life work, and which was the root and essence of Israelite monotheism. According to this view, Yahwism is the first point in human history at which deity is conceived of in moral terms (*Moses* [Detroit: Wayne State University Press, 1975] esp. 172, 193–211). Siegfried Herrmann

Subsequent critical scholarship moved away from a fascination with the "historical Moses,"[8] as well as from a focus on the role of the formative individual in society, and began to focus instead on literary forms, social settings, tradition complexes, and broader institutional and social patterns. This shift in perspective brought with it a change in the way Mosaic authority has been perceived. It is well known, for example, that Martin Noth reduced the historical Moses to a grave site in Transjordan and Gerhard von Rad divorced the Sinai traditions from the exodus-settlement traditions, locating both complexes deep in Israel's institutional cultic life. Such studies have had a dramatic impact on research in the last forty years both in terms of shifting away from the historical to the tradition-historical question and in terms of understanding the institutional nature of what has often come to be considered the "Mosaic *office*."

Whereas earlier scholarship had stressed Moses' charismatic authority, principally focusing on his being the charismatic religious "founder" and national leader, or the prototypical charismatic prophet or judge, more recent scholarship has tended to seek the *institutional offices* that lay behind these roles. So H.-J. Kraus has argued that Moses, in his role as "charismatic prophet" in Deuteronomy 18, really is serving as the prototype of a central Israelite cultic *office*—that of the amphictyonic covenant mediator.[9] Similarly, Rolf Knierim has

---

combines the concern for Moses' historicity with the disputed notion that decisive impulses are generated by strong personalities ("Mose," *EvT* 28 [1968] 301–28). Walther Eichrodt distinguishes between "charismatic" and "institutional" leaders in Israel, placing Moses as *Religionsstifter* in the former (*Theologie des Alten Testaments*, vol. 1 [Leipzig: Hinrichs, 1933] esp. 150–54). Edward F. Campbell, Jr., regards Moses as "a theological architect" not only for Yahwism but for Old Testament theology in general ("Moses and the Foundations of Israel," *Int* 29 [1975] 141–54). Dewey M. Beegle, *Moses, the Servant of Yahweh* (Grand Rapids: Eerdmans, 1972) 344–45; see the critical assessment by George W. Coats, "What Do We Know of Moses?" *Int* 28 (1974) 91–94. Eva Osswald, *Das Bild des Mose in der kritischen alttestamentlichen Wissenschaft seit Julius Wellhausen* (Berlin: Evangelische Verlagsanstalt, 1962) 340.

   [8] E.g., Geo Widengren, "What do we know about Moses?" in *Proclamation and Presence: Old Testament Essays in Honour of Gwynne Henton Davies* (ed. J. I. Durham and J. R. Porter; London: SCM, 1970) 21–47. Widengren admits to being able to attempt only a "minimum interpretation of available facts," which focuses on the decalogue (for which he is willing only to maintain a very general Mosaic inspiration of some of the commandments), the dispensing of the land, and Moses' levitical background.

   [9] Hans-Joachim Kraus, *Gottesdienst in Israel* (2nd ed.; Munich: Kaiser, 1962) 126–33.

seen behind the "charismatic judge" of Exodus 18 the central office of the royal judiciary introduced during the reign of Jehoshaphat.[10] Others have taken Moses to represent the germinal foundations of the institution of kingship in Israel, which accounts for his connection with the dispensation of law and justice. Given this view of Moses, it was not infrequent that rabbinic literature understood the reference to kingship in Deut 33:5 ("There arose a king in Jeshurun") to refer to Moses' kingship rather than to God's. Accordingly, behind the portrait of Moses lay the ideal of the king.[11] Moses now became the prototype of the institution rather than the exemplar of charismatic empowerment. Such a shift in focus has given rise to a protracted debate over whether Moses was, in fact, the founder of Yahwism. For good reasons such a premise has been disputed by Klaus Koch and Rolf Rendtorff,[12] though not without protest.[13]

Is Moses' authority that of "charismatic empowerment" or rather that of "institutional legitimation"? Does he symbolize the stable inertia of stasis or does he instead represent the potential dynamism of change? Does he speak for divine freedom against Israel's attempts to institutionalize religion or does he speak for those central institutions themselves? The question, phrased in this way, leads to the impasse in which the history of scholarship presently finds itself. James Muilenburg has attempted to bring charisma and office into closer relationship by arguing that, precisely in the "Mosaic office" of prophetic covenant mediator, we see a "charismatic *office*" at work.[14]

---

[10] Rolf Knierim, "Exodus 18 und die Neuordnung der mosäischen Gerichtsbarkeit," *ZAW* 73 (1961) 146-71.

[11] Johannes Pedersen, *Israel, Its Life and Culture* (London: Oxford University Press, 1940) 3:102-4. See also Aage Bentzen, *King and Messiah* (2nd ed.; Oxford: Basil Blackwell, 1970); and Joshua R. Porter, *Moses and Monarchy: A Study in the Biblical Tradition of Moses* (Oxford: Basil Blackwell, 1963). For the intertestamental and rabbinic literature as well as Philo, see especially Wayne A. Meeks, *The Prophet-King: Moses Traditions and the Johannine Christology* (Leiden: E. J. Brill, 1967) 107, 153, 188-89, 195-96.

[12] Klaus Koch, "Der Tod des Religionsstifters: Erwägungen über das Verhältnis Israels zur Geschichte der altorientalischen Religionen," *KD* 9 (1962) 100-123; Rolf Rendtorff, "Mose als Religionsstifter? Ein Beitrag zur Diskussion über die Anfänge der israelitischen Religion," in *Gesammelte Studien zum Alten Testament* (Munich: Kaiser, 1975) 152-71.

[13] Friedrich Baumgärtel, "Der Tod des Religionsstifters," *KD* 9 (1963) 223-33.

[14] James Muilenburg, "The 'Office' of the Prophet in Ancient Israel," in *The Bible in Modern Scholarship* (ed. J. P. Hyatt; London: Carey Kingsgate, 1966) 88, 94-97.

The very notion of having charismatically empowered functionaries located in what have come to be called central offices, however, raises the immediate question of how charisma is to be understood as it functions in relation to social cohesion and organization.

When we ask about Mosaic authority, we are not interested primarily in who Moses was, what he did, what offices he held, or how he acted as an authority figure in his own day. Lists of such "Mosaic functions" have often been produced with dissatisfying results. Moses has been seen to function as priest and Levite, prophet, "servant" and "man of God," charismatic leader, magician, judge, lawgiver, religious or cult founder, national founder, mythological figure, literary hero, chief intercessor, suffering servant, divine healer, and so on.[15] Such attempts to identify who Moses was are generally concluded with the admission that "he is all of these things and more." Our interest is not in asking who Moses was or with what "office" Moses was associated.[16] R. Smend has asked the much more important question: What is it that encounters us in Moses?[17]

See also J. Kenneth Eakins, "Moses," *RevExp* 74 (1977) 461–71, who argues that Moses is, on the one hand, the prophet and deliverer (charismatic) while, on the other hand, also exercising two interrelated offices: those of covenant mediator and lawgiver. Eakins, however, does not attempt to resolve the tension.

[15] Herbert Schmid, *Die Gestalt des Mose: Probleme alttestamentlicher Forschung unter Berücksichtigung der Pentateuchkrise* (Darmstadt: Wissenschaftliche Buchgesellschaft, 1986) esp. 66–83; Patrick D. Miller, "The Many Faces of Moses: A Deuteronomic Portrait," *Int* 41 (1987) 245–55. On the relationship of Moses as "suffering servant" and "healer," see George W. Coats, "Healing and the Moses Traditions," in *Canon, Theology, and Old Testament Interpretation: Essays in Honor of Brevard S. Childs* (ed. G. M. Tucker et al.; Philadelphia: Fortress, 1988) 131–46.

[16] Coats has reacted against a "sociological" approach to the issue, because evidence for tying Moses to specific institutions does not present a consistent or clear picture (*Moses: Heroic Man, Man of God* [JSOTSup 57; Sheffield: JSOT Press, 1988] 25–26). Even Gottwald, who is often accused of viewing Moses as the charismatic founder of Yahwism, is ultimately only able to speak of the "Moses group" in his discussion of the "socio-historic horizons" of the Moses traditions. Moses as an individual never appears (*The Hebrew Bible: A Socio-Literary Introduction* [Philadelphia: Fortress, 1985] 223–27. Sociological questions go far beyond the simple question of origins, however, and relate to how a symbol functions to shape, reflect, and interpret social values. A sociological study asks not simply what "office" lies behind the figure of Moses but rather what social function(s) did the symbol "Moses" have in Israelite society, regardless of origins.

[17] Smend, *Mosebild*, 69.

Moses in Old Testament Tradition _____

The question of how "Mosaic authority" functioned socially in ancient Israel is immediately confronted by the obvious fact that little seems to be made of Moses outside the pentateuchal sources until the development of the Deuteronomic traditions. The eighth-century prophets refer to Moses only twice, and both of these texts are, for good reason, considered to be later additions.[18] By the end of the seventh century, in the traditions known to Jeremiah (Jer 15:1), Moses appears in the role of the prototypical intercessor.[19] Nonetheless, even Jeremiah prefers to refer more generally to "the fathers" when considering the wilderness generation, and Moses' absence from chapter 11 and similar passages is striking. Moses appears more frequently in the psalms, but here too an advanced stage of the tradition is presented which shows Priestly editing and later theological reflection.[20] This lack of appeal to Moses for legitimation outside of the Pentateuch suggests that much of the discussion concerning his role results from later theological reflection in the course of the development of Israel's central institutions.

Nevertheless, an early connection of Moses with Israel's cult has often been found both in the Mosaic genealogy lying behind the priesthood at Dan (Judg 18:30) and in the ascription to Moses of the cultic object Nehushtan, which suffered its ultimate disgrace during the purge of Hezekiah (2 Kgs 18:4). The Deuteronomistic historian would have had no reason to invent either the fact that

[18] Contra Widengren, "What do we know about Moses?" 40. On the problem of Hos 12:13, which only alludes to Moses though not by name, see Lothar Perlitt, "Mose als Prophet," *EvT* 31 (1971) 604. Cf. Mic 6:4.

[19] Cf. Moses' intercessory role in Ps 106:23. Such an intercessory function is likely what lay behind the later ascription of the intercessory communal complaint psalm, Psalm 90, to "Moses, the man of God."

[20] Thus the equal billing given to Aaron and Moses in Ps 77:21; 99:6; 105:26; 106:16. The mention of Moses in 106:32 reflects the later Priestly tradition in which Moses is punished for his own failure rather than for the failure of the people, though there is an attempt here to bring the two conflicting accounts together by saying that it went ill with him "on account of" the people. See the discussion of this problem in Thomas W. Mann, "Theological Reflections on the Denial of Moses," *JBL* 98 (1979) 481–94. Psalm 103 is also often ascribed to a later time, not least because of the presence of Aramaisms (see Leslie C. Allen, *Psalms 101–150* [Waco: Word, 1983] 21). In any event, the psalm reserves no special place for Moses in distinction to the people in general (v. 7) and cannot serve to illuminate our question.

the Danite cult might be traced back to Moses or the fact that an apostate cult image in the Jerusalem Temple might have been ascribed to him. In fact, that he did not censor the information about Nehushtan deriving from Moses is rather striking, given the high regard in which Moses was held in the Deuteronomistic tradition. The text suggests, rather, that the Mosaic legitimation of the cultic object must predate Hezekiah, and speaks for some form of authority attributed to Moses reaching deep into the history of the Jerusalemite and possibly the Danite cults.

Any such connection between the historical Moses and particular institutions now lies buried under layers of tradition. Even given such possibilities, it is in the late traditions of Ezra-Nehemiah and the Chronicler that Moses appears prominently, by which time he is fully regarded as the mediator of the Torah.[21] What will assist in discussing the nature of the authority ascribed by the canonical tradition to Moses is, first of all, a consideration of texts relating to the "transference" of Mosaic authority and, second, a discussion of texts relating to challenges leveled against such authority.

Moses and the Transference of Authority _____

There are two groups of texts that speak of the transference of Mosaic authority: the first relates to the sharing of Mosaic authority with other members of the community (Exod 18:13–27; Num 11:16–30), and the second concerns the passing on of such authority to Moses' successor, Joshua (Num 27:12–23; Deut 31:14–15, 23; 34:9). There are two interrelated questions before us. First, what role is played by Moses in these texts, and how does his person or action relate to the nature of the authority conveyed? Second, how do issues of "charismatic empowerment" on one hand and "institutional authorization" on the other relate to one another?

---

[21] Although Moses is already the mediator of Torah in dtr tradition, Chronicles and Ezra-Nehemiah heighten this status. See 2 Chr 8:13 and 24:6, 9, where Moses is credited with legislation with which the source material in 1 Kgs 9:25 and 2 Kgs 12:4–8 does not credit him. No preexilic passage independent of the pentateuchal tradition speaks of "the Law of Moses" (Widengren, "What do we know about Moses?" 27).

Of all the texts mentioned above, the role of Moses in Exod 18:13–27 is perhaps most direct and straightforward. Moses must choose certain persons to assist him in governing the people, and he does so based on certain criteria: they must be of high stature (*'anšê ḥayil*), fear God, be trustworthy, and hate bribery. In this text there is no mention of any "charismatic" empowerment, and the persons chosen are selected because of the position they *already* hold in the community. It is a straightforward case of Moses selecting the community's natural leaders to serve with him. Their gifts have long been apparent, and their appointment by Moses to serve as "officers" is but confirmation of their natural qualifications. They may be "charismatic" in the sense of exhibiting personal magnetism and charm, but the text lacks any note of a force of divine empowerment which breaks into the normal course of events to seize upon a person unexpectedly thereby thrusting him or her into a position of divinely charged leadership.

Turning to Num 11:16–30, however, we are presented with a much more interesting case. Here too Moses is invited to select a group of people with whom his labors can be shared. As was the case in Exodus 18, here too there are certain qualifications that serve as the basis for the selection: the candidates are to be the "elders" of the community as well as its "officers" (*šōṭěrîm*). What is new here, however, is the clear reference to spirit-empowerment which these seventy are to receive: God will take some of the spirit that is upon Moses and will place it upon them. God does so, with the result that the seventy begin to prophesy, that is, "fall into an ecstatic trance," including Eldad and Medad, who had remained in the camp. When informed of the actions of Eldad and Medad, Joshua protests to Moses that he should forbid such activity. Moses chides Joshua, wishing instead that such power might be even further distributed to include everyone.

This text is riddled with problems and peculiarities that can be treated only in the most cursory fashion. Most scholars agree that the story of the seventy was originally unrelated to the story of the quail in Num 11:1–15, 18–24a, and 31–35, which now serves as the framework into which the story of the seventy has been embedded.[22]

---

[22] The tension is reflected in the fact that in the story of the quail Moses' "aloneness" is focused on his inability single-handedly to provide meat for the people (v. 13).

At the same time, most view the story of the seventy as one redactional piece. Though some would argue that the episode about Eldad and Medad (vv. 26–29) was a later addition to protest a narrow confinement of a supposed "prophetic office," there seems to be no convincing reason to accept such a proposal.[23]

More important for our study are two questions: What is the significance of the ecstatic "prophesying" into which the seventy fell, and whose spirit is it that was conveyed to them? It is reported in v. 25 that "when the spirit rested upon them, they prophesied." Then is added the curious note: "But they did not do so again." As it stands, the text suggests that the "prophesying" described here is a one-time experience. It likely intended to mean no more than that, as confirmation of their having been appointed to lead Israel, these persons fell into a momentary ecstatic trance. "Prophesying" in this sense (*hiṯnabbî'*) relates strictly to the ecstatic phenomenon itself rather than to a portrayal of any actual "prophetic activity." The seventy did not serve as a cadre of prophets under the prophetic leadership of Moses, and the text intends no connection between Moses or the seventy and such prophetic groups.[24] They served rather as leaders of the people, and their leadership was confirmed by this singular and momentary ecstatic outburst.[25] It is only in later tradition that the story was understood to relate to the institution of a permanent prophetic guild of which Moses and the seventy were prototypes.[26]

In the story of the seventy the solution envisions a more or less permanent institution totally unrelated to the issue of who will provide the meat. The seventy will help Moses "bear the burden" (*nāśā' bĕmaśśā'*) of the people (v. 17). But in the story of the quail it is the people itself, not their "burden," that Moses is incapable of bearing (v. 14, contra RSV). For a review of the difficulties, see Philip J. Budd, *Numbers* (Waco: Word, 1984) 126–27.

[23] Johann Gamberoni, "': . . . o, wenn doch das ganze Volk Jahwes Propheten wären . . . !' (Num 11,29b)," *TGl* 67 (1977) 116.

[24] Contra Schmid, *Gestalt des Mose*, 69. On this point, see Perlitt, "Mose als Prophet," 601–3.

[25] Ze'ev Weisman, "The Personal Spirit as Imparting Authority," *ZAW* 93 (1981) 229–30.

[26] In Num 11:25 the targumic tradition, confusing the roots *ysp* and *swp*, read the phrase *wĕlō' yāsāpû* ("They did not continue [prophesying]") as *wĕlō' yāsupû* ("They did not cease [prophesying]"), with the effect that the seventy now represent a permanent prophetic cadre in Israel's midst.

The crucial question relates to the nature of the "spirit" that was conveyed to the seventy. According to vv. 17 and 25, it was clearly "some of the spirit that is on" Moses (*min-hārûah ʾăšer ʿālêkā/ ʿālāw*). It is not at all clear whether this spirit, which is referred to simply as *the* spirit (*hārûah*) in vv. 17, 25, and 26, was Moses' *own* spirit or rather the *divine* spirit.[27] The reference in v. 29 to the Lord putting "his spirit" upon all would seem to argue for the latter position. The spirit referred to here is God's own spirit, the *rûah YHWH*. The significant fact, however, is that even though it is the spirit of God it does not fall directly upon the seventy. It is clearly mediated through Moses. It is the divine spirit as filtered through Moses' own body and spirit. Two characteristics stand out. First, it is only a "portion" of this mediated spirit (*min-hārûah*) that serves the purpose, so that Moses' power is not diminished in the transference. Moses is understood to be the ever-plentiful source, reservoir, or repository of God's empowering spirit. Second, Moses does not participate in the ecstatic outburst of the seventy but remains outside of their experience as though standing apart from and over against it.

The text is trying to hold two notions of power in tension. The one would understand the force that empowers the seventy to be God's spirit, discontinuous with human experience and with the human spirit. Such charismatic empowerment would be regarded as standing over against human conveyance, institutions, and limitations. It is God's *own* spirit. Accordingly, Moses would serve simply as the channel through which such divine power passed, untouched, on its way to its final destination. The other, however, refuses to allow such a notion of utter discontinuity to pass unchallenged. That empowering spirit is at one and the same time precisely *the* spirit that is Moses' very own. Here Moses is conceived not simply as a mere accessory or funnel who plays at best a passive role. Rather Moses is himself the repository of "the spirit." The spirit that the seventy receive is not discontinuous with human experience or with the human spirit. This spirit does not stand over against the human spirit, but is at one with it.

---

[27] So Perlitt ("Mose als Prophet," 601) and Weisman ("Personal Spirit," 226, 234) insist that the spirit is that of Moses' own person.

Moses is being presented in this text as symbolic of both the generative force of the empowering spirit and its mediatory agent. Moses is symbolic of the empowering spirit in terms of both its discontinuity and its continuity with human engineering; in terms of both its generative and its mediatory nature; in terms of both its formative and its preservative quality;[28] in terms of both its unique and utterly nonrepeatable quality, which stands outside of and over against human experience, and its paradigmatic quality, which is ever repeated precisely within human experience; in terms of both its "charismatic" quality and its "institutional" form. This text allows no tidy dichotomy between the "power of charisma" on one hand and the "form of institution" on the other.

A second group of texts concerns the "bequeathal" of Moses' authority to his successor, Joshua. In Deut 31:14–15, 23 we read of a cultic ceremony during which God charges (*ṣwh*) Joshua to be strong and courageous and designates him as the one who will lead the people into the land of promise. Two points must be stressed here. First, there is no "charismatic" transference of the spirit in this text, whether God's or Moses'. Second, God's "commanding" of Joshua is a repetition of, and therefore a ratification of, the "commanding" that Moses himself has already effected. In 31:6 Moses "charges"[29] all the people to "be strong and bold" (*ḥizqû wĕ'imṣû*), and then in v. 7 he gives the same charge to Joshua in a public ceremony. Therefore, when God repeats the ceremony one more time, this time privately in the tent of meeting (vv. 14, 23), it is a simple ratification of what has already taken place through Moses' public performances.

In fact, this text is but a ratification of what has already been reported in Num 27:12–23, since it is there that the transference of Moses' authority to Joshua is described. Joshua is presented there as "a man in whom is the spirit" (*'îš 'ăšer-rûaḥ bô*). In a public ceremony Moses lays his hands on Joshua with the result that some of Moses' "majesty" (*hôd*) is transferred to Joshua.

The action reported in this text, which on the surface seems quite uncomplicated, is confounded by Deut 34:9, which intends to report on the same event. Deut 34:9, however, reports that Joshua "was full

---

[28] E.g., Herbert Schmid, *Mose: Überlieferung und Geschichte* (Berlin: Alfred Töpelmann, 1968) 112.

[29] Note the use of *ṣiwwîtî* in v. 5.

of the spirit of wisdom, because Moses had laid his hands on him (*mālē' rûaḥ ḥokmâ kî-sāmak mōšeh 'et yādāyw 'ālāyw*). The obvious problem is that the texts report a varied sequence of events. Num 27:18–23 reports the sequence as follows: Joshua already possesses spirit prior to Moses' ritual of laying on of hands. As a result of the ritual action, Moses imparts to Joshua his "authority" (*hôd*). Deut 34:9 seems to reverse this sequence. The reception of the spirit follows upon the ritual of laying on of hands rather than preceding it.

This inversion has led to a debate as to whether there are two fundamentally different notions of authority at work in these texts: one marked by a charismatic concern in which the spirit is primary and in which the ritual laying on of hands serves as simple confirmation of what the spirit has already accomplished (Num 27:12–23); and one marked by an institutional concern in which the ritual action itself conveys the essential authority, and in which the imparting of the spirit is confirmation of what the institution has already effected (Deut 34:9). Walter Vogels tried to resolve the tension by proposing that there is no conflict. Both texts, he argued, reflect a charismatic understanding of authority. The confusion, Vogels suggested, results from misunderstanding the syntax of Deut 34:9, which he reads as follows: "Now Joshua the son of Nun was full of the spirit of wisdom. *When* (*kî*) Moses laid his hands on him the Israelites obeyed him. . . ." In both cases, Vogels argues, the order is *first* charismatic spirit empowerment and *second* institutional ritual action. Human ritual, he says, merely identifies the person who is already charismatically endowed.[30]

However, the Masoretic Text (MT) does not understand the syntax of Deut 34:9 in the manner suggested by Vogels. The accentuation of the verse clearly divides it according to the traditional rendering, linking the phrase "Moses had laid his hands on him" to what precedes rather than to what follows. Further, Vogels's attempt to drive a wedge between charisma and institution has already been shown to be not only impossible but based on commitments that lie in the mind of the reader rather than in the text itself. It is rather a matter of identifying further what is meant by "spirit" in these two texts and how the bestowal of this "spirit" is related to the person of Moses.

[30] Walter Vogels, "The Spirit in Joshua and the Laying on of Hands by Moses," *LavTP* 38 (1982) 3–7.

When it is said of Joshua in Num 27:18 that he is a man "in whom is the spirit" (*'āšer-rûaḥ bô*), reference is being made more likely to a personal quality of Joshua characterized as "courage" or "fortitude" than to any charismatically endowed presence of the "spirit of God." The simple term *rûaḥ*, without the definite article and without a modifying noun or pronominal suffix (*hārûaḥ, rûaḥ 'ădônai, rûḥî*), is regularly used to refer to a personal quality of the individual quite apart from "divine inspiration." This *rûaḥ* is often used to refer to personal courage, fortitude, or strength, which can be both lost[31] and restored.[32] What Num 27:18 likely means is that Joshua is a man known for his courage, vitality, and strength of character. It does not mean that he has been overcome by the *rûaḥ 'ădônai*. Thus, the order here is very similar to that of the texts we have already considered: based on personal qualities (his *rûaḥ*) that are recognizable by social custom and conventions Joshua is confirmed by ritual ceremony as a result of which he receives Moses' "authority."

This "authority" (*hôd*) which Joshua receives functions identically to the way "the spirit that is on Moses" functioned in Num 11:17, 25. It is not the entirety of Moses' *hôd* that Joshua is given but, as with the spirit imparted to the seventy, it is a portion taken *from* Moses' unlimited reservoir of such power (*mēhôdĕkā in Num 27:20=min-hārûaḥ 'āšer 'ālêkā* in Num 11:17, 25). It is this "Mosaic" *hôd* that empowers Joshua for his task. Joshua may be "a man in whom there is *rûaḥ*," but it is only after the reception of this *hôd* that Joshua can gain the unquestioned obedience of the people (Num 27:20). The possession of *rûaḥ* is what *qualifies* Joshua for his task, much as Exodus 18 and Numbers 11 reported the qualifications of those chosen by Moses. But it is the *hôd* rather than the *rûaḥ* that conveys ultimate authority so that Joshua can lead.

Deut 34:9 reports that Joshua was "full of the spirit of wisdom" as a result of Moses' laying on of hands. Here we have a different way of saying much the same thing: Moses' authority is conveyed to Joshua. That this empowering agent is referred to as *rûaḥ ḥokmâ* shows the ambiguity of how this empowering spirit was conceived. It is not simply an indeterminate personal *rûaḥ*, as was Joshua's *rûaḥ*

---

[31] E.g., Josh 2:11; 5:1; 1 Kgs 10:5; Prov 18:14.
[32] E.g., Gen 45:27; Judg 15:19; 1 Sam 30:12.

mentioned in Num 27:18. Rather, it is a quite specific and trans-personal *rûaḥ*, namely, the *rûaḥ ḥokmâ*. By using such language the text avoids saying that this spirit was the *rûaḥ 'ădônai*. The reference here is to an empowering spirit that is both fully connected to the spirit of God and to Moses' own generative power. There is no way to ferret out what it is about this empowering spirit that pertains to God and what it is that pertains to Moses.

The Mosaic *hôd* in Num 27:20 is the functional equivalent of the *rûaḥ ḥokmâ* in Deut 34:9.[33] Once again, Moses is symbolic of that which is generative, unique, and nonrepeatable. For this reason the canonical form of Deuteronomy attached to the report of Moses' transference of authority in 34:9 the further note in v. 10 that *never* arose anyone again like Moses, who was the generative source of power for Israel's institutional life. Whether this power is con-ceived of as *rûaḥ* or *hôd* is ultimately immaterial. At the same time, however, Moses represents that power which is sustaining, para-digmatic, proto*typical*, and ever incarnated in those who are charged with his very own *hôd*. As in the story of the seventy, so here too a divine empowerment is at work that comes inextricably linked to human arrangement—a charismatic force that achieves its shape precisely through human configuration. One can only use the language of paradox to describe Moses' symbolic function: he is a "nonrepeatable archetype"[34] who is "paradigmatically unique." His persona symbolizes the convergence of the forces of "charisma" and "institution." To suggest that such empowerment can be reduced either to charisma or institution, to the discontinuity of transcendence or the continuity of immanence, to the uniquely generative or the typically sustaining, would be to force our texts in ways they simply will not permit.

---

[33] Contra Eduard Lohse, *Die Ordination in Spätjudentum und im Neuen Testament* (Göttingen: Vandenhoeck & Ruprecht, 1951) 20. Schmid considers the two to be similar concepts (*Mose,* 69).

[34] Weisman suggests much the same thing when he refers to Moses as a "charismatic archetype." At the same time, however, Weisman weights the equation in favor of the arche*typical* function of Moses when he insists that the "spirit" in Num 11:25 is *strictly* related to the person of Moses and is not at all related to the transcendent spirit of God ("Personal Spirit," 228, 234).

Challenges to Mosaic Authority _____

Notions of "Mosaic authority" are evidenced also in stories that narrate challenges leveled against Moses as leader of the people. Three texts in particular stand out as informative. Num 12:1–16 relates a confrontation between Moses and the combined forces of Aaron and Miriam, who protest Moses' sole right to leadership; Num 16:1–40 reports a conflict between Moses and Aaron on one side and people gathered around Korah, Dathan, and Abiram on the other; and Deut 18:15–22, though not reporting on a conflict as such, discusses the authority of Moses within the context of aberrant forms of divine intermediation.

Num 12:1–16 relates a confrontation between Miriam, Aaron, and Moses in which Miriam and Aaron accuse Moses of malfeasance and the improper usurpation of authority. There are serious redactional questions as to whether the narrative comprises one homogenous tradition or two originally independent conflict narratives that have been intertwined: one concerning a charge based on laws regulating intermarriage (v. 1) and a second pertaining to Moses' monopoly on divine revelation (v. 2).[35] If there once was an independent tradition concerning the charge of Moses' intermarriage with "the Cushite," it has been so thoroughly truncated and so deeply buried as to make impossible any independent analysis.[36] Nowhere in this text is there an attempt to identify this woman with Zipporah, and nowhere else is Moses censured for such a marriage. Whether the tradition originated in a polemic either against Moses[37] or in favor of mixed marriage, it appears to be impervious to scrutiny, at least for our

[35] E.g., Gressmann, *Mose und seine Zeit*, 264, 271; Auerbach, *Moses*, 105.

[36] Gressmann takes the note concerning Moses' marriage to the Cushite to have been the core of the original tradition, since otherwise its presence could not adequately be explained (*Mose und seine Zeit*, 271).

[37] Trent C. Butler sees behind a number of such narratives a widespread movement aimed at undermining Moses' authority. This "anti-Moses" movement, which Butler suggests operated on a number of fronts, sought to show that the "real" Moses was unsuited for any position of leadership, thus undermining certain social groups that depend on Moses for their legitimation ("An Anti-Moses Tradition," *JSOT* 12 [1979] 9–15). Coats is correct, however, when he insists that such conflict narratives do not serve the narrative intention of undermining such authority, but rather serve to heighten the heroic stature of the protagonist who is able to overcome great odds to succeed (*Moses*, 123).

purposes. Much more important is the issue concerning Moses' sole right to mediation of divine revelation.

A second question concerns the roles played by Miriam and Aaron in this narrative, and whether or not one or both are essentially involved in the charge against Moses relating to his abuse of power. Many scholars have focused on the person of Aaron and have concluded that what lies behind this conflict narrative is a struggle of competing groups of priests for control of Israel's cultic life. That such struggles took place is undeniable, and that certain later priestly groups traced their ancestry back to Moses while others traced theirs back to Levi, Phinehas, or especially Aaron has led many to see reflected in this text a struggle for supremacy between Aaronide and Mosaic priests.[38]

The text, however, nowhere suggests that Moses is locked in competition with Aaron over a matter of priestly prerogatives. The conflict concerns who, in a more general and encompassing way, is the medium of divine revelation—through whom "God speaks." The tent of meeting, where the confrontation is to take place, is in this tradition (J or E) a place of divine revelation, not a place for priestly ritual. Furthermore, the text clearly focuses on prophecy (v. 5) rather than priesthood. The presence of Miriam and her connections with prophecy (Exod 15:20) also speak for this association. The text relates to conflicting claims about how one "speaks" for God, that is, how "prophetic" revelation receives its own legitimation and authorization.

If Moses does not serve here as the paradigmatic priest, however, neither does he function as the archetypical prophet according to which all future prophecy is to be measured.[39] We will briefly discuss the relationship of Moses to prophecy below. Here it is quite apparent that Moses stands in a position outside of and over against Israel's

---

[38] Gressmann, *Mose und seine Zeit*, 275; Auerbach, *Moses*, 22; G. Fohrer, "Tradition und Interpretation im Alten Testament," *ZAW* 73 (1961) 14; Horst Seebass, *Mose und Aaron, Sinai und Gottesberg* (Bonn: H. Bouvier, 1962) 32–60; F. M. Cross, "The Priestly Houses of Early Israel," *Canaanite Myth and Hebrew Epic* (Cambridge, MA: Harvard University Press, 1974) 195–215; Schmid, *Gestalt des Mose*, 58–59; idem, *Mose*, 86–98.

[39] See the remark that Moses, in speaking face to face with God, is demonstrating the ultimate prophetic experience (H. W. Robinson, *Inspiration and Revelation in the Old Testament* [Oxford: Clarendon, 1946] 186).

prophetic experience. God's revelation comes to prophets in one way, but to Moses in quite another and obviously superior way. The difference is clearly articulated in vv. 6–8: Moses represents an immediacy to God ("mouth to mouth") that is qualitatively different from and superior to the expected form of prophetic mediation (visions and dreams). Moses achieves his authority over against prophecy by serving not as its prototype or archetype but rather as its *antitype*.

If Num 12:1–8 is not about priestly or prophetic authority, then some have found here a prototype of royal authority: Moses symbolizes the king, who is the final legitimator of all priestly and prophetic activity.[40] Though somewhat closer to the intent of the text, this suggestion is still wide of the mark. The text itself is quite clear on the matter. The first thing that the narrator tells us through the divine address is that Moses is "entrusted with God's entire house" (*bĕkol-bêtî ne'ĕmān hû'*, v. 7). He is to God as one who was "over the house" (*'ăšer 'al habbayit*), the technical phrase used to refer to a "chief steward."[41] Moses' authority is analogically described as that of the "chief steward" of a person's household. It was not only the king who would have such a chief administrator. Such an office was as domestic as it was royal. Since it is God's house, however, perhaps we ought to think in terms of the royal court and see in Moses the sort of authority that the king's chief steward would have possessed— full authority over household affairs, particularly in the absence of the king, accountable to no one apart from the king himself, having direct access to the king at any time, needing no appointment or mediation. It is this office which serves as the social metaphor for Moses' authority as seen in the following phrase: "With him I speak face to face . . . and he beholds the form of the Lord." As Joseph had with Pharaoh ("only as regards the throne will I be greater," Gen 41:40), so Moses has full authority to administer, dispose of, and regulate the affairs of God's household—Israel.

The picture of Moses as "chief steward" does not represent the vested interests of some narrowly defined social group, whether priests, prophets, or royal administration. The analogy of the "chief steward"

---

[40] Budd, *Numbers*, 130, 138.
[41] Gen 39:4; 44:1, 4; 1 Kgs 4:6; 16:9; 18:3; 2 Kgs 10:5; 15:5; Isa 36:3.

can result only from theological reflection, which in fact *refused* to allow Moses to be domesticated or co-opted by any single group or party. His authority is not simply unique: it is *singularly* unique and is identifiable with no institution—neither the "word" of the prophet nor the "law" of the priest nor the "counsel" of the elder nor the "judgment" of the king. To come in contact with Moses was to come in contact with the very primal form of legitimation itself.[42]

Moses functions in a similar way in the narrative of the conflict between Aaron, Dathan, Abiram, and the Korahites (Num 16:1–40). In this text, too, the redaction-critical and tradition-historical questions are considerable. In very general terms, most scholars distinguish between an early epic tradition (JE) focusing on the political charge leveled by Dathan and Abiram against Mosaic leadership and a later priestly tradition detailing the rebellion of the Korahite Levites against Aaronide priestly control.[43] Because of its brevity, the earlier tradition tells us little about the nature of how Mosaic authority was perceived or symbolized, except for the fact that he is accused by Dathan and Abiram of wanting to "make himself a prince" (*hiśtārēr*) over the people (vv. 12–14). What exactly this entails, and whether or not it is a gross misrepresentation of Mosaic authority or an accurate assessment, makes it difficult to evaluate the epic layer of the text. More likely the epic tradition invested Moses with the authority of the one who had "brought Israel up," though even this datum is perverted to reshape Egypt itself as the "land flowing with milk and honey" (v. 13).

Much more instructive is the tradition concerning the conflict between the Korahites and Aaron for the priesthood. What is striking is that Moses is the spokesperson for Aaron and provides him with his essential support.[44] It is Moses who gives the ritual

[42] Perlitt, "Mose als Prophet," 601.

[43] Auerbach, *Moses*, 109–11. For a somewhat different interpretation, see George Coats, *Rebellion in the Wilderness: The Murmuring Motif in the Wilderness Traditions of the Old Testament* (Nashville: Abingdon, 1968) 165–84. Coats sees not separate traditions but rather a common tradition underlying the two complexes in which the struggle originally concerned nonpriestly issues. Nonetheless, Coats too allows that the Korah material now reflects a later reworking by the priestly tradition by means of which Korah and the 250 represent levitical interests over against Aaron's priestly control. For a review of the issues involved, see Budd, *Numbers*, 181–86.

[44] Gressmann argues that originally Aaron was the leader of the rebels and that this story too concerned an inner-priestly conflict between Aaronides and Mosaic

command to Aaron and the Korahites to "fire up" their censors, even
though Moses is given no priestly status in the story whatsoever.[45]
He does not engage in the ritual action himself. Rather, he defines,
commands, warns, and invokes judgment, and all the while Aaron
is utterly silent. The passive silence of Aaron and the active and commanding presence of Moses contrast in the strongest measure. This
battle for priestly prerogatives is finally settled by Moses—and settled
by the very one who stands *outside* the priestly circles.

Here again Mosaic authority comes to expression as though from
the outside, yet is the source of final legitimation for those who stand
inside. Just as the Chronicler would later position David as the cult
founder who designed the details of the cult (1 Chronicles 23–28)
but who himself stood irrevocably outside (1 Chr 22:6–10), so already
in earlier tradition Moses had become the primordial cult founder
who mediated the details of the inside while standing irrevocably
outside.[46] The power of his authority derived from the very fact
that he stood outside the cult, above it, beyond it, even over against
it. Had Moses picked up a censer he would have brought ruin upon
the cult just as surely as, for the Chronicler, David would have had
he picked up a hammer to build the Temple. But though David could
not pick up a hammer, every nail hole had been conceived in his
mind's eye. And even though Moses did not dare pick up a censer
in the struggle against Korah he was the mediating source for the
design of every grain of incense. Irrevocably outside, and yet intimately inside.

The tension between the one who is irrevocably outside yet
intimately inside is also clearly expressed in what are perhaps the
most intriguing texts: those that concern the raising up of a "prophet
like Moses." In Deut 18:15–22 the promise is twice stated that God

---

priests (*Mose und seine Zeit*, 269–70). There is no hint of any such conflict in the
present text.

[45] Contra Auerbach, who argues that originally Korah represented a nonlevitical
attempt to wrest priestly control from the Levites, represented equally by Moses
and Aaron (*Moses*, 111).

[46] Simon J. De Vries, "Moses and David as Cult Founders in Chronicles," *JBL* 107
(1988) 619–39. De Vries argues that Moses' authority as "cult founder" was a traditional datum that was accepted without question by the Chronicler, though the
Chronicler now tries to place a similar mantle over David's shoulders (pp. 626, 635).

would raise up for the people a prophet like Moses. This text is commonly taken to refer to a "prophetic office" which traced its origins back to Moses, and which also came to expression in such persons as Samuel, Elijah, and Jeremiah, who according to Christopher Seitz was the last in this succession.[47] The question, however, of whether Moses represents the authority of God's free and charismatically endowed prophetic spirit[48] or rather the properly constituted and institutionally organized authority of a prophetic "office" immediately interposes itself. To understand the issue of "charisma" and "authority" as evidenced in this text it is necessary to compare the text to others with which it is tradition-historically related.

In Deut 18:16–18 God's promise to raise up a prophet like Moses is placed within the context of Moses' mediation of God's word at Horeb. But where does such a tradition come from, and what is the purpose of this remark? In Exod 20:19–22 there is a report of how Moses first came to serve as a mediary for the people at Horeb. The people, who were terrified by God's theophanic presence, begged Moses to mediate the divine word. Moses responded, "Do not be afraid; for God has come only to test (*nsh*) you and to put the fear of him upon you. . . ." When on the mountain, God instructs Moses, "Thus you shall say to them, 'You have seen for yourselves that I have talked with you from heaven.'" The text reports no divine approval or endorsement of the people's fear. Rather their fear is *required* as part of the "testing" or "refining" process which their presence at the mountain entails. There is no hint that Moses stands in for them in this testing process. Quite the opposite. They must face their fear, as it is the divine presence *itself* which encounters them. This encounter with God's refining presence is not to be mitigated by having Moses stand in for them. When Moses goes onto the mountain, he is not taking their place. Rather he is *modeling* for them what the nature of this testing involves. He models for them in a prototypical way what it is that they themselves must experience, and they are to share in his experience *in their own hearing* of God's word (see Exod 19:9). Yet already the note is sounded that

[47] Christopher Seitz, "The Prophet Moses and the Canonical Shape of Jeremiah," *ZAW* 101 (1989) 3–27; cf. Muilenburg, "Office of the Prophet," 86–88.

[48] See, e.g., Martin Noth, "Office and Vocation in the Old Testament," in *The Laws in the Pentateuch and Other Studies* (Philadelphia: Fortress, 1967) 229–49.

Moses is not *simply* a model. It is precisely *in their hearing* that the people come to *believe* in Moses, that is, to receive him as one set apart from their experience, standing outside of and over against their own reality.[49]

When this early epic tradition is taken up in Deut 5:24–31, there are significant changes made. Again the people are afraid and ask Moses to go alone (vv. 24–27). However, the note of the people's fear is not countered by an admonition not to fear. Quite the opposite. Their fear is acknowledged as appropriate! The note of a necessary "testing," so prominent in Exod 20:19–22, is totally lacking in Deut 5:24–31, and its place is taken by a divine endorsement of their trepidation: "They are right in all that they have spoken" (v. 28). It is precisely this *fear* that now exemplifies true faith (v. 29). They are duly dismissed from any further necessary encounter with the divine, and it is Moses who alone is to remain at God's side (*wĕ'attâ pô 'ămōd 'immādî*, vv. 30–31). Moses is to do that *which the people are not permitted to do.* He alone is to receive God's word. He now is not their archetype but rather their antitype. He is not their model but rather their other self, which stands over against them and their experience.

This tradition is then taken up in Deut 18:15–22, where it is placed in an entirely different context. Again the people are afraid and want Moses to go alone (v. 16). Again God praises them for the propriety of their insight (v. 17). Now, however, a peculiar note is added that was not a part of any earlier tradition: "I [God] will raise up for them a prophet like you from among their own people." Now for the first time Moses' mediation is interpreted to refer to a prophetic form of such mediation. The author's intent is to answer a question that has been posed by the surrounding context: How is it that Israel is to receive *on a continuing basis* the divine word? The nations around them receive such words through wizards, mediums, necrologists, and the like (vv. 9–14). Israel, however, is to receive such communication through prophets.

---

[49] On the significance of the word "believe" (*'mn*) as applied to Moses, see Heinrich Gross, "Der Glaube an Mose nach Exodus (4. 14. 19)," in *Wort-Gebote-Glaube: Beiträge zur Theologie des alten Testaments. Walther Eichrodt zum 80. Geburtstag* (ed. H. J. Stoebe et al.; Zurich: Zwingli, 1970) 57–65.

Is Moses understood to function in this text as the "fountainhead" of Israelite prophecy? Likely so, but there are several mitigating factors. First, the syntax of 18:18 itself is instructive. It does not report about a "prophet like Moses." Rather, what is "Mosaic" about this prophet is more generally related to the entire clause: "A prophet shall I raise up for them from among their kin like you" (*nābî* '*āqîm lāhem miqqereb 'ăḥêhem kāmôkā*, v. 18; similarly v. 15). The physical distance between the word "prophet" and the expression "like you" mitigates any essential connection between Moses' person and any such prophet. Second, even the phrase "a prophet like Moses" is extremely ambiguous. It might mean "a prophet, like Moses," that is, casting Moses as "your average prophet." More likely, however, we should read "a prophet like Moses," suggesting that Moses is not the prototypical prophet. Rather Moses relates to a *special* form of prophecy in the same way that the figure of Melchizedek relates to a special form of the priesthood when the king is given the title "a priest forever, after the order of Melchizedek" (Ps 110:4). The purpose is to represent not a typical order but rather a unique order which stands over against that which is typical and gives the typicality its authenticity and legitimation. Finally, the context demands that the attention is on the *fact* of prophetic mediation, and not on its Mosaic character. With this caveat in mind, what in Deuteronomy 5 was taken to be Moses' *unique* status before God now serves as a model or canon for successive generations. He becomes prototypical once again, now serving as the model for the legitimate mediation of the divine word over against other aberrant forms.

The tradition was not satisfied to rest here, however. If Deut 18:15–22 understood this "Mosaic prophet" to be prototypical of Israel's mediation then Deut 34:10 pointed once again back to its normative and unique status. The final word on this subject is that "never again did there arise a prophet in Israel like Moses, who knew Yahweh face to face" (author's translation; *wělō'-qām nābî' 'ôd běyiśrā'ēl kěmōšeh 'ăšer yēdā'ô YHWH pānîm 'el-pānîm*). This tradition, which began at the foot of Horeb, now ends on the banks of the Jordan, where the "never again" sounds a finality that gave a canonical stamp to Moses' position within Israelite religion. It was only much later, under the impetus of eschatological fervor, that the "never again" of Deut 34:10 was reinterpreted to mean "never since,"[50] thereby allowing for the hope that "there may yet be. . . ." This later reinterpretation led to the hopes for a Moses redivivus expressed in the New Testament (Acts 3:22–26).

Moses: Power Taking Usable Shape

Throughout this material there is a pulsating beat generated by the Old Testament's view of Moses as "the intimate outsider." Mosaic authority was expressed in the paradox of his "paradigmatic uniqueness." He is the "nonrepeatable prototype." He embodies both continuity and discontinuity with historical consciousness. He is the paradigm for Israel's life, so intimately identified with it that he comes to be known in tradition as the exemplar of intercession.[51] Yet he is the unique and nonrepeatable one who stands outside and over against Israel's experience.[52] The narrative material, too, drives this point home with fierce determination. Moses comes to his slave people as an Egyptian prince, yet he is a Hebrew by birth. His chief place of revelation is "outside the camp" or "alone on the mountain," and his very presence must be veiled before the people. Yet he is continuously in their midst as one of them. He parcels out the promised land at the threshold of Israel's existence, but yet he does not participate in it, himself becoming a fixed part of that threshold. His own authority does not come by "spirit empowerment," but he is the source of such spirit. He is the leader of Israel by divine appointment, yet he leads at the people's request. He is the "divine

[50] On the translation "never again" for *wĕlō'* . . . *'ôd* rather than "not yet," see BDB, 729. On the issue of the use of Deut 34:10 in later tradition, see Meeks, *Prophet King*, 169–74, 199–200.

[51] On the nature of Mosaic intercession in this regard, see George W. Coats, "The King's Loyal Opposition: Obedience and Authority in Exodus 32–34," in *Canon and Authority: Essays in Old Testament Religion and Theology* (ed. G. W. Coats and B. O. Long; Philadelphia: Fortress, 1977) 97–103, 109.

[52] Coats locates this paradox not in psychosocial realities but rather sees it as two distinct foci of separate literary complexes: one concerning "Moses the man of God," which would correlate to our "charismatic" pole, insofar as it stresses discontinuity with human experience; and the other relating to "Moses the popular hero," which would correlate to our "institutional" pole insofar as the stress is on continuity with popular experience (*Moses*, esp. 131–43, 155–56).

mediator like no other" (mouth to mouth), yet he is the pattern by which all mediation is to be measured. He stands over against revelation, yet encompasses all revelation within himself. He is the cult founder without himself being a priest. He symbolizes the generative force behind Israel's very existence, and yet he represents God's sustaining presence in the midst of history. He represents at one and the same time the substance of divine charismatic empowerment and the ordered form which that empowerment takes. Moses is paradigmatic and prototypical of Israel's institutions. But of equal importance, he is the nonrepeatable focal point of God's gracious action for Israel.[53]

In Christian tradition Jesus has been understood simultaneously as "a sacrifice for sin" and "a model of the godly life." The first focuses on the power of Jesus' ministry, which is discontinuous from our experience and generative of the gift of grace. The second represents that which is continuous with and sustaining of our own lives of faith. On one hand, Jesus' ministry is understood to be fully sufficient for our salvation, the single nonrepeatable action of one who was "fully God." On the other, his ministry was the work of one who was "fully human," serving paradigmatically for our own faithful living.

Whether or not this theological language of paradox is intrinsic to the Judeo-Christian tradition, what we have seen is that in many ways the figure of Moses paved the way for an understanding of the life that Christ would lead among us,[54] for the same tension that gives the gospel its driving beat is already heard, if in muted tones, in the symbolic presentation of Moses. Moses cannot be reduced to symbolizing the unfettered charismatic power of the "prophets." Nor can he be limited to an embodiment of Israel's institutional forms or to the ordering principle of Torah. Moses symbolizes the force

---

[53] For similar language on the dialectical function of Moses, see James Nohrnberg, "Moses," in *Images of Man and God: Old Testament Short Stories in Literary Form* (ed. B. O. Long; Sheffield: Almond, 1981) 47, 57.

[54] It is only with some difficulty that Moses' death can be understood as "a sacrifice for sin," but certainly it was so understood by some. See Miller, "Many Faces of Moses," 253–54; Rodney R. Hutton, "Moses on the Mount of Transfiguration," *HAR* (forthcoming), but cf. the caution of Mann, "Theological Reflections on the Denial of Moses," 486.

that is generated when power takes usable shape, when a bolt of electricity is directed into the high-voltage line, when energy is transferred into physical form. But the issue of charisma and institution is ultimately not even a simple question of how power is mediated. It is rather a question that concerns continuity and discontinuity. It is about issues of substance and form, of generation and sustenance, of being both prototype and antitype, of being intimately inside and yet irrevocably outside, and about the utter inability to have one without the other. His is the story of an intimate outsider and the gift of life he brought to Israel.

3

⌗

The Judges:
Charisma and Qualification

Judges and Charisma:
Common Assumptions _____

TURNING FROM MOSES to the judges, we encounter a form of leadership that is crucial for our conversation, since the judges are often
regarded as ideal paradigms of charismatic leadership. Before discussing the nature of such charisma, however, it is necessary to consider
in some detail two common assumptions that have provided the basis
for most conversation on the matter. The first assumption is that
there was in Israel's history a discrete period lasting for approximately
two hundred years (ca. 1240 to 1040 B.C.E.) that can be designated
as "the period of the judges." This historical period, which bridges
those of the settlement and the monarchy, is generally characterized as a distinct period of transition from seminomadic to agrarian
and urban social organization. Based on a distinction often made
between a "community" (*Gemeinschaft*) and a "society" (*Gesellschaft*),
Israel's social development has characteristically been understood
as a unilinear development from the former to the latter. Winfried
Thiel, for example, understood Israel's roots to be anchored in
nomadic forms of community (*nomadische Gemeinschaftsformen*),
which stood in direct opposition to the Late Bronze Age class society
(*Klassengesellschaft*), but which eventually and precipitously veered
in the direction of the latter.[1]

---

[1] Winfried Thiel, *Die soziale Entwicklung Israels in vorstaatlicher Zeit* (Neukirchen-
Vluyn: Neukirchener Verlag, 1980) 88, 102, 146–47, 161.

43

The second common assumption is that leadership during this period was exercised jointly through the "traditional" rule of the elders and the "charismatic" rule of the "judges." Accordingly, this form of leadership was not only distinct from that which followed in the period of Israel structured as "society," characterized by the "legal/rational" rule of the monarchy, but was in many ways diametrically opposed to it. Furthermore, the "institutional" or "legal/rational" leadership of the monarchy was already prefigured in the days of the tribal confederation by the formal leadership exercised by the so-called minor judges.[2] These persons were "officeholders" whose institutional status was often understood to be the antithesis of the more or less pure form of charismatic rule of the "deliverer heroes." The leadership of the former was marked by stability, ordered appointment, lengthy duration, and bureaucratization, while that of the latter was marked by spontaneity in the midst of crisis, divine selection through spirit empowerment, limited duration, and resistance to ordered forms of bureaucracy. These two forms of leadership, one charismatic and the other institutional, were understood to be in nearly polar opposition.[3] The task of this chapter is to consider these two assumptions and to evaluate the impact they have had on the conversation concerning the interplay of charisma and institution in the emergence of Israel's state structures.

The So-called Period of the Judges

By the time that the book of Ruth was written the author could refer directly and with no further elaboration to a specific time "in the days when the judges ruled" (*bîmê šepōṭ haššōpēṭîm*, Ruth 1:1) and assume that the audience would immediately understand to what period reference was being made. The history of Israel had to some extent already been carved into discrete periods. Within this framework the Deuteronomistic historian further subdivided the period of the judges into segments comprised of a well-known recurring

---

[2] Roland de Vaux, *The Early History of Israel to the Period of the Judges* (London: Darton, Longman & Todd, 1978) 757.

[3] Already clearly articulated by Oskar Grether, "Die Bezeichnung 'Richter' für die charismatischen Helden der vorstaatlichen Zeit," *ZAW* 57 (1939) 120.

cycle of popular apostasy, divine rejection, cry of anguish, the raising up of a "deliverer judge," and rest, most clearly articulated in Judg 2:11-19.[4] Can it be assumed, however, that such a periodization of Israel's history was part of its historiographical consciousness from the very beginning? How far back can such a historical consciousness be traced in the records of the Old Testament?

The subdividing of the period of the judges into segments of recurring apostasy and deliverance reflects a historiographical interpretation that is scarcely attested outside of the Deuteronomistic History itself. Even such a late text as Isa 63:9-14 reflects only the rudiments of such a pattern (redemption→rebellion→rejection→remembrance), but not without considerable variation and lack of specificity. It is only the extremely late theological reflection expressed in Ezra's prayer (Neh 9:26-30) which alludes clearly to the often-recurring pattern (*rabbôt 'ittîm*, v. 28) of the period of the "saviors" (*môšî'îm*, v. 27). Earlier historiographical reflection seems unfamiliar with such a schematization. At least there is no attempt to subdivide Israel's history into such an interpretative framework.

Amos 2:9-12 and Hos 9:10 provide perhaps the earliest available interpretation of Israel's past. These texts refer simply to an undifferentiated and continuous state of rebellion following the "possession of the land of the Amorite," which began as soon as the people "came to Baal-peor."[5] The more Yahweh called to them the more they apostatized (Hos 11:2-4; 13:4-6). Similarly in Jeremiah (2:6-7; 7:21-26; 11:2-10; 31:31-34; 32:20-23) and Ezekiel (16:1-34; 20:27-28; 23:1-4), which display a much more developed historical consciousness, there is a constant insistence on the continuous and *non*-recurring nature of Israel's apostasy. Once Israel had rebelled in the land of Canaan, there were never any periods of grace between "rounds." The same lack of subdivision is found also in the psalms, which, because of their cultic provenance, may best of all reflect Israel's common historiographical self-consciousness. One might expect references to repetitive apostasy and deliverance in the historical review provided by Ps 78:54-72. Instead, there is reference simply

---

[4] But contrast the historical survey in 2 Kgs 17:7-18, which does not place Israel's past onto the grid of such a recurring pattern.

[5] See the references to the apostasy at Adam (Hos 6:7), Gilgal (9:15), and Gibeah (10:9).

to an undifferentiated period of apostasy followed by Yahweh's forsaking of Shiloh and Joseph and his selection of Judah/Zion. The historical reviews contained in Psalm 105 and Ps 135:8–12 show no concern at all in discussing the theme of apostasy in Canaan. There may be a vague allusion to a recurrent pattern of apostasy and grace in Ps 136:23–24, assuming that the references to the "low estate" and the "rescue from the foes" refer to the traditions recorded in Judges 3–16. However, they may as easily refer to some more contemporary crisis and cannot be adduced as evidence for a historiographical subdividing of the period of the judges.

Only in Ps 106:34–46 is there any clear recollection of a pattern of recurrent apostasy followed by popular outcry and divine deliverance. Here we have the same late pattern reflected to some extent in Isa 63:9–14, but especially in Neh 9:26–30. All three of these texts share an identical cultic setting: a public ritual of penitence. It is very likely this association of literary theme (the subdividing of Israel's early apostasy) and setting (public penitence) that accounts for the employment of the theme by the Deuteronomistic Historian in structuring his history of Israel's early apostasy to provide a theological interpretation for this period. There is no way of determining the extent to which such subdividing may have reflected a popular understanding of the past. It may as easily have reflected a radical departure from Israel's common historiographical consciousness.

The notion that the period of the judges was subdivided into recurrent segments of apostasy and deliverance is most likely a later historiographical interpretation of Israel's history either developed or newly employed by the Deuteronomistic Historian to provide a theological interpretation of Israel's early history. This interpretative grid was itself associated with the ritual setting of public penitence, and therefore endowed the period of the judges with the character of a "judgment doxology." When approaching the period of the judges from a historical perspective, the reader must be aware that the primary source has the character more of a theological treatise than of a historical document.

If such subdividing of the period of the judges into fragments is at least historiographically questionable, what can be said about the period of the judges taken as a whole? The primary division of Israel's history into the discrete periods of the judges and the monarchy is attested, not surprisingly, principally in the Deuteronomistic History. The reference in 2 Sam 7:11 (=1 Chr 17:10), though obscured by a troublesome text, certainly reflects on a period of time in which Yahweh had "appointed judges" (*ṣiwwîtî šōpĕṭîm*) over Israel.[6] Even clearer is the reference in 2 Kgs 23:22 to "the days of the judges who judged Israel," particularly significant because it is counterpoised to "the days of the kings of Israel or of the kings of Judah." The Deuteronomistic History clearly divides Israel's existence in Canaan into discrete periods: the period of the judges and the period of the kings.

Once one leaves the Deuteronomistic History, however, it is difficult to find evidence for the tradition that a discrete "period of judges" preceded that of the monarchy. There are genealogical references and brief notes referring to some of the figures of the book of Judges, such as Othniel (Josh 15:17), Tola (Gen 46:13; Num 26:23; 1 Chr 7:1-2), Jair (Num 32:41; Deut 3:14; Josh 13:30; 1 Kgs 4:13; 1 Chr 2:22), and Elon (Num 26:26). Such vague references, however, never suggest that there was a discrete period during which these persons lived, and apart from the book of Judges we would have little evidence to suggest that any of the "major judges" ever lived.

Two texts, however, might be taken as evidence for the existence of such a tradition predating the work of the Deuteronomistic historian. The first, Isa 1:26, makes reference to the "restoration of Israel's judges as at the first" (*wĕ'āšîbâ šōpĕṭayik kĕbāri'šōnâ*), which on the surface seems to refer to an existent tradition of such a periodization of Israel's history. It is doubtful, however, that such is the case. The word "judge" is used elsewhere by Isaiah with reference to specific contemporary officeholders alongside the military leader, the soldier, the prophet, and the elder (3:2). Furthermore, the association of the judge with the counselor (*yō'āṣayik*) in 1:26, repeated in 3:2-3, is likely a traditional association. Job 12:17 lists the two "officeholders" together alongside others such as kings, priests, elders, and princes. Finally, the structure of the text itself suggests that the reference in Isa 1:26 is not to any premonarchic leader but rather

---

[6] Similarly, in 2 Sam 7:7 Yahweh makes reference to "the tribes (*šibṭê*) of Israel whom I appointed." Following 1 Chr 17:6, however, we should read "the judges (*šōpĕṭê*) of Israel whom I appointed." Cf. NRSV "The tribal leaders of Israel, whom I commanded."

to a contemporary officeholder. As J. Watts has pointed out, the chiastic arrangement of Isa 1:21–26 associates the restoration of these Isaianic judges (v. 26a) with the implementation of full justice and righteousness once characteristic of the faithful city (v. 21b).[7] Isa 1:26 thus has in mind not the restoration of premonarchic leaders in Israel but rather the restoration of forensic judges in Jerusalem who will once again implement the justice and righteousness originally (*bārī'šōnâ*) lodged in the faithful city.

The second text, Obad 21, similarly makes reference to deliverers (*môšî'îm*) "who shall go up to Mount Zion to judge (*lišpōṭ*) Mount Esau." On the surface, Obadiah seems to be reflecting an existing tradition that spoke of "deliverers" functioning as "judges" in Israel's past. This historical reflection seems to be supported by the context of the text, wherein copious references to "possessing" the land (*yāraš*) precede the mention of such judges (vv. 17, 19–20). References to the conquest tradition seem to be followed by a reference to "saviors" who functioned as "judges." There are difficulties, however, with taking Obad 21 as evidence for the existence of such a tradition. First, as is generally accepted by commentators, the reference in v. 21a is likely not to "deliverers" but rather to "those who are delivered."[8] Second, whereas the "saviors" in the book of judges "judge Israel," the persons mentioned in Obad 21 will "judge *Mount Esau*."[9] For these reasons the text in Obad 21 cannot be accepted as evidence that Israelite historiography traditionally conceived of there being a "period of the judges."

It is only the Deuteronomistic History that provides any information concerning such a conception. The problem is even further complicated by asking when precisely this period of the judges was

---

[7] John D. W. Watts, *Isaiah 1-33* (Waco: Word, 1985) 24.

[8] Following the Greek *sesǫsmenoi*, presupposing either Hebrew *nôšā'îm* or, more likely, *mûšā'îm*. So Hans Walter Wolff, *Obadja und Jona* (Neukirchen-Vluyn: Neukirchener Verlag, 1977) 40, 42, 50; Wilhelm Rudolph, *Joel, Amos, Obadja, Jona* (Gütersloh: Gerd Mohn, 1971) 314–18; Artur Weiser, *Das Buch der Zwölf Kleinen Propheten: Hosea-Micha* (Göttingen: Vandenhoeck & Ruprecht, 1956) 213.

[9] R. G. Boling finds a reference to Ehud "judging Moab" in Judg 3:30, which might be taken as a parallel example. However, he has to reconstruct the Hebrew text at this point by adding an extremely dubious and ambiguous note based on the LXX *kai ekrinen autous Aōd heōs hou apethanen*, "and Ehud judged *them* until he died" (*Judges* [Garden City, NY: Doubleday, 1975] 87).

thought to have occurred in the Deuteronomistic historian's scheme of events. Who are these "judges" to whom the historian refers in 2 Sam 7:11 and 2 Kgs 23:22? 1 Sam 12:11 states, "the Lord sent Jerubbaal and Bedan and Jephthah and Samuel, and delivered you out of the hand of your enemies on every side" (contra NRSV). The problems with this listing are obvious. First, the reference to Samuel in the third person is surprising since it is Samuel himself who is speaking. Such a rhetorical miscue simply indicates that the speech represents more the words of the narrator than it does those of Samuel. Second, reference is made only to a few of the figures mentioned in Judges 3–16. What about Othniel, Ehud, Shamgar, Deborah, and Samson, not to mention the so-called minor judges? Third, who is this Bedan to whom reference is made? Is this a scribal error for "Barak," as the Septuagint would suggest? Is it a variant form of Abdon? Or does mention of him reflect an alternate tradition which recalls an otherwise unknown "judge"?[10] Assuming that the narrator intended the list to conform to a received chronological order, the mention of Bedan becomes all the more troublesome. Between Jerubbaal and Jephthah come only Abimelek and the so-called minor judges Tola and Jair, none of whom make good candidates for association with "Bedan" or inclusion in the list.

Perhaps the most confusion results from the inclusion of Samuel in the list, since it seems to suggest that the Deuteronomistic historian understood the "period of the judges" to extend not simply through Samson but through Samuel. This perspective, however, is fully consistent with the historian's note in 1 Sam 7:15 that "Samuel judged Israel all the days of his life." It is further supported by the note in 2 Chr 35:18 which refers to "the days of the prophet Samuel" as an equivalent substitution for "the days of the judges who judged Israel" (2 Kgs 23:22).

The historiography of "the period of the judges," therefore, is limited to a particular perspective shared by the circles surrounding the Deuteronomistic historian. There is little way of knowing to what extent the picture presented of this period, together with its being

---

[10] So Abraham Malamat, "Charismatic Leadership in the Book of Judges," in *Magnalia Dei: The Mighty Acts of God. Essays on the Bible and Archaeology in Memory of G. Ernest Wright* (ed. F. M. Cross et al.; Garden City, NY: Doubleday, 1976) 154–55. There is a Bedan listed as a Manassehite or Gileadite in 1 Chr 7:17.

subdivided into discrete periods or recurrent segments, conformed to the actual course of history. Nor can it be determined whether the period as presented by the historian corresponded to a common historiographical consciousness that predated his work. Both the "period of the judges" and its recurrent segmentation represent the grid-work on which the author constructed his historical work in order to give theological expression to a particular view of history. Any discussion of issues pertaining to the judges, particularly those of a historical or social-scientific nature, must take into account not only the "literary" nature of the sources but more importantly their tendentious nature, which seeks to provide a shape to the past that makes "theological sense."[11]

Warrior and Judge: Charisma and Office _____

The second common assumption relates to the "style of leadership" exhibited by the judges. The primary difficulty is that the texts have generally been read as though they could provide accurate information pertaining to the real shape of leadership in Israel's premonarchical period. It has further been supposed that, when viewed against Weberian social analysis, the texts reveal a society focused on charismatic leadership. The best illustration of this assumption is the work of Abraham Malamat, who was so optimistic about the equation that he lamented Weber's lack of attention to the judges. Had Weber considered the judges, argued Malamat, he would have discovered the "ideal type" of such charismatic leadership.[12] The "true charismatic leadership" of Gideon, for example, was contrasted by Malamat to the rule of Abimelek, which was characterized by an "absence of all charismatic flavor" as seen in his recourse to mercenaries

_____

[11] On the problem of whether there was a discrete "period of the judges," see Niels Peter Lemche, *Early Israel: Anthropological and Historical Studies on the Israelite Society Before the Monarchy* (Leiden: E. J. Brill, 1985). Lemche is clear not only in discounting the existence of any such period but also in discounting the book of judges as a historical source: "we have no way whatsoever, to determine whether any historical tradition at all underlies the narrative . . . so long as we lack other sources" (pp. 383–84, 416).

[12] Malamat, "Charismatic Leadership," 157.

and his bureaucratization.[13] Malamat is obviously applying Weber's "rational/legal" and "charismatic" forms of domination to differentiate between some leaders who were purely charismatic and other leaders who possessed not the least shred of charisma. Malamat is so convinced by Weber's analysis that he even employs Weber's concepts of "routinization" to understand the leadership of Gideon and Jephthah.[14] For Malamat, the judges evidence a "pure concentrated form" of charismatic leadership, which ceased to function only with its institutionalization (read "routinization") within the framework of the Israelite monarchy.[15]

The question of forms of leadership in the period of the judges revolves around one of the most often rehearsed debates of the century relating to the book of judges—namely, the relationship of those figures reported in the major narrative blocks, often referred to as the "major judges," to those mentioned in the brief annalistic notes in 10:1–5 and 12:7–15, generally referred to as the "minor judges." Since the debate has been rehearsed so often, only the main lines of the debate will be summarized as they relate specifically to the issue of charisma and institution in the judges.[16]

By the time Martin Noth developed his seminal theory regarding the "major" and "minor judges" there was already a long-standing tradition, represented by the study of Albrecht Alt,[17] that the former were "charismatic tribal hero/deliverers" and the latter were "institutional and official proclaimers of the law." It had also already been proposed that both of these groups eventually were referred to as "judges," even though it was an inaccurate assessment of history and a missapplication of the title, which originally belonged only to the "officials." O. Grether accounted for the misapplication of the title by suggesting that when the notion of "savior/deliverer" was withdrawn from the profane realm, the title "judge" was awarded to the

---

[13] Abraham Malamat, "The Period of the Judges," in *The World History of the Jewish People*, vol. III (ed. Benjamin Mazar; Tel-Aviv: Massada, 1971) 148–51.

[14] Ibid., 147–48.

[15] Malamat, "Charismatic Leadership," 164.

[16] The best recent summary is provided by Hartmut N. Rösel, 'Die 'Richter Israels': Rückblick und neuer Ansatz," *BZ* 25 (1981) 180–203.

[17] See Albrecht Alt, "The Origins of Israelite Law," in *Essays on Old Testament History and Religion* (Garden City, NY: Doubleday, 1968) 130–33, whose analysis was based on comparative study of medieval Icelandic society.

deliverers as a consolation prize.[18] In contrast, Noth popularized
what came to be the received tradition: the misapplication was due
to the presence of the figure of Jephthah in the lists both of the
charismatic hero/saviors and of the official judges. Because of
Jephthah's membership in the ranks of the judges, Noth argued, the
historian mistakenly reasoned that all such heroes should carry the
title.[19] The more crucial thesis proposed by Noth concerned the social
location of these "official" minor judges. With some modification
of A. Alt's view,[20] Noth proposed that these persons occupied the
central amphictyonic office of the "judge of Israel." This office
represented an unbroken succession of supreme pan-Israelite judicial
arbiters which continued into the period of the monarchy. Noth
found references to these juridical officials in Mic 5:1 and Deut
17:8–13.[21]

After some interval Noth's thesis met with severe criticism from
a number of perspectives. On the one hand were those who sought
to expand the list of Noth's "official administrators" by including
in their ranks others whom Noth had defined as charismatic saviors.
H. W. Hertzberg, for example, stretched the number of these officials
to twelve,[22] and W. Vollborn brought the list to a more modest nine.[23]
The effect was to level the distinction between the various "types"
of judges, allowing Vollborn to attribute to them both charismatic[24]

---

[18] Grether, "Die Bezeichnung 'Richter,'" 121.

[19] Martin Noth, "Das Amt des 'Richters Israels,'" in *Festschrift Alfred Bertholet zum 80. Geburtstag* (ed. W. Baumgartner et al.; Tübingen: J. C. B. Mohr, 1950) 406–7.

[20] Whereas Alt had understood the minor judges to be proclaimers of the "casuistic" law received from Israel's Canaanite setting, Noth considered them to be the proclaimers of Israel's indigenous legal tradition.

[21] Noth, "Das Amt," 413–17. See also H. J. Kraus, *Die prophetische Verkündigung des Rechts in Israel* (Zollikon-Zurich: Evangelischer, 1957) 18, who likewise regarded the "minor judges" as executors of a cultic office, namely, that of "Mosaic prophet."

[22] Adding to the list of the so-called minor judges Tola, Jair, Jephthah, Ibzan, Elon, and Abdon, the figures of Othniel, Deborah, Abimelek, Gideon, Eli, and Samuel (H. W. Hertzberg, "Die kleinen Richter," *TLZ* 79 [1954] 285–90).

[23] Deleting from Hertzberg's list Eli, Abimelek, and Gideon (Werner Vollborn, "Der Richter Israels," in *Sammlung und Sendung: Vom Auftrag der Kirche in der Welt: Festschrift D. Heinrich Rendtorff* (ed. J. Heubach and H.-H. Ulrich; Berlin: Christlicher Zeitschriftenverlag, 1958) 23–24.

[24] Ibid., 27; of Tola, Jair, and Othniel he speaks of the "special invasive power of God."

and institutional[25] properties. On the other hand, there were those who undermined Noth's theory by arguing that its primary presuppositions concerning the "judge of Israel" were faulty, namely, the definition of what it meant to "judge" and the idea that lay behind the notion of "Israel." F. C. Fensham and A. van Selms attacked the theory that the primary meaning of "judge" related to a strictly judicial office. The verb *šāpaṭ* had a double meaning that related both to "ruling" and to "judging," and thereby both to the charismatic and to the institutional dynamic of Israel's leaders, making any distinction between major and minor judges superfluous.[26] The term "judge," argued van Selms, was in fact applied anachronistically to Israel's premonarchical leaders and had been drawn from a later antiroyal republican movement throughout the Mediterranean.[27] Alongside many others, W. Richter attacked the notion that a pan-Israelite federation could possibly have provided the political backdrop for the functioning of the judges, since it was the city rather than any supposed amphictyony that was their primary power base.[28] Thus, there was no pan-Israelite office and therefore no unbroken succession of "officeholders."[29] The judge was the civil administrator of a city and its surrounding countryside who was appointed to office by tribal elders.[30]

On another front K.-D. Schunck and T. Ishida attacked the notion that "military heroes" and "civil officials" operated in functionally different worlds. Though Schunck followed Noth in seeing the judge as a central official of the tribal confederation,[31] he understood part of the job description to be leadership in warfare. Military heroes in particular evidenced the empowerment of Yahweh's spirit and

---

[25] Ibid., 27–28, 30. Selection of wealthy or influential, perhaps by lots or by the naming of one's successor; the appointment of persons who had proven themselves successful in war; in general, persons "whose opinion was weighty."

[26] F. C. Fensham, "The Judges and Ancient Israelite Jurisprudence," *Die Ou Testamentiese Werkgemeenskap in Suid-Afrika* 2 (1959) 18, 20–21.

[27] A. van Selms, "The Title 'Judge,'" *Die Ou Testamentiese Werkgemeenskap in Suid-Afrika* 2 (1959) 48–50. A different application of the "Republican" background for the term *šāpaṭ* is provided by Jan Dus, "Die 'Sufeten Israels,'" *ArOr* 31 (1963) 444–69.

[28] Wolfgang Richter, "Zu den 'Richtern Israels,'" *ZAW* 77 (1965) 42–44.

[29] Ibid., 55–56.

[30] Ibid., 71.

[31] K.-D. Schunck, "Die Richter Israels und Ihr Amt," in *Volume du Congrès: Genève, 1965* (VTSup 15; Leiden: E. J. Brill, 1965) 256–58.

seemed destined for the office of judge.[32] As with Hertzberg and Vollborn, such leveling of distinctions allowed Schunck to reconstruct a list of twelve such judges, beginning with Joshua and concluding with Samuel.[33] Ishida also leveled all distinctions between major and minor judges, viewing them as military leaders who arose when Yahweh's spirit came upon them and who organized local tribal confederations. Following their victories in the field, they commonly assumed the rulership of the tribal league which they organized, holding the office for life. Ishida envisioned a series of such charismatic leaders who, on the basis of their exploits, assumed institutional offices.[34] D. McKenzie followed Noth at several points, especially concerning the limitation of šāpaṭ to a strictly judicial meaning and the pan-Israelite and successive nature of the office.[35] Even given this limitation, however, he nonetheless extended the list to include Othniel, Deborah, Samson, and Samuel. Given such leveling, he too ascribed both institutional (legal experts) and charismatic (supernatural insight) qualities to these judges.[36]

In spite of the protests lodged against making distinctions between two fundamentally different styles of leadership in premonarchical Israel, most scholars continued to represent the Alt-Grether-Noth theory in some modified form. Reference was made above to two studies by A. Malamat on the question of the charismatic and institutional nature of the judges, and it will suffice here to mention his rather inconsistent treatment. Following the general protest against the Alt-Grether-Noth theory, Malamat too suggested that the differences in the presentation of war heroes and official judges in the book of Judges likely was due to a mere difference in literary sources utilized—one annalistic (Judg 10:1–5; 12:7–15) and the other narrative.[37] Quite possibly even the so-called "minor judges" were also military figures, and there was "no essential difference between major and minor judges, except for the . . . variant manner in which they are portrayed in the Book of Judges."[38] Nevertheless, in the later

[32] Ibid., 259–61.
[33] Ibid., 254–55.
[34] Tomoo Ishida, "The Leaders of the Tribal League," *RB* 80 (1973) 514–30.
[35] Donald A. McKenzie, "The Judge of Israel," *VT* 17 (1967) 118–20.
[36] Ibid., 121.
[37] Malamat, "Period of the Judges," 131.
[38] Ibid.

article he reversed himself, stating that the major and minor judges were clearly distinct from one another.[39] As mentioned above, he so thoroughly associated a Weberian notion of "pure charisma" with the major judge that, although he does not discuss the matter, one can only assume that he ascribed a wholly noncharismatic institutional quality to the minor judge. Such a conviction is a rather startling reversion to the Alt-Grether-Noth theory, given the history of scholarship that had seriously undermined it.

More recent treatments have also generally tried to maintain some sort of distinction between the "major" and "minor" judges, usually along the lines of Noth's differentiation between temporary charismatic deliverer and permanent institutional official, while also blurring the distinction by mixing the two lists. Though denying the pan-Israelite nature of the "office of judge," A. D. H. Mayes followed Noth more closely than have other recent scholars. He held tightly to the clear difference between the charismatic deliverers and the officials, insisting that there is no evidence to suggest that any of the charismatic deliverers apart from Jephthah ever came to hold an office.[40] Mayes took Samuel, whom he grafted onto the annalistic lists of the minor judges, to be the model for reconstructing the "office of the judge."[41] Roland de Vaux too retained the distinction between the temporary "greater judge (Ehud, Gideon, Jephthah, Samson, and Shamgar) and the permanent "lesser judge" who was "an instrument of government." However, he struck Othniel from the list of the former and added Samuel to the list of the latter. Furthermore he argued that Jephthah and Gideon were both originally "saviors" who, on the basis of their war exploits, later became "judges."[42] Once again such confusion allowed de Vaux to speak obliquely of "charismatic inspiration" as the major quality of the "greater judge," but also to see this charisma as a major criterion in later being selected to serve as "lesser judge."[43]

Z. Weisman introduced a creative twist into the argument. Weisman

[39] Malamat, "Charismatic Leadership," 152.
[40] A. D. H. Mayes, *Israel in the Period of the Judges* (London: SCM, 1974) 57–59.
[41] Ibid., 66.
[42] De Vaux, *Early History of Israel*, 757–72.
[43] So de Vaux can speak of the "charisma" of the prophet Deborah and of the inspired seer Samuel (ibid., 762, 764).

also maintained a strict distinction between major and minor judges. He ascribed charismatic qualities to the military heroes, who, he argued, stood in nearly constant conflict with the civil/traditional leadership of the elders. Into the turbulence of this conflict, argued Weisman, waded the minor judges, whose function was to mediate and ensure the balance between the other two systems.[44] Weisman denied the label "charismatic leadership" to the period of the judges, since the charismatic heroes did not provide what one could call "leadership" in the strict sense.[45] Nevertheless, more than many others he applied Weber's theory concerning the types of domination to the period and clearly distinguished charismatic from noncharismatic persons. What is unclear about Weisman's treatment is how he understood the authority of the minor judge. Using Weberian terminology he associated "legal/rational" leadership with the elders and "charismatic" leadership with the war heroes, leaving the minor judges to mediate between these two opposed forms. Thus, Weisman apparently considered the minor judges symbolic of the coalescence of or dialectical tension between charisma and office.

Finally, Hartmut Rösel has also maintained the distinction of major from minor judges. For Rösel, the clue to understanding the authority of these two functions is seen in the narrative of Jephthah: he is first offered the position of military leader (*qāṣîn,* Judg 11:6) and upon his refusal is then offered the office of ruler (*rō'š,* 11:8). Rösel saw in these two terms references to the function of the major judge as war leader (*qāṣîn*) and the minor judge as local ruler (*rō'š*).[46]

There have, however, been a few contemporary voices that reject any strict distinction between "charismatic" and "institutional" forms of authority as exercised in the period of the judges. J. Alberto Soggin further undermined the existence of the so-called minor judges by calling into question the historical value of the annalistic lists in Judg 10:1–5 and 12:7–15. He suggested that these lists preserve mere fragments of an official chronology used to designate periods according to the lives of eponymous figures, in much the same way that

---

[44] Ze'ev Weisman, "Charismatic Leaders in the Era of the Judges," *ZAW* 89 (1977) 407–8.

[45] Ibid., 402.

[46] Hartmut N. Rösel, "Jephtah und das Problem der Richter," *Bib* 61 (1980) 253–54; idem, "Die 'Richter Israels,'" 203.

similar lists of eponymous figures served in Mesopotamia.[47] Martin Rozenberg also questioned the historical applicability of the material in Judges, particularly with regard to the ascription of charisma to some of Israel's premonarchic rulers. Though the authority of the judges (and here he makes no distinction of various types) was highly personal and ad hoc, it was exercised as a normal form of leadership that was military, religious, and political in nature. The ascription of charisma to these leaders reveals less how the people felt about the judges than how the author theologically evaluated them.[48] Finally, Alan Hauser rejected any distinction of the major from the minor judges on the premise that the only legitimate distinction is of a literary nature. Taking up the argument of Malamat, he insisted that there is nothing to indicate that the minor judges had a radically different role to play from that of the major judges. Such categories serve no useful function apart from indicating the length and style of the literary traditions in which the memory of these leaders was preserved.[49]

Redefining the Arena of Debate

The concern for a "literary" understanding of the figures in the book of Judges was taken up in the commentary by Robert Boling, which set the pace for a dramatic recasting of the question as pertains to the major and minor judges. The question now shifted to a consideration of the "literary function" that was served both by the narratives of the "major judges" and the annalistic notices of the "minor judges." Rather than focusing on whether or not the one was charismatic and the other institutional, the conversations have generally focused on authorial intention relating to the moral character of the persons depicted. In the ordering of the "judges" Boling understood Othniel's position at the beginning to serve as the "model" judge, who was then followed by "major and minor malfunctions, deviations from the Othniel standard." The rest of the history of the judges

---

[47] J. Alberto Soggin, "Das Amt der 'kleinen Richter' in Israel," *VT* 30 (1980) 247.

[48] Martin S. Rozenberg, "The *šōfĕtim* in the Bible," *Eretz Yisrael* 12 (1975) 82–84.

[49] Alan J. Hauser, "The 'Minor Judges'–A Re-Evaluation," *JBL* 94 (1975) 190, 199–200.

alternated between good and problematic examples, with Samson representing the near collapse of the entire system.[50] The literary function of the lists of "minor judges" was that of providing periods of peaceful interludes through exemplary administration.[51] For Boling, the ordering is strictly literary and achieves the purpose of the author, namely, a propagandistic attempt to legitimate Josiah's policies in the seventh century.[52]

The notion that the "minor judges" serve the literary function of providing "peaceful interludes" was followed by B. Webb in his recent treatment.[53] Webb saw these periods as so peaceful, in fact, that he suggested the plot of the book threatened "to peter out into a mere chronicle of the careers of judges who were so undistinguished that scarcely anything about them could be recalled—a chronicle of trivialities."[54] Their function, Webb argued, was to provide periods of "truce" in the struggle between Yahweh and the people of Israel, a struggle occasioned by the continual downward slide of the "major judges."[55] Thus, though there is a differentiation to be made between the major and minor judges, the issue is not charisma versus institution but rather effective versus ineffective leadership. Similarly, Lillian Klein has recently seen in the "minor judge paradigm" a literary way to "ease the tension," to "invoke an interlude," or to "provide a breather," allowing the reader to relax for resumption of the downward course of the "major judge paradigm."[56] For Klein, however, the "minor judge paradigm," which includes *all* the judges after Abimelek, also symbolizes the fragmenting of Israelite cohesion from within.[57]

Whereas Boling, Webb, and Klein associated the literary function of the minor judges with that of providing a slowing down of the action relating to Israel's disintegration, E. Mullen chose the reverse route. For him the literary function of the minor judges was that

[50] Boling, *Judges*, 83.

[51] Ibid., 187–89.

[52] Ibid., 184–85.

[53] Barry G. Webb, *The Book of the Judges: An Integrated Reading* (Sheffield: JSOT Press, 1987) esp. 160–79.

[54] Ibid., 162.

[55] Ibid.

[56] Lillian R. Klein, *The Triumph of Irony in the Book of Judges* (Sheffield: Almond, 1988) 81–83.

[57] Ibid., 99, 104–6.

of *quickening* the narrative pace toward the Samson cycle.[58] The annalistic notes served two other literary purposes as well. They destroyed the predictability of the cyclical scheme of the book and formed an inclusio around Jephthah, who is the theological focus of the book.[59]

The very fact that the minor judges can be seen to symbolize a "slowing down" of action, whether due to stable administration (Boling), their trivial nature (Webb), or the author's desire to invoke an interlude (Klein), as well as the "speeding up" of action (Mullen), is only one point that raises doubts about the ability of a "literary" reading of the text to provide unambiguous insights. Other questions could also be raised about these recent studies. For example, according to Mullen the two annalistic notices of the "minor judges" serve to accelerate the motion forward to Samson as well as to form an inclusio around Jephthah. Is it likely, however, that both could be the case? This would have the effect of forcing the reader into phenomenal mental gymnastics, not knowing which way to "lean" when reading the second annalistic note in Judg 12:7–15. Does the reader "point back" to Jephthah, "hurry on" to Samson, or try to do both at the same time?

Nevertheless, these most recent studies have the effect of radically recasting the question concerning the charismatic or institutional nature of Israel's leadership during the so-called period of the judges. The question has nothing to do with whether they were or were not charismatic, whether they were war heroes, officials, or both. Rather, the question of the distinction of "major" from "minor judges" is concerned first of all with the moral qualities of the so-called "major judges" (perceived by all the studies to be in a more or less continuous slide into malfeasance and apostasy) and second with the literary function served by the "minor judges." These recent studies remind us that if there is a distinction at all it is very likely one that is a literary creation designed to serve a literary function.

The question is whether the book of Judges can provide us empirical data upon which to reconstruct the forms of leadership

---

[58] E. Theodore Mullen, Jr., "The 'Minor Judges': Some Literary and Historical Considerations," *CBQ* 44 (1982) 196, 200.

[59] Ibid., 198, 201.

in premonarchic Israel. More likely, the best we can hope is that it will provide glimpses of how leadership in premonarchic Israel came to be understood centuries after it had passed from the scene. To admit this limitation, however, is not without benefit. Our review of the literature shows that most of past scholarship was oriented toward the historical task of reconstructing something that was a figment of later imagination. The result was that, in one form or another, a "period of charismatic leadership" was constructed on principles laid down by Weber and others and then relegated to a discrete location in Israel's past. Any discussion concerning charisma and institution as relating to the judges could only have related to this discrete period.

What the recent studies on the judges suggest, however, is that the book of Judges gives us entry into the world of the *author*. We are not interested, therefore, in determining whether or not there was a particular charismatic leader active during the period of the judges. We are interested, rather, in understanding how the *readers* of the book of Judges were intended by the author to understand the dynamics of divine inspiration and regularized appointment at work *in their own lives*.

The Judges and the Deliverers

The review of literature on the topic of the relation of major to minor judges illustrates the fact that, as detailed as the investigation might be, there is no adequate solution to the problem. It seems highly unlikely, however, that the Deuteronomistic historian himself understood any essential difference between the two. The simplest solution is to assume that the names in the annalistic notes (Judg 10:1–5; 12:7–15) were drawn from an independent source. Since most of these figures, unlike the "war heroes," appear in genealogical lists elsewhere,[60] it is easiest to postulate that the Deuteronomistic historian culled their names from such a list, whether from family chronicles[61] or an official chronology based on eponymous figures.[62]

---

[60] Tola (Gen 46:13; Num 26:23; 1 Chr 7:1–2); Jair (Num 32:41; Deut 3:14; 1 Kgs 4:13); Elon (Gen 46:14; Num 26:26). Lacking only for Ibzan and Abdon.

[61] Malamat, "Period of the Judges," 131.

[62] Soggin, "Das Amt der 'kleinen Richter' in Israel," 247.

The reason why the historian incorporated these persons into his list likely had less to do with fleshing out the total to a representative number such as twelve[63] than with adding a certain number of years for chronological purposes.

The annalistic notes themselves provide no information whatsoever for speculation concerning some original social location of the "minor judges." In fact, the Deuteronomistic historian evidently considered them to be military heroes alongside the figures who appeared in his narrative source. The tradition that Tola was the eponym of a clan of skilled warriors (1 Chr 7:1–2), as well as the traditional association of Jair with the conquest of Gilead (Num 32:41; Deut 3:14), makes it likely that these persons were included by the historian because of the tradition of their military prowess. As for Elon, his association with Tola in Gen 46:13–14 and Num 26:23–26 could easily account for his incorporation into the list. The notes concerning the progeny of Ibzan and Abdon, the first symbolizing the power of marriage alliances (Judg 12:8–9) and the second representing the military power of riding on asses (12:13–14), certainly suggests that to these persons also were ascribed the trappings of a "valiant warrior" (*gibbôr ḥayil*).

Hauser is correct in insisting that there was no essential difference between the two types of leaders.[64] The Deuteronomistic historian intended the reader to view them as though fashioned from the same mold and serving the same function – that of "delivering" Israel from its foreign enemies in situations of crisis. In this regard it is extremely doubtful that Tola's "deliverance" of Israel (Judg 10:1) was to be understood simply as delivering from the domestic chaos of Abimelek's reign, as maintained by Boling and Webb.[65] The story of Abimelek's "rule," along with the resolution of its disastrous effects, is brought to full completion by the summary notes in Judg 9:56–57. Twice the author uses the verb *šwb* (return, restore, requite) to bring the story to a close. Abimelek's actions had come full circle, and the curse of Jotham had found its target. There remained nothing,

---

[63] So already C. F. Burney, *The Book of Judges* (London: Rivingtons, 1918) 289–90; cf. Hertzberg, "Die kleinen Richter," 285–90; Schunck, "Die Richter Israels und Ihr Amt," 255.

[64] See p. 57 above.

[65] Boling, *Judges*, 187; Webb, *Book of Judges*, 160.

as far as the reader is concerned, that required further "deliverance."
That in 10:1 the historian makes no reference to the foreign enemy
from whom Tola delivered Israel is indicative only of the fact that
such information was not available in the annalistic source from
which the Deuteronomistic historian culled these names. He introduced Tola as the first of the members of this list, since it was Tola
who according to tradition was most clearly a man of war. That he
used the verb "deliver" of Tola was simply the author's rhetorical
device for tying these names into the overall theme of the work.

The judges, therefore, present a homogenous form of leadership
from the perspective of the Deuteronomistic historian and his
audience. As shown above, considerable attention has been given
to the question of what it means that these persons "judged Israel,"
but with few firm results. Very little attention has been given to
the significance of their "delivering" (*hôšîaʿ*) Israel. This was by no
means a special type of action relegated to these few legendary figures
from the book of Judges. In fact, the action of "delivering" a city
or nation from foreign oppression was a common and popular
literary motif ascribed to a broad spectrum of persons including
Joshua (Josh 10:6), Saul (1 Sam 9:16; 10:27), David (1 Sam 23:2, 5),
Joab and Abishai (2 Sam 10:11), and warriors or kings in general
(1 Sam 11:3; 2 Kgs 6:27; 13:5; Isa 19:20; Jer 14:9; Hos 13:10). Even
foreign kings could be spoken of as "deliverers" (2 Sam 10:19; 2 Kgs
16:7). Beyond the cases that speak of a military confrontation, the
term "deliver" could also be used of Moses rescuing the women at
the well (Exod 2:17), of one rescuing a woman being raped (Deut
22:27), and of David giving legal relief to a woman (2 Sam 14:4).

With such widely attested and varied uses of the term *hôšîaʿ*, the
Deuteronomistic historian could not have understood the style of
leadership of the judges to have been bound to a specific period of
time. Such "saving" was a common motif in Israel's epic literature.
We conclude from this observation that if there was a particularly
"charismatic" dynamic to the leadership of the judges it was not a
style relegated by the author to some long-lost legendary past cut
off to access by contemporary leaders. The historian drew upon common shared experience and was reflecting current notions of "charismatic" empowerment as exhibited in all such actions of deliverance.

Spirit and the Ratification of Social Designation _____

The final concern is to discuss the nature of "charisma" in relation to leadership and to consider the adequacy of applying the notion of charisma to the judges of Israel. Weber's typology of domination has not been accepted by all. Stewart Clegg is representative of those who reject any attempt to distinguish discrete types of authority, insisting that "power is not a thing like a cat or a dog. . . . There are no breed standards to determine what type of thing it is . . . and no criteria which even allow us to recognize species."[66] Most, however, have accepted Weber's basic approach of distinguishing such discrete types of authority as "traditional," "legal/rational," and "charismatic," but have sought to refine the distinctions. Such "neo-Weberians" are not unmindful of the pitfalls with Weber's approach. William Friedland is well aware that Weber's primary problem in discussing charisma was a confusion of psychological and sociological criteria. Though Weber was a sociologist studying a sociological problem he nevertheless focused on the psychological dimension of the individual possessed by extraordinary capacities of authority that are not subject to social confirmation.[67] Similarly, even though Dankwart Rustow speaks of "pure charisma," he admits that the phenomenon of leadership is "three parts setting and one part personality."[68]

Some "neo-Weberians" have followed Weber's system fairly consistently, however. Bryan Wilson clearly distinguishes types of leadership, contrasting charisma sharply with other forms. He speaks of the charismatic as being "a disruptor of the prevailing order, a man who abrogates and transcends convention, who creates discord, coming, as it were, to put the world to the sword."[69] Charisma for Wilson implies a radical break in the existing structure of social and

[66] Stewart Clegg, *Power, Rule and Domination: A Critical and Empirical Understanding of Power in Sociological Theory and Organizational Life* (Boston: Routledge & Kegan Paul, 1975) 2.

[67] William H. Friedland, "For a Sociological Concept of Charisma," *Social Forces* 43 (1964) 19–20.

[68] Dankwart A. Rustow, *A World of Nations: Problems of Political Modernization* (Washington, DC: The Brookings Institution, 1967) 166–68, 153.

[69] Bryan R. Wilson, *The Noble Savages: The Primitive Origins of Charisma and Its Contemporary Survival* (Berkeley: University of California Press, 1975) 9.

power relationships and fractures the order of the prevailing system.[70]

Most others, however, have been more cautious about so clearly distinguishing ideal forms of domination. Dennis Wrong modifies Weber's system by making further distinctions of the ideal types of authority, drawing them out to five: coercive, induced, legitimate, competent, and personal.[71] Charisma as a type of domination is reduced in significance by being subsumed as a minor form of personal authority, but one that exhibits personal authority in its most extensive form.[72] Wrong maintains the distinction of such charismatic-personal authority from other forms when he argues that such authority is not restrained by the limits of "tradition" or of "legal statute,"[73] code words for Weber's other two types of domination.

The most insightful critique of Weber's theory of domination has come from E. Shils. If the "neo-Weberians" were well aware of the slide of the various forms of domination into one another (referred to most often as "diffusion," "office charisma," or "routinization"), Shils sharpened the debate by insisting that charisma as such not only disrupts social order but, more importantly, maintains or conserves it.

> The charismatic quality of an individual as perceived by others, or himself, lies in what is thought to be his connection with (including possession by or embodiment of) some very central feature of man's existence and the cosmos in which he lives. . . . The centrality is constituted by its formative power in initiating, creating, governing, transforming, maintaining, or destroying what is vital in man's life.[74]

For Shils, charismatic attribution always focuses on that "vital layer" at the center of human existence which expresses itself in the need for order. Whatever embodies, expresses, or symbolizes the essence of an ordered cosmos awakens the disposition of awe and reverence,

[70] Ibid., 10. Wilson, however, was studying native American and African communities in extreme conflict with encroaching European culture and would obviously find such conflict to be central to leadership, whether charismatic or not.

[71] Dennis H. Wrong, *Power: Its Forms, Bases and Uses* (Oxford: Basil Blackwell, 1979) 21–24.

[72] Ibid., 62–63.

[73] Ibid., 64.

[74] E. Shils, "Charisma, Order, and Status," *ASR* 30 (1965) 201.

that is, the charismatic disposition.[75] This understanding of charisma allows Shils to see institutions themselves as "charismatic" by virtue of the tremendous power concentrated in them. In order to claim charisma or to have charisma attributed to it, however, the institution must appear to be fully integrated with a transcendent moral order, a standard of justice referring to an order beyond that which is exhibited in the limited structures of the institution itself.[76] It is this moral order which for Shils is the primary "centering" principle that lies at the foundation of any claims of charisma.

The effect of Shils's theory, which seems extremely valid in view of this study, is to reject any notion that charisma represents an intrusive disordering principle that is in social tension with a "legal/rational" or "traditional" form of authority. The attribution of charisma is based on the perception of contact of leadership *as such* with the centering principles of cosmic justice and order. Charisma does not refer to a distinct form of authority. It relates, rather, to the legitimating function attendant on all authority insofar as it is perceived as being anchored in core social values which themselves are thought to reflect cosmic order.

Such an understanding of charisma is also hinted at even by those more closely tied to Weber's theory. Friedland emphasizes that, for charisma to be attributed, the message of the charismatic must be relevant and meaningful within the social context of the audience. The charismatic must embody values and sentiments that are inchoate in society.[77] Talcott Parsons speaks of charisma as a mechanism of "reintegration" which gives disorganized persons orientation and meaning to their lives.[78] Wrong sees such charismatic authorization as embedded in the need for moral justification, as anchored in a larger collective goal or system of values, and as part of a larger cosmos based on moral principle.[79] Even Wilson admits that such charismatic attribution is itself culturally determined and that it depends less on the quality of the leader than on a "will to believe."[80]

[75] Ibid., 203–4.
[76] Ibid., 206–7.
[77] Friedland, "For a Sociological Concept of Charisma," 21–23.
[78] Talcott Parsons, *Politics and Social Structure* (New York: Free Press, 1969) 110.
[79] Wrong, *Power: Its Forms, Bases and Uses,* 103–11.
[80] Wilson, *Noble Savages,* 29, 87, 95.

Given this understanding of "charisma," what can be said about the attribution of charisma to the judges of Israel? Two points seem to be clear. First, when we say that the judges exhibit charisma, we mean that the author portrayed them as leaders who were fundamentally "supercharged" by commitments to core values of Israelite society. Since they are also epic protagonists, they are naturally portrayed as also displaying behavior understood to result from greed, passion, or some tragic flaw, best illustrated in the case of Samson but also seen in the cases of Gideon and Jephthah. But beyond the flaws of such normal epic characterization they are persons who represent the struggle for the establishment and preservation of Israelite national identity and the commitment to solidarity and cohesion. In spite of their forays into lamentable behavior and near disastrous mishaps, they were received by the reader as representative of the centering of cosmos and order in the life of Israel. As soon as the note of a judge's death was announced, the next movement in the plot was once again in the direction of disorder and chaos. The attribution of charisma to the judges does not relate strictly to the note of spirit empowerment, as will be demonstrated by what follows. It is the other way around. Spirit empowerment serves as one symbol among others of confirmation of the attribution of charisma.[81]

The second point to be made is that any charisma as it manifests itself in the person of the judge is not understood to be an intrusion into the normal ordering principles of social leadership. The "charisma" of the judge was not exclusively located in some extraordinary incursion of divine power into the otherwise orderly management of "business as usual." To the extent that the judges can be spoken of as charismatic, such charisma is not associated with divine empowerment—that is, with the momentary explosion of the "spirit of God" in the person's life. The point can be easily and briefly demonstrated with each of the major characters.

When the spirit of Yahweh empowers Othniel to fight against Cushan-rishathaim (Judg 3:10), this empowerment cannot be divorced from earlier notes regarding Othniel's qualifications and social location. The reader of Judges 3 is already aware, from a canonical per-

---

[81] Rozenberg, "The *šōfĕtim* in the Bible," 84.

spective, that Othniel had a significant reputation. He carried the distinction of being the younger brother of Caleb (as well as Caleb's son-in-law!) and had already been credited with the conquest of Kiriath-sepher (Josh 15:17; Judg 1:13). When the reader is informed in Judg 3:10 that the spirit of the Lord came upon Othniel, it can hardly be taken as an illogical choice for which the reader is unprepared. Othniel, through his credentials of social position and military prowess, was in position to receive further confirmation of his leadership.

With Ehud the situation is no different. The fact that "the Lord raised up . . . a deliverer" for Israel (Judg 3:15) is clarified by the statement that it was the people of Israel *themselves* who had already selected Ehud to carry tribute to Eglon, King of Moab, representative of Ehud's consequential social position.[82] Ehud is further qualified for his task by not only being a Benjaminite, that is, a "son of the right (hand)" (*ben-haymînî*), but also by being "bound up in his right hand" (*'îš 'iṭṭēr yad-yĕmînô*, Judg 3:15), that is, by being left-handed. Rather than a mark of disqualification, as Klein interprets it,[83] this note appears to be what particularly suits Ehud for the mission ahead.[84] There is, in fact, no note at all of Yahweh's spirit coming upon Ehud. This lack of spirit intervention cannot be taken as a negative valuation resulting from the "silence" of Yahweh.[85] Rather it attests to the simple fact that the author was not bound to strict literary conventions such as spirit empowerment in order to portray leadership as divinely appointed.

The notice concerning Shamgar (Judg 3:31) is universally considered hopelessly opaque. The fact that he is probably not Israelite and that the narrative context itself treats him almost as if he did not exist[86] makes it difficult to evaluate his presence, except that the reference in 5:6 may account for his having been placed in close proximity

[82] Malamat, "Charismatic Leadership," 162.

[83] Klein, *Triumph of Irony*, 37.

[84] So Webb, *Book of Judges*, 131.

[85] Klein, *Triumph of Irony*, 37–40. The reference to Yahweh's "raising up" (*wayyāqem*) Ehud is sufficient to compensate for any supposed "silence." Cf. Vollborn, "Der Richter Israels," 27.

[86] Judg 4:1 continues with the note concerning the death of Ehud rather than Shamgar. On the question, see Wolfgang Richter, *Die Bearbeitungen des 'Retterbuches' in der Deuteronomischen Epoche* (Bonn: Peter Hanstein, 1964) 92–97.

to Deborah. As for Deborah, she clearly was already exercising some
sort of prophetic activity associated with the dispensing of oracles
at a sacred grove (4:4–5). The text suggests that her oracles were issued
in matters of legal counsel, but the reference to her "judging Israel"
may have been secondarily ascribed by the author. In any event, she
too has a clearly defined social status and, as with Ehud, there is
no reference to her receiving the spirit of Yahweh. To the extent
that as a prophet and judge she was charismatic, there is no isolating
any such charisma from her prior qualifications and social position.

The case of Gideon is intriguing for a number of reasons, not least
because he protests his inadequacy for the job, claiming to be the
weakest member of the weakest family in the land (Judg 6:15). Such
inadequacy is often regarded as proof that "charismatically endowed
persons" are the least suited, are "outsiders," or are socially marginalized
from central institutions. Malamat, for example, cites Deborah's
gender, Gideon's kinship, and Jephthah's social marginalization as
characteristic requisites of "charismatic endowment."[87] It is "outsiders"
who are the subjects of charismatic designation. The association of
charisma with outsiders, however, has been disproved in sociological
analysis. In order for charisma to be attributed to them, persons
must be enabled to act within the bounds of legitimacy as defined
by society as a whole on the basis of credentials accepted by society
in accordance with social conventions.[88] It is not outsiders who are
the proven charismatic leaders; rather those to whom charisma is
most effectively attributed are "the most inside of the outsiders" in
coalition with "the most outside of the insiders."[89] In the case of
Gideon, his claims of inadequacy have nothing at all to do with his
real social status, which was that of a "mighty man of valor" (6:12)
from a prestigious and wealthy family of royal proportions (6:27;
8:18). His protestation is simply a typical narrative motif also
demonstrated in the case of Saul, who, though being the obvious
candidate (1 Sam 9:2), protested his inadequacy (9:21). Far from being
an "outsider" Gideon's attribution of charisma related to his social
location as "most outside of the insiders." He had already established

---

[87] Malamat, "Charismatic Leadership," 160.

[88] Friedland, "For a Sociological Concept of Charisma," 23.

[89] Rustow, *World of Nations*, 161.

himsel˙ with his credentials and his mighty acts, and only then did the spirit of Yahweh "clothe itself" with Gideon (Judg 6:34)[90] as confirmatory of his leadership.

The same observation applies to Jephthah. According to many, his "outsider" social location as the son of a prostitute with a checkered past associated with a band of freebooters (Judg 11:1–3) makes him a perfect choice for charismatic endowment. Again, however, such "Robin Hood-esque" characterization results from the conventions of narrative style and cannot be taken to relate to his "charismatic attribution." Further, the fact that he is the son of a prostitute does not detract from the fact that he *is*, after all, the son of Gilead. Further, he is immediately introduced as a "mighty warrior" (*gibbôr ḥayil*), which associates his credentials with those of Gideon (6:12). Jephthah is not recruited by the "spirit" but rather by the elders of Gilead, with whom he makes a contract concerning leadership (11:9). From a Weberian perspective this narrative represents the combination of "traditional" (elders) and "legal/rational" (contractual) domination rather than "charismatic." It is not until 11:29, long after his installation as "head" (*rō'š*, 11:11), that the spirit of Yahweh comes upon him, as though to confirm what had already taken place through other means.

Finally, Samson presents perhaps the most peculiar case of all. The Lord's spirit is said to stir Samson for momentary bursts of superhuman strength in 13:25; 14:19; and 15:14. In fact, however, Samson had been designated from his birth as a "candidate" for such power by virtue of his consecration as a nazirite (13:5); and from the perspective of the narrative it was the vow and the length of his hair that were as much the source of his "charisma" as was any occasional and fleeting spirit empowerment. Here again, the spirit empowerment appears to serve as the ratification of something already in process rather than the extraordinary breaking in of the unexpected.

None of the judges was depicted by the Deuteronomistic historian as possessing a "charismatic empowerment" that stood over against other, more ordinary forms of legitimation. If one can legitimately

---

[90] Klein totally misunderstands the text when she finds here a reference to Gideon's "wearing" the spirit and then takes this as a negative evaluation of Gideon (*Triumph of Irony*, 55, 68). It is the opposite: the spirit "puts on Gideon" (*wĕrûaḥ YHWH lābĕšâ 'et-gidʿôn*)!

speak of the judges as "charismatic," it is only in the sense that they represent the centering principles of cosmic justice and order in the mind of the author and his intended audience. In spite of their flawed characterization, a result of traditional epic narrative style, these judges fight for Israel and for solidarity in the face of chaos and dissolution. Their struggles are perceived as being anchored in core social values which themselves are thought to reflect cosmic order.

The attribution of charisma to the judges is understandable only from the perspective of the literary character of the narratives. If we are to understand such leadership as a historical phenomenon, it must be done on the basis of analyses of Israelite history laid down by social historians such as N. Gottwald, F. Frick, W. Lemche, R. Coote, and K. Whitelam.[91] Because of negative evaluations concerning the applicability of the Deuteronomistic History for reconstructing a "period of the judges," however, this chapter was confined to reflections on "charisma" from literary perspectives. Any discussion of the topic of "charisma" as manifest in the historical emergence of Israel's state structures could only be engaged following a discussion of the literary nature of the sources. Attention will now be turned to charisma as it relates to Israel's monarchy, with attention given to leadership in transition from a pre-state to a state society.

---

[91] Gottwald, *Tribes of Yahweh;* Frank S. Frick, *The Formation of the State in Ancient Israel: A Survey of Models and Theories* (Sheffield: Almond, 1985); Lemche, *Early Israel;* Robert B. Coote and Keith W. Whitelam, *The Emergence of Early Israel in Historical Perspective* (Sheffield: Almond, 1987).

4

The Kings and Charisma: Foundations of Royal Authority

Charisma, Kingship, and Paganism _____

THE DEBATE over the relationship of charismatic empowerment and official and institutionalized forms of authorization has provided much of the driving force behind the study of the Israelite monarchy, particularly since the publication of Albrecht Alt's seminal studies on Israel's history. No two works have had such impact on studies pertaining to the development of monarchy in Israel as have his investigations into Israel's state formation and into the particular character of monarchy in Israel and Judah.[1] In the former study Alt argued that Israel was definitively and constitutively stamped by its nomadic past and its tribal organization. The eventual development of a state form of government was therefore regarded by Alt as a foreign invasion of Israel's body politic which, if not malignant, was at least benignly tumorous. Alt regarded the charismatic principle as essential to premonarchic Israel's self-understanding and argued that Saul's monarchy was faithful to this charismatic ideal. Saul's rule was divinely appointed and nondynastic, based on his war leadership as commander of the popular militia. With David, however, there was a radical departure from Israel's indigenous charismatic

---

[1] On Israel's state formation, see Albrecht Alt, "Die Staatenbildung der Israeliten in Palästina," *Kleine Schriften zur Geschichte des Volkes Israel* (Munich: C. H. Beck, 1959) 2:1–65 (originally published in 1930). On the monarchy, see Albrecht Alt, "Das Königtum in den Reichen Israel und Juda," *Kleine Schriften zur Geschichte des Volkes Israel,* 2:116–34 (originally published in 1951).

ideal. David was a career soldier whose basis of authority was not that of the spontaneous charismatic appointment of God ratified by popular support but rather that of personal conquest. With the transition to Davidic monarchy, argued Alt, Israel assumed a typically Canaanite form of state administration, which was antithetical to its Yahwistic (i.e., charismatic) roots.

In the second study Alt pursued the thesis further. Whereas monarchy in Judah continued along this aberrational path, argued Alt, in Israel the charismatic principle once again surfaced following Solomon's death. Kingship regained its indigenous charismatic, nondynastic character, with a brief lapse during the Omride dynasty. Jehu, however, restored Israel to its charismatic nondynastic base with a vengeance, and it remained so to the end of Israel's history. The best Alt could say for charisma in Judah was that a ghost of the principle survived in the notion that divine legitimation was lent to the dynasty as a permanent possession.

The clear implications of Alt's studies are twofold: first, that kingship as such was a foreign aberration and wholly an invasion of Israel's self-conscious commitment to its authentic tribal league identity; second, that kingship in the north returned to the charismatic ideal whereas kingship in Judah continued in its radical departure from its constitutive roots.[2] These two theses have had a tremendous impact on scholarship over the last thirty years, not least because they were adopted and championed by the histories of Israel produced by both John Bright and Martin Noth. Furthermore, they have had a vital influence in the common tendency radically to divorce charisma from institution/office and to apply one to Israel and the other to Judah.

Though based on fundamentally different perspectives, the more contemporary studies of G. Mendenhall and N. Gottwald have yielded surprisingly similar results to those of Alt. As is well known, the "revolt model" of Israel's origins as advocated by Mendenhall and Gottwald also proposed a radical distinction between the tribal/ peasant constituency that comprised "Israel" and the urban monarchi-

---

[2] In the second study Alt allowed for the survival of "office charisma" in Judah ("Das Königtum," 132), but already in the first study made it clear that in the Judean system there was no longer any room for the charismatic principle ("Die Staatenbildung," 62).

cal city-states against whose repressive policies the peasants eventually revolted. With the peasant revolt came a thoroughgoing reorientation toward egalitarian social principles, convictions that were coordinate with the egalitarian principles of Yahwism. The subsequent introduction of monarchy in Israel, therefore, represented a radical reversion to Canaanite paganism, which was antithetical to Israel's egalitarian ethos.

The revolt model, similar to the model proposed by Alt, makes a decisive distinction between the form of organization that was genuinely Israelite and that which was a foreign imposition. Alt saw charisma as that which was identifiably Israelite, whereas Gottwald focused on an egalitarian social ethos as Israel's constitutive feature. Both, however, stressed the fact that kingship represented a radical departure from Israel's authentic and constitutive identity and an unfortunate encumbrance upon its historical aspirations. The primary concern of this chapter is to evaluate the broader issues raised by Alt and Gottwald with regard to the nature of kingship in Israel, particularly how it was authenticated, legitimated, and anchored in Israel's social world. Appraising the interplay of charisma and office first requires asking questions about the transition from pre-state to state forms of government in Israel. Second, we will consider the determining character of monarchy in Judah and Israel in order to establish what differences may have existed and why. Third, we will explore texts pertaining to the rise of Saul as paradigms for discerning charismatic and institutional impulses in Israel's monarchy. Finally, we will evaluate the role of the community in the process of charismatic endowment, attribution, and recognition.

From Judge to Monarch: The Question of Transition

The thesis proposed by Alt was that Davidic kingship represented a radical break with Israel's indigenous charismatic experience, represented by Saul, who ruled in the spirit of the judges. Alt's proposal met with some initial support, and Saul has often been regarded as not significantly more than a charismatic leader whose authority rested in the "ideal power of the Yahweh amphictyony,"[3] and whose rule was utterly nondynastic. David's authority, on the other hand, has often been viewed as based on the power of his private army and his personal conquests, his rule regarded as entirely dynastic, noncharismatic, and characteristically non-Israelite.

However, Alt's proposal has also met with resounding critique. Walter Beyerlin challenged Alt's thesis at two points. First, the type of "nebiistic" charisma exhibited by Saul was of an entirely different sort from that exhibited by the judges. Second, Saul's monarchy was most certainly understood to be dynastic, as is indicated by 1 Sam 13:13–14 and 20:31.[4] For Beyerlin, Saul already represented a fully monarchic form of charisma distinct from that of the judges. Similar objections were issued by G. Buccellati and, more recently, by T. Ishida, both of whom also insisted on the dynastic character of Saul's monarchy.[5] The question remains, however, what form the transition took from pre-state to state form of government. Did this dynastic character, whether attributable first to David, Solomon, or already to Saul, represent a fundamental break with premonarchic forms of leadership, or was it continuous with Israel's earlier experience? In other words, was the dynastic principle of monarchy fundamentally a foreign aberration, or, as argued already by A. Soggin, did it have its direct antecedents in the doctrine of the charismatic endowment of the judges?[6]

The desire has persisted to find in the progression from pre-state to state government a radical disruption setting kingship off from an earlier, more authentic form of government. Shmuel Abramski,

---

[3] Karl-Heinz Bernhardt, *Das Problem der altorientalischen Königsideologie im Alten Testament* (Leiden: E. J. Brill, 1961) 160–61. See also L. Schmidt, "König und Charisma im Alten Testament: Beobachtungen zur Struktur des Königtums im alten Israel," *KD* 23 (1982) 77–79. Where Schmidt principally differed from Alt was in placing the radical shift from personal charisma to office charisma not with David but first with Solomon, whose only legitimation was the will of his father.

[4] Walter Beyerlin, "Das Königscharisma bei Saul," *ZAW* 73 (1961) 187–88, 197.

[5] George Buccellati, *Cities and Nations of Ancient Syria: An Essay on Political Institutions with Special Reference to Israelite Kingdoms* (Rome: University of Rome, 1967) 195ff.; Tomoo Ishida, *The Royal Dynasties in Ancient Israel: A Study on the Formation and Development of Royal-Dynastic Ideology* (New York: Walter de Gruyter, 1977) 51–54.

[6] J. Alberto Soggin, "Charisma und Institution im Königtum Sauls," *ZAW* 75 (1963) 64.

for example, has followed Beyerlin in locating the rift between the judges and Saul.[7] Frank Crüsemann has followed Alt in finding the break between Saul and David, contrasting Saul as a *primus inter pares* of free egalitarian Israelites with David, whose base of power was located in his development of client relationships as well as in his status as foreign ruler over Israel.[8] W. Thiel and N. Gottwald have located the fracture between the reigns of David and Solomon, focusing on the differences regarding land tenure and tribal privileges. Whereas David respected the traditional Israelite system of land tenure[9] and the individual's status as a free agrarian,[10] Solomon made the essential move away from the old system. So Gottwald can speak of a "surge toward Solomonic triumphalism."[11]

The view that regards Israel's early history as comprising two or more radically discontinuous epochs, however, is not convincing. Based on insights gained from recent sociological studies, there has been a decisive movement away from a revolutionary model of Israel's origins, whether that of Albright, Alt, or Gottwald, toward what is regarded as an evolutionary model of Israel's state origins which sees the antecedents of monarchy already located deeply within the "period of the judges" itself.[12] On the basis of such a model, Robert

---

[7] Shmuel Abramski, "The Beginning of the Israelite Monarchy and Its Impact upon Leadership in Israel," *Immanuel* 19 (Winter 1984–85) 8.

[8] Frank Crüsemann, *Der Widerstand gegen das Königtum: Die antiköniglichen Texte des Alten Testaments und der Kampf um den frühen israelitischen Staat* (Neukirchen-Vluyn: Neukirchener Verlag, 1978) 212–14.

[9] Winfried Thiel, "Soziale Auswirkungen der Herrschaft Salomos," in *Charisma und Institution* ed. T. Rendtorff; Gütersloh: Gerd Mohn, 1985) 302, 310.

[10] Norman K. Gottwald, "The Participation of Free Agrarians in the Introduction of Monarchy to Ancient Israel: An Application of H. A. Landsberger's Framework for the Analysis of Peasant Movements," *Semeia* 37 (1986) 82–83.

[11] Ibid., 92.

[12] Crüsemann seems to have been the first to apply such insights (*Der Widerstand gegen das Königtum*, 201–17). Though he still sought to distinguish between strictly discrete stages in the emergence of state, he freely drew upon studies by E. Durkheim, M. Fortes, E. Evans-Pritchard, and C. Sigrist in distinguishing between the premonarchic period, which he identified as a "segmentary society" (i.e., an acephalous tribal society characterized by the "fission" and "fusion" of its segments), and the monarchy of David, which he identified as a "segmentary state."
The distinction between separate "Gideon" and "Jerubbaal" traditions, proposed by Barnabas Lindars simply indicates the difficulty ("Gideon and Kingship," *JTS* 16 [1965] 315–26). For a dynastic assessment of Gideon's rulership, see Ishida, *Royal*

Coote and Keith Whitelam have challenged the common assumption made by the "revolutionary" model that the monarchy was a foreign aberration in Israel's political life.[13] Quite the contrary, the monarchy "is fundamentally determined by the nature of the origins of Israel in the hill country and is the result of internal stimuli in response to social and environmental circumscription."[14] In other words, the monarchy was a product of Israel's own inherent impulses, given the peculiarities of its specific economic and social condition. Similarly, Frank Frick campaigned against the "abrupt mechanical" explanation of the origins of Israel's monarchy, insisting that it resulted from internal processes of cultural change in response to Israel's distinctive environmental situation.[15] Kingship developed not simply as an ironic imitation of the Canaanite city-state (so Gottwald) but rather in relation to Israel's own environment.[16] Finally, James Flanagan has also argued that Israel's state formation resulted from the gradual evolution (with occasional devolution) from segmentary system through the chiefdoms of Saul and the early David to an early form of state with the later David and Solomon.[17]

Significant for our purposes is the consensus that these studies have reached concerning two specific issues: first, the assumed egalitarian nature of Israel's pre-state society; and, second, the often-accepted notion of the foreign origins of Israel's kingship. The popular notion

---

Dynasties, 2. For a consideration of Abimelek's kingship, see also Baruch Halpern, "The Rise of Abimelek Ben-Jerubbaal," *HAR* 2 (1978) 79–110.

[13] Robert B. Coote and Keith W. Whitelam, "The Emergence of Israel: Social Transformation and State Formation following the Decline in Late Bronze Age Trade," *Semeia* 37 (1986) 107–47; more fully developed in Robert B. Coote and Keith W. Whitelam, *The Emergence of Early Israel in Historical Perspective* (Sheffield: Almond, 1987). See already Keith W. Whitelam, *The Just King: Monarchical Judicial Authority in Ancient Israel* (Sheffield: JSOT Press, 1979) 72, in which he argued that the difference between Saul's rule and rule in the premonarchic period was simply one of degree. Saul sowed the seeds that were brought to fruition in the reigns of David and Solomon.

[14] Coote and Whitelam, "Emergence of Israel," 130–31; Coote and Whitelam, *Emergence of Early Israel*, 139–49.

[15] Frank S. Frick, "Social Scientific Methods and Theories of Significance for the Study of the Israelite Monarchy: A Critical Review Essay," *Semeia* 37 (1986) 19, 23, 25, 29.

[16] Frank S. Frick, *The Formation of the State in Ancient Israel: A Survey of Models and Theories* (Sheffield: Almond, 1985) 196.

[17] James W. Flanagan, "Chiefs in Israel," *JSOT* 20 (1981) 47–73; idem, *David's Social Drama: A Hologram of Israel's Early Iron Age* (Sheffield: Almond, 1988) 291, 304.

is that pre-state Israel, as a segmentary society, possessed social structures that were acephalous and egalitarian.[18] It has also commonly
been assumed that this native Israelite egalitarianism, expressed fundamentally in its land-tenure system, collided with an antithetical
system of prebendal retainerships common among the Canaanites
with their highly stratified class society, resulting in the perversion
of the former with the adoption of the latter by Israel's monarchs.[19]

That segmentary societies are by definition egalitarian, however,
has come under considerable critical attack. At most it can be said
that segmentary societies are overlaid with a patina of egalitarian
rhetoric but in fact exhibit the characteristics both of hierarchy and
of class differentiation.[20] To the extent that segmentary societies do
happen to exhibit characteristics of egalitarianism, any such characteristics are as easily attributable to other factors such as environment
and ecology.[21] In fact, it is hardly deniable that social stratification
was inherent in Israel during the pre-state period and in principle
goes back to its very origins.[22] To speak of pre-state Israel as egalitarian, therefore, reflects ethnocentrist Western notions of what
constitutes leadership[23] and cannot be sustained by the evidence
present in the texts themselves.

Nor is the notion of kingship as a foreign imposition forced upon
Israel by external threat regarded as satisfying in the current debate.
The thesis that kingship was a "consolation prize" that Israel was
forced to accept because of the breakdown of the tribal arrangement
in the face of the Philistine threat[24] has been resoundingly dismissed

---

[18] Crüsemann, *Der Widerstand gegen das Königtum,* 209. According to this view,
Israel's self-conscious egalitarianism was accompanied by a classless economy.

[19] E.g., Thiel, "Soziale Auswirkungen der Herrschaft Salomos," 302–3; Marvin L.
Chaney, "Systemic Study of the Israelite Monarchy," *Semeia* 37 (1986) 61, 68–70.

[20] N. P. Lemche, *Early Israel: Anthropological and Historical Studies on the Israelite
Society Before the Monarchy* (Leiden: E. J. Brill, 1985) 223; Flanagan, *David's Social
Drama,* 281. See especially the critique by J. W. Rogerson, "Was Early Israel a
Segmentary Society?" *JSOT* 36 (1986) 17–26, who asks whether the label "segmentary
society" can even be applied to Israel.

[21] David Fiensy, "Using the Nuer Culture of Africa in Understanding the Old
Testament: An Evaluation," *JSOT* 38 (1987) 77–79.

[22] Coote and Whitelam, "Emergence of Israel," 138. Note their distinction between
bandits, nomads, peasants, and urban elite in *Emergence of Early Israel,* 90–114.

[23] Fiensy, "Using the Nuer Culture," 77–78.

[24] E.g., Crüsemann, *Der Widerstand gegen das Königtum,* 212; Gottwald, "Participa-

by Frick, Coote and Whitelam, and Finkelstein, all of whom stress the multifaceted reasons that contributed to the origins of the state in Israel.[25] Rejecting the supposed Philistine threat as the "prime mover" of Israelite statecraft, all three authors focus instead on economic aspects of the agricultural and trade base of ancient Palestine. They argue in unison that a centralized state emerged in response to the needs for agricultural specialization in the face of social and environmental circumscription. Whether this economic crisis was brought on by a simple need and desire to maximize and extend the capabilities of the labor supply,[26] by a general collapse of trade in the eastern Mediterranean,[27] or more directly by the particular topographical features of Palestinian soil,[28] the end result is the proposal of a radically new model for Israelite state origins.

This model, which is adopted here, is one that regards kingship not as something foreign and inimically antithetical to a supposed pristine Israelite charismatic/egalitarian ideal, but rather considers the monarchy to have emerged from economic and social forces welling up from within Israel's own constitutive identity. The very same socioeconomic forces that essentially gave rise to Israel itself also eventuated in the rise of Israel's monarchy. The two were not generated by conflicted and competing forces, as is so often assumed. Israel's emergence, then, is to be understood as the coherent and gradual evolution of a state under the pressure of social and economic forces, a state that developed consistent to and in tandem with the peculiarities of Israel's specific ecological setting. Gone are the Philistines as the singular cause of Israel's kingship. The peasant's revolt, too, though a historical possibility, cannot be regarded as generative of Israel's national identity.

---

tion of Free Agrarians," 80, 88; Cris Hauer, Jr., "From Alt to Anthropology: The Rise of the Israelite State," *JSOT* 36 (1986) 9–10.

[25] Frick, "Social Scientific Methods," 23; idem, *Formation of the State,* 26, 180–81; Coote and Whitelam, "Emergence of Israel," 125–31; idem, *Emergence of Early Israel,* 139–43; Israel Finkelstein, "The Emergence of the Monarchy in Israel: The Environmental and Socio-Economic Aspects," *JSOT* 44 (1989) 43–74.

[26] Frick, *Formation of the State,* 197–202.

[27] Coote and Whitelam, "Emergence of Israel," 116; idem, *Emergence of Early Israel,* 129.

[28] Finkelstein, "Emergence of the Monarchy," 58–60.

Most importantly, gone too is the distinction between a charismatic/egalitarian impulse constitutive of pre-state Israel and an institutionalized, bureaucratized and canaanized monarchy standing over against it. In fact, the ideology undergirding kingship reinforced the very charismatic nature of the monarchy itself. As the theoretical focal point of the administration of justice in Israel,[29] the king was the symbolic point of integration with the transcendent moral order of the universe. The king symbolized the fundamental centering principles and values expressive of Israel's view of social reality, that "vital layer" at the center of its corporate existence. He mythically represented (and some would insist that he theoretically maintained) the very principles of cosmic coherence and cohesiveness. It was this perceived social function that constituted the basis for the attribution of royal charisma.

Charisma and Institution
in Jerusalem and Samaria

The preceding discussion was directed to Alt's thesis that the rise of monarchy in Israel perverted an indigenous Israelite impulse toward charisma. The task now is to consider Alt's second thesis—that kingship in the north reverted back to the principle of charismatic leadership, thereby constituting an essentially different type of kingship from that evidenced in Judah. As mentioned above, Alt's thesis has found broad support because of its being championed by the popular histories of Bright and Noth, and generations of students of the Bible have cut their theological teeth on the distinction between monarchy in the north, faithful to Israel's charismatic instincts, and kingship in the south, thoroughly paganized and institutionalized.

Alt's thesis has often been reapplied in creative fashion, building on the distinction between Israelite "personal charisma" and Judean "office charisma"[30] or between a more faithful and conservative

---

[29] Of course the "ideal symbolization" of such charismatic attribution would often have been contradicted by common experience. Nevertheless, the ideal was never wholly discontinuous with popular expectations or actual experience. See Whitelam, *Just King,* 37, 119, 136, 219.

[30] Schmidt, "König und Charisma im Alten Testament," 73–87. Schmidt regarded

manifestation of monarchy in the north and a more innovative and less traditional manifestation in the south.[31] Here again, however, convincing arguments have been leveled against Alt's thesis, so that the drawing of any qualitative distinction between kingship in Judah and in Israel seems out of the question. T. C. G. Thornton rightly insisted that "charismatic" kingship in Israel cannot be contrasted to "dynastic" kingship in Judah since kingship in Israel was every bit as dynastic in intent as that of its southern neighbor. In fact, Thornton pointed out, all of Alt's supposed "charismatic" kings were the founders of dynasties, even if short-lived. Ahijah himself promised Jeroboam a dynasty which he only later retracted, and Jehu too was pledged a dynasty of four generations. Furthermore, the very fact that successful usurpers would kill the remaining children of the former king attests to their awareness of the powerful dynastic claims that were expected to be made and possibly accepted by a willing populace.[32] Alt's rationalization that such murder simply "lay in the nature of things" is uncritical and verges on the macabre.[33] To follow Alt's theory would be to excuse the chaos, anarchy, and murder caused by dynastic instability in Israel as divinely willed, when in fact such instability was viewed as a manifestation of human sin.[34]

A related question has been why there was such dynastic instability in the north as opposed to the stability of the Davidic dynasty. Alt and those who have followed him attributed dynastic stability in

---

"personal charisma" as an endowment already evidenced prior to a person's becoming king, which the one endowed had for life, at which point it lapsed. "Office charisma," however, was bequeathed during the act of anointing. Schmidt presents confused arguments, however, on whether such charisma could or could not be inherited. Though suggesting it could not be inherited (p. 80), he nevertheless speaks elsewhere of an "inherited charisma" (pp. 76, 82).

[31] Flanagan unconvincingly argues that "chieftaincy" survived longer in the north because of innate northern conservatism (*David's Social Drama*, 304). Whereas Judah had already begun referring to David as a king, in Israel he was still regarded as a chieftain.

[32] T. C. G. Thornton, "Charismatic Kingship," *JTS* 14 (1963) 1–11. The basic critique is followed also by G. W. Ahlström, "Solomon, the Chosen One," *HR* 8 (1968–69) 93–110; Buccellati, *Cities and Nations*, 195ff.; Ishida, *Royal Dynasties*.

[33] Alt, "Das Königtum," 121.

[34] The prophet Hosea (Hos 8:4), who provides the most direct perspective on northern concepts of Israel's dynastic chaos, clearly attributes it to the sin of the people, not to divine plan or to national ideology.

Judah to the loss of the traditional charismatic principle. The new concept of "charisma of office" rendered the Judean king untouchable.[35] Such a theory immediately flounders, however, given the clear indication that already Saul was considered untouchable by no one less than David himself (1 Sam 24:6, 10; 26:9; 2 Sam 1:14–16). Rather than attributing dynastic instability in Israel to the persistence of the doctrine of charismatic leadership, it is much more likely that such instability was due to a number of other factors, including the extreme intertribal competition suffered by Israel; the lack of focus on one central site for both cultic and political matters; the immediate proximity and involvement of Israel in international struggles; better agricultural land, which could sustain a larger and more diverse population and a more interactive economy; and the lack of opportunity and sheer breathing room for the full development of a "dynastic mystique."[36]

Every indication is that Saul's monarchy was every bit as dynastic in principle and intention as that of David, and that it was so understood not only by Saul himself (1 Sam 20:31) but also by Abner, his general (2 Sam 2:8–9), and by the Deuteronomistic historian, who recognized the legitimacy of Ishbaal's succession with a full regnal formula (2 Sam 2:10). Only by assuming the accepted principle of dynastic succession can one intelligibly understand the narrative of David's treatment of Jonathan's son Mephibosheth, a possible claimant to the throne of his grandfather. Following the deaths of Saul and Jonathan in warfare and of Ishbaal by circumstances from which David took his usual pains to distance himself (2 Sam 4:1–12), David summoned Jonathan's son Mephibosheth to Jerusalem, so the text purports, in order to show him kindness for the sake of his father (2 Sam 9:1–8). One can only surmise that David also intended to keep Mephibosheth under close surveillance. That the Saulides continued to harbor dynastic ambitions, and that David continued to perceive such aspirations as a constant threat, is clear from David's reaction to Mephibosheth's rumored plot to regain his grandfather's throne (16:3; 19:26–30). As soon as the opportunity conveniently

---

[35] Schmidt, "König und Charisma im Alten Testament," 84.
[36] Thornton, "Charismatic Kingship," 9–11; Ishida, *Royal Dynasties*, 171–79.

presented itself David disposed of the remaining Saulides – including the most direct claimant, Mephibosheth himself.[37]

Nor did kingship in Israel following the revolt of Jeroboam revert to some imagined pristine form of charismatic designation. Alt contended that the two-year reigns of Nadab and Elah simply represented the expected pause following the death of the charismatic leader until a proper charismatic successor could be designated by Yahweh.[38] Such reasoning shatters on the fact that the descendants of Jehu, who according to Alt reconstituted the charismatic monarchy, ruled for approximately seventy years, somewhat long for such an interregnum. Those who argue that Omri's kingship was a reversion to dynastic monarchy cite as evidence the fact that, whereas charismatic kingship functioned with no fixed location or bureaucratic administration, Omri copied David's strategy by acquiring his own city, Samaria, and by outfitting it with all the normal trappings of dynastic rule.[39] The problem with this argument is that it overlooks the simple fact that Omri first ruled in the old capital of Tirzah for six of his twelve years before moving the capital to Samaria. Are we to assume, therefore, that his rule somehow became dynastic only after his move to Samaria? And why is it that Samaria was maintained as the administrative center of Israel throughout the period of the supposed charismatic kings following Jehu's revolt? Besides Omri's connection to Samaria, a connection that was thoroughly maintained by Jehu, the argument concerning the dynastic nature of Omri's reign

[37] Though 21:7 continues the fiction of David's kindness to Mephibosheth, in 21:8 Mephibosheth is directly listed among those handed over by David to the Gibeonites. The difficulty is that the *mĕpibōšet* mentioned in 21:8 is listed as the son of Saul and his concubine Rizpah, whereas the *mĕpibōšet* of 21:7 is presented as the son of Jonathan, in agreement with the broader narrative. The two are most likely the same, however. The remark in v. 8 reflects an annalistic note that presents a different genealogy, and the note in v. 7 reflects the later narrative intent to tie the material back to the theme of David's covenant with Jonathan (1 Sam 20:15–16; 2 Sam 9:1–13). Much depends on who Jonathan's mother was. If it was Ahinoam (1 Sam 14:50), then Mephibosheth's relationship to Rizpah would be difficult to explain. If, however, Jonathan's mother was Rizpah herself, then the tension in 2 Sam 21:7–8 is minimized. If so, Rizpah was both the mother of Ishbaal (accounting for Ishbaal's strong reaction to Abner's rumored usurpation of the harem in 3:7) and the grandmother of Mephibosheth.

[38] Alt, "Das Königtum," 121.

[39] Ibid., 123.

is also based on the fact that he did not receive prophetic/divine legitimation as the "charismatic" Jehu did. However, apart from Jeroboam, none of the other supposed charismatic kings received such prophetic legitimation, so its absence can hardly serve as evidence for what does or does not constitute charismatic appointment. The fact that Alt would have considered Omri dynastic and Jehu charismatic is extremely arbitrary and led to the fact that Bernhardt considered Jehu to be no less dynastic than Omri.[40]

There is no convincing reason to consider monarchy in the north to have been essentially different ideologically from that in Judah. If there was a difference, it was one of degree. Furthermore, such differences were due not to any underlying divergence in ideology but rather to the specific and peculiar situation in which the kings of Israel and Judah found themselves. Thus, any severing of charismatic from dynastic principle as manifest in the monarchies of Israel and Judah is to be rejected. Below we will consider more fully the relationship of divine and popular legitimation of the king. Before proceeding to that stage, however, several texts will be considered that bear on the nature of the problem in relation to the rise of Saul.

The Rise of Saul: Narrative Models of Empowerment

To insist, as have many, that Saul's charismatic empowerment was directly expressive of the charisma of the premonarchic judges overlooks the obvious fact that the cycle of narratives relating the selection of Saul in 1 Sam 9:1–11:15 presents a highly variegated portrait of Saul's charismatic endowment. These narratives concerning the rise of Saul to the monarchy provide an important source for discussing the popular conception of royal charismatic empowerment.

Though there have been attempts to reconstruct an original sequence of events leading to Saul's enthronement,[41] most have been

---

[40] Bernhardt, *Das Problem der altorientalischen Königsideologie,* 171.

[41] See the complicated rearrangement of the units required by J. Maxwell Miller, "Saul's Rise to Power: Some Observations Concerning 1 Sam 9:1–10:16; 10:26–11:15 and 13:2–14:46," *CBQ* 36 (1974) 172.

content to assume that one or another of the narrative traditions represented in the material constitutes an earlier and/or more reliable basis for historical reconstruction. It is most frequently argued that the narrative of Saul's deliverance of Jabesh (1 Sam 11:1–15) comes closest to providing an actual historical basis for Saul's rise.[42] Such an assumption, however, is usually based on an ideological desire to maintain the connection of Saul's charisma with that of the judges, since in this narrative Saul is most closely credited with a "judge-type" charisma. Our study has clearly demonstrated that for a number of reasons the conception of such a charisma is purely a literary and theological device. In fact none of the traditions reflected in 1 Sam 9:1–11:15 can serve as a historical source for reconstructing the actual advent of monarchy in Israel.[43] They can, however, serve to inform us of how the issue of charisma and legitimation was understood by those who produced and consumed such literature, and for our purposes that is a more crucial issue than is the question of historical fact.

1 Sam 11:1–15:
Saul as Successor to the Judges

A quick overview of the material suggests that there are several originally independent traditions reflected in 1 Sam 9:1–11:15, although the point has been heatedly debated. T. Veijola, for example, argued that the entire complex of material developed as one piece in a tradition historical process and was not created by combining originally independent narrative units. Crüsemann likewise maintained that the complex as a whole was already closely interwoven at a fairly early stage, with the exception of the story of the selection by lots (10:17–21).[44] Veijola and Crüsemann are virtually alone

---

[42] E.g., A. D. H. Mayes, "The Rise of the Israelite Monarchy," *ZAW* 90 (1978) 18; Tryggve N. D. Mettinger, *King and Messiah: The Civil and Sacral Legitimation of the Israelite King* (Lund: Gleerup, 1976) 87. For discussion, see Volkmar Fritz, "Die Deutung des Königtums Sauls in den Überlieferungen von seiner Entstehung 1 Sam 9–11," *ZAW* 88 (1976) 357–58.

[43] Clearly stated, e.g., by Fritz, "Die Deutung des Königtums Sauls," 361. Diana Edelman, too, considers the material a "literary fiction," though she attempts to reconstruct an underlying historical sequence ("Saul's Rescue of Jabesh-Gilead [1 Sam 11:1–11]: Sorting Story from History," *ZAW* 96 [1984] 203–7, 209).

[44] Timo Veijola, *Das Königtum in der Beurteilung der Deuteronomistischen Historiographie: Eine redaktionsgeschichtliche Untersuchung* (Helsinki: Suomalainen

in this conviction, however, and since the days of Wellhausen there has been a nearly unanimous distinction drawn between the story of Saul's search for the asses, which led to his anointing (1 Sam 9:1–10:16), generally regarded as early and promonarchical, and the story of Saul's designation by lots and the Jabeshite campaign (1 Sam 10:17–11:15), a continuation of the narrative in 8:1–22, generally considered to be late and antimonarchical.[45]

A further question, however, has been whether or not the tradition of the Jabeshite campaign in 11:1–15 is part of one of the two major tradition complexes or whether it forms a third independent narrative strand. Some, following Wellhausen, have connected 11:1–15 to 9:1–10:16 as part of the early source, especially because of their common focus on spirit empowerment.[46] Others have taken 11:1–15 to form a unit with 10:17–27, principally out of a desire to understand the peculiar nature and relationship of 10:26–27 and 11:12–13.[47] Increasingly, however, 11:1–15 has been understood to represent a third independent tradition relating to the rise of Saul, one that reflects a different perspective on the nature of the charisma with which he was endowed.[48]

Several details support the conclusion that the story of Saul's elevation to kingship following the Jabeshite campaign was indeed an independent unit that was taken up in later redaction to complement the fuller narrative cycle. The story of Saul's Jabeshite rescue

Tiedeakatemia, 1977) 39–40; Crüsemann, *Der Widerstand gegen das Königtum,* 55–58.

[45] Though how late and how antimonarchical are debated. Wellhausen considered the material in 10:17–27 to be Elohistic. Noth, however, argued that it was first the dtr historian who articulated such an antimonarchical position so clearly. For a review, see Mayes, "Rise of the Israelite Monarchy," 4–6.

[46] For fuller discussion of the issue, see Bruce C. Birch, *The Rise of the Israelite Monarchy: The Growth and Development of 1 Samuel 7-15* (Missoula, MT: Scholars Press, 1976) 54.

[47] Baruch Halpern argues form-critically on the basis of a supposed two-part pattern of royal designation and confirmation (*The Constitution of the Monarchy in Israel* [Chico, CA: Scholars Press, 1981] 154–55); also Walter Dietrich, *David, Saul und die Propheten: Das Verhältnis von Religion und Politik nach den prophetischen Überlieferungen vom frühesten Königtum in Israel* (Stuttgart: W. Kohlhammer, 1987) 106, 145–46.

[48] Birch, *Rise of the Israelite Monarchy,* 58–59; Fritz, "Die Deutungen des Königtums Sauls," 359; Ishida, *Royal Dynasties,* 48–49; Mayes, "Rise of the Israelite Monarchy," 15–16; Mettinger, *King and Messiah,* 87; Miller, "Saul's Rise to Power," 171; Soggin, "Charisma und Institution im Königtum Sauls," 58, 61.

cannot likely have been a constituent part of the narrative in 9:1–10:16 since, at least in its present form, the latter presupposes its continuation in 13:7b. The chronology of the present text betrays such editorial activity. In 10:8 Samuel instructs Saul to proceed to Gilgal to wait for seven days. In 11:4–5, however, Saul is found at his home in Gibeah plowing as though nothing had happened. Only after the Jabeshite campaign does he proceed to Gilgal (11:14–15), but not *before* Samuel, and not for the seven-day wait. The actual compliance report to Samuel's command in 10:8 to go to Gilgal and wait for seven days is postponed until 13:7b, following not only the Jabeshite campaign itself but also Samuel's farewell address (12:1–25) and Jonathan's defeat of the Philistine garrison at Geba (13:3). The redundancy of Saul's trips to Gilgal, plus the delay of the compliance report in 13:7b–8, makes any connection between 9:1–10:16 and 11:1–15 extremely unlikely.[49]

It is equally unlikely that 11:1–15 was organically connected to the story of the selection by lots in 10:17–27, since the people respond to Nahash's threat in 11:2–3 as though totally unaware of what had transpired in 10:20–24. The ignorance of the Jabeshites themselves might be overlooked, particularly if they were foreigners.[50] However, the even more extreme reaction of Saul's fellow Gibeahites in 11:4–5 is completely unintelligible had the narrative presupposed Saul's elevation before all Israel already in 10:24. Only by assuming that there was as yet no obvious candidate for the job of liberating Jabesh does their reaction make sense. The report of the rescue of Jabesh-gilead is an independent tradition that bears its own depiction of the "charismatic" appointment of Saul.

As noted above, the narrative of Saul's rescue of Jabesh-gilead has frequently been accepted as the earliest available tradition concerning the rise of monarchy in Israel, and thus a reliable source for historical reconstruction. It must be insisted, however, that the text is engaged in a significant theological interpretation rather than a historical appraisal. The charismatic endowment portrayed in 11:1–15 clearly seeks to establish Saul's continuity with the charisma of Israel's

---

[49] This is particularly true if the Septuagint correctly preserved the note at 11:1 that the Jabesh campaign occurred "about a month later," a datum that cannot be correlated with Saul's seven-day wait.

[50] As proposed by Edelman, "Saul's Rescue of Jabesh-Gilead," 202–3.

premonarchic leaders.[51] Kingship *as such*, and not simply the kingship of Saul, is regarded as the logical and ultimate expression of the imagined leadership of the premonarchic period. The narrative conforms so closely with the tradition of Gideon that they must reflect the same perspective on leadership. Gideon too was engaged in his normal agricultural livelihood when he was commissioned to deliver Israel from the Midianites (Judg 6:11–16), was possessed by the spirit (6:34), summoned the militia by sending messengers throughout the land (6:35), defeated the enemy, and as a result of a stunning victory was offered the throne (8:22). The narrative of Saul's relief of Jabesh may well have circulated along with the tradition of Gideon in order to establish a progression from kingship legitimately and rightly refused (Judg 8:23) to kingship legitimately and rightly accepted (1 Sam 11:15). In spite of the role of the populous in v. 15 the focus of the story is not on the role of the assembly in promoting or confirming Saul as king but rather is on the divine empowerment of the leader who is charismatically equipped as a deliverer of his people.[52] Such expectations fed into the general ideological pool pertaining to kingship, and the king was regarded as the community's defender and deliverer, empowered by the spirit of God to wage its battles. It may be Yahweh who has "wrought deliverance in Israel" (11:13), but it is the king, charismatically supercharged by Yahweh's own spirit, through whom Yahweh's deliverance is effected (11:3).[53]

[51] The unity of 11:1–15 itself is debated. Many argue that vv. 12–14 (or even v. 15) are later additions to bridge the story with the note in 10:26b–27. The issue, however, is not significant for our purposes. For discussion, see Birch, *Rise of the Israelite Monarchy*, 59–60; Fritz, "Die Deutungen des Königtums Sauls," 357; Mayes, "Rise of the Israelite Monarchy," 15–16; Miller argues that 10:26b–27 was already part of the Jabesh story ("Saul's Rise to Power," 165–70).

[52] Contra those who see in 11:1–15 an emphasis on election of the king by the popular assembly, e.g., Ishida, *Royal Dynasties*, 48; Mettinger, *King and Messiah*, 111.

[53] See 1 Sam 19:5; 2 Sam 3:18; 2 Kgs 14:27. The king is specifically viewed as the "deliverer" both of the nation (1 Sam 23:2–5; Ps 18:50; 144:10) and of the individual (2 Sam 14:4; 2 Kgs 6:26). Even the prophetic reproach in Hos 13:10 reflects the theoretical ideal of king as "savior."

1 Sam 9:1–10:16:
Saul and the Spirit of Prophecy _____

The story of Saul's anointing by Samuel (10:1–13) illustrates an entirely different perception of charismatic empowerment from that of the narrative just discussed, although again there has been considerable debate on the matter. Mettinger has rejected any distinction between the type of "shophetic" charisma represented in 11:1–15 and the "nebiistic" charisma reflected in 10:1–13. The crucial question is whether the effect of Saul's charismatic endowment is to be seen principally in his prophetic outburst (10:10) or whether the charisma has some broader goal in view, as claimed by Mettinger. Since this point is fundamental for understanding the nature of the charismatic endowment in the story, the issues involved must be discussed in some detail.

Mettinger argued that, because 10:5 refers to the Philistine *nĕṣîb* (garrison, outpost, administrative center?) and 10:8 refers to Saul proceeding to Gilgal for a seven-day wait, the command in 10:7 to "do whatever you see fit to do"–and the *real goal* of Saul's charismatic endowment–relates to the pending battle with the Philistines in 13:2–14, which likewise mentions the Philistine *nĕṣîb* and Saul's seven-day wait. Thus, the promised charisma of 10:6–7 cannot simply be reduced to the prophetic outburst of 10:10. Like the charisma of 11:1–15, it equips Saul for eventual battle. The two types of charisma illustrated in these narratives, argued Mettinger, are therefore the same.[54]

Of course the fact that it is Jonathan who defeats the *nĕṣîb* in 13:3, that the *nĕṣîb* is located in Geba rather than Gibeah, and that the *nĕṣîbê* are plural in 10:5 but singular in 13:3, forces any such interpretation into a frenzy of reconstruction. The crucial issue, however, is whether Saul's being equipped for battle against the Philistines at Gilgal in 13:3–15 relates directly to the spirit empowerment reported in 10:10 as a "shophetic" type of charisma, as suggested by Mettinger, or whether the charismatic endowment of 10:10 is limited to Saul's experience at Gibeath-elohim.

Mettinger's proposal is doubtful for at least three reasons. First,

---

[54] Mettinger, *King and Messiah*, 236.

any connection between Saul's charismatic endowment in 10:10 and his being equipped for battle, as suggested by Mettinger, depends on taking the phrase "do whatever you see fit to do" in 10:7 as relating to the subsequent events at Gilgal, alluded to in 10:8. However, the phrase *'ăśēh lĕkā 'ăšer timṣā' yādekā* in 10:7 may mean nothing more than "you will be able to do whatever you want."[55] Or likewise it may refer to some event following immediately on the report of the signs in 10:9–13. What this event might be depends on the problematic reading in 10:13. The Masoretic Text reports that Saul went to the "high place" (*habbāmâ*), allowing the possibility that some otherwise unreported event took place there. The Septuagint reports that Saul went to the "hill" (*bounos*), the same designation used for Gibeath-elohim in 10:5 and 10, suggesting an original reading of *haggib'ātâ*, referring to the city (*'îr*, v. 5b) nearby. Some commentators suggest that Saul went to his "home" (*habbaytâ*), preparing for the exchange with his uncle which follows. If the latter is the case, perhaps the phrase "do whatever your hand finds to do" anticipates Saul returning in total silence and doing *nothing*. In any case, it is unclear that the command in 10:7 relates to the events reported only in 13:3–15.

Second, if Saul's charismatic endowment near Gibeah is a "shophetic" type equipping him to "deliver" Israel, it is indeed a strange case, since Saul delivers nothing at Gilgal in 13:3–15. He only manages to fall from Samuel's good graces. Accordingly, if the charismatic endowment near Gibeah is related to Saul's action at Gilgal, it could only be the *antithesis* of a shophetic type of charismatic appointment.

Third, and most significant, the narrative in 10:1–13 clearly depicts the charismatic endowment in 10:6 and 10 as being but a feature of one of the three "signs" by which Saul will know that he is the anointed ruler. The three signs transpire at Rachel's tomb (10:2), the oak of Tabor (10:3–4), and Gibeath-elohim (10:5–6). The aspect of spirit of endowment reported in 10:10 is limited to the third of these signs. When 10:9 reports that "all these signs were fulfilled that very day" (*wayyābō'û kol-hā'ōtōt hā'ēlleh bayyôm hahû'*), we can only

---

[55] Furthermore, were the phrase in 10:7 to relate to the similar phrase in 10:8bβ, one would expect 10:8bβ to read *wĕhôdaʿtî 'ēt 'ăšer taʿăśeh lĕkā* rather than *wĕhôdaʿtî lĕkā 'ēt 'ăšer taʿăśeh*.

assume that the spirit empowerment was a temporary phenomenon that had no effect after the prophetic frenzy, which ceased in 10:13. No aspect of these signs looks any further ahead than to the conclusion of Saul's experience at Gibeath-elohim.

Furthermore, there is a clear distinction to be made between the spirit empowerment, which leads directly to the subsequent prophetic ecstasy (vv. 6, 10), and the mighty act itself (v. 7), which is clearly not part of the sign but is rather subsequent to it. The charismatic prophetic outburst was itself one of the *signs*, which were limited to "that very day" (v. 9). Even if Mettinger were right about the mighty act referring to the Philistine battle, this could not overcome the clear chasm that is invariably fixed between a "sign," which is a self-sufficient element in such narratives, and its referent. It seems unlikely, therefore, that Saul's spirit empowerment could originally have been connected with the battle report in 13:3-15. The charismatic prophetic outburst was itself but one of the *signs*, which were limited to "that very day."

The fact that we have here to do with a "sign" is the key to understanding the nature of the charisma attributed to Saul in 10:1-13. It is this fact above all else that sets this form of empowerment off from the shophetic charisma recorded in 11:1-15. The empowerment attributed to the judges and to Saul in 11:1-15 is nowhere understood to be a sign that points to some more significant fact. The charisma of the judges and of Saul in 11:1-15, though always of a temporary nature, has no referent in view other than its own effectiveness. It is the momentary energizing of the savior to effect the deliverance of the people within the framework of a specific crisis. In 10:1-13, however, the charismatic endowment, though again temporary, is not an end in itself. It is simply a sign that attests to a more comprehensive endowment, namely, the fact that God is perpetually with Saul in a particularly significant way, which sets him apart from all others (10:7).

The depiction of charismatic empowerment described here has its closest analogue in the story of the seventy elders who "prophesy" in Num 11:25. There too, as was argued above,[56] the prophetic ecstasy did not convey a prophetic charisma as such. In both cases it vanished

---

[56] See chapter 2 above.

as quickly as it had appeared. Rather it served to signify the perpetual leadership of the one so endowed. Though momentary, it was the public demonstration of the legitimation and divine consecration of Israel's leaders.[57]

1 Sam 10:17–27:
Saul and Divine Providence

A third, and again distinct, tradition regarding Saul's elevation to kingship is recorded in 1 Sam 10:17–27. In this tradition Saul the Matrite[58] is selected to be Israel's king by a procedure using lots. It has long been generally accepted that the story originally resumed the narrative cycle that left off in 8:22. What has been of more debate is whether or not the story of the selection by lots is unitive or was made up of two separate traditions—one concerning the selection by lots itself (10:20–21bα) and a second concerning the securing of a verbal oracle regarding the stature and whereabouts of the one selected (vv. 21bβ–24). Many have followed O. Eissfeldt in distinguishing between two such sources,[59] principally on three grounds. First, the lot procedure absolutely requires the presence of Saul, yet he is absent from the gathering. Second, the reference in 10:22 to "inquiring again" presupposes not only a different form of divination from that of casting lots but also suggests that there had already been one such request for a verbal oracle which has been displaced by the subsequent connection of the oracle story with the story of the lots.[60] Third, the question in 10:22, "has any other man come by here?" (contra NRSV; cf. Hebrew *hăbā' 'ôd hălōm 'îš*), suggests

---

[57] In spite of the fact that the use of *nibbā'* (*niphal*) and *hitnabbē'* (*hiphil*) can often have negative connotations, Beyerlin's contention ("Das Königscharisma be Saul," 192) that the form of nebiistic ecstasy evidenced here together with the manner of authority it connotes is "non-Israelite" is to be firmly rejected.

[58] Note the conflict with the genealogical information provided in 9:1, which makes no reference to Matri, supporting the conclusion that an independent narrative tradition is presented in 10:17–27.

[59] Otto Eissfeldt, *Die Composition der Samuelisbücher* (Leipzig: J. C. Hinrichs, 1931) 7. For opposed positions, see Mettinger, *King and Messiah*, 180–81; Ishida, *Royal Dynasties*, 45.

[60] This general solution is proposed, e.g., by Birch, *Rise of the Israelite Monarchy*, 42–47.

an aborted initial search. The text was altered by the LXX to read "Did the man come this way?" (*ei erchetai ho anēr entautha*) in order smooth over the conflict, but the MT is to be maintained.[61] Modern commentators who distinguish between two such sources have generally proposed that the story of Saul's selection by oracle, in which God revealed that the one who was tallest would be king, was the older tradition and was reworked by the Deuteronomistic editor to produce a story of selection by a lot procedure.[62]

Such efforts to discriminate between two separate traditions in this text are perhaps overly zealous. The major difficulty is assumed to be Saul's absence from the lot procedure. However, if we choose to abide by the MT, which seems to be more difficult to understand than the LXX, what is surprising is the lack of any reference in 10:21 to the family of the Matrites being brought near by its households as a result of which Saul was selected. Of course the LXX thinks it is doing the reader a favor by providing the expected information; but perhaps there was a solid reason for its absence from the MT. The MT informs us that the lot procedure involved the physical presence of the participants through the selection of the Matrites, but at that point the MT suddenly shifts gears. Before readers can prepare for the next round, they are precipitously informed in 10:21b that Saul was selected. Was he there or not? It is nowhere said that the family was brought near! In spite of the question of procedure, the reader seems to be invited to assume that, in fact, the family *was not* brought near and the selection of Saul occurred in some way other than by his personal presence. As soon as he got wind of what had happened, however, he looked for the nearest cover. Understanding the story in this way allows us to maintain the basic unity of the tradition while avoiding the clumsy textual emendation required by Mettinger as well as the presumed relationship with 10:1–16 suggested by Veijola.[63]

---

[61] So Hans Jochen Boecker, *Die Beurteilung der Anfänge des Königtums in den deuteronomistischen Abschnitten des I. Samuelbuches: Ein Beitrag zum Problem des "deuteronomistischen Geschichtswerks"* (Neukirchen-Vluyn: Neukirchener Verlag, 1969) 46.

[62] Ibid., 47–48; Crüsemann, *Der Widerstand gegen das Königtum*, 55–56; Mayes, "Rise of the Israelite Monarchy," 10.

[63] Mettinger, *King and Messiah*, 181; Veijola, *Das Königtum in der Beurteilung der Deuteronomistischen Historiographie*, 39, 51.

Unlike the traditions in 9:1–10:16 and 11:1–15 this story nowhere makes reference to the spirit empowerment of Saul. In fact he hides – quite the opposite of what one might expect from God's charismatically designated and endowed leader. Such observations have led to a negative view of the text, seeing nothing at all charismatic in this irrational story of Saul's appointment.[64] The point of the story, however, focuses on the divine charisma, which is at work in two directions. First, Saul's charismatic legitimation is seen in the fact that his selection was by means of lots. Far from being a "neutral" means of selection whereby everyone has an equal and random chance of being arbitrarily chosen, the method presupposed the most intimate involvement of deity imaginable. God caused the lot to fall upon the very one on whom the divine eye rested. Second, Saul's charismatic empowerment is evidenced in the note regarding his stature. Just as David's beauty betrayed his charismatic presence (1 Sam 16:12, 18), so Saul's sheer size made him absolutely unique. There was no one else like him among all the people (10:24)!

But Saul's charisma is also seen in something quite the opposite. Just as it is said of David that God's standards of selection are different from human standards (1 Sam 16:7), so here too God looks in ridiculous places – such as among the baggage – to find the one who is right for the job.[65] While others might have thought it logical to select among those who postured and paraded their achievements, God rummaged among the supplies to find the chosen one. God's choice was precisely the one who tried to hide, but precisely the one whose very stature made such hiding utterly unimaginable. The humor of the situation could hardly have been lost on the audience and ought not be overlooked by the reader.

Saul's Charisma in Literary Context

These three stories of Saul's charismatic endowment have often been lined up in a supposed chronological sequence progressing from popular election, presumably the earliest and most primitive form,

---

[64] Soggin, "Charisma und Institution in Königtum Sauls," 57.
[65] Dietrich, *David, Saul und die Propheten,* 143.

to divine election, the latest and most theologically reflective form. Ishida, for example, regards 11:1–15 as the earliest of the narratives, stressing Saul's election by the popular assembly. The story in 9:1–10:16 is taken by Ishida to be the latest of the three, accenting the divine designation of the anointed. The tradition of selection by lots in 10:17–27 is a middle stage, balancing popular involvement with divine designation.[66] The fact that Soggin could take 10:17–27 to be illustrative of a democratic *Tendenz*,[67] however, suggests the inadequacy of any such attempts.

Any effort to discriminate chronologically between popular election and divine appointment simply reflects the common desire to perpetuate the distinction between divine charisma and human institution. Clearly, the three stories before us allow no such neat differentiation. If there is any differentiation in these three texts it is not to be reconstructed from some presumed chronological order but rather established on the basis of the present shape of the text. Edelman's attempt to find in the present form of the text a pattern of divine designation (9:1–10:27), testing (11:1–11), and popular confirmation (11:15) moves in the right direction, though her argument is too neatly construed.[68] First, any scheme that attributes at least one if not two full chapters to the divine designation but one scant verse to public confirmation certainly suggests that no such pattern determined the present structure of the text. Second, Edelman is not able to distinguish between the narratives in 9:1–16 and 10:17–27 and must subsume both under her rubric of divine designation. It ought not be overlooked, however, that already in 10:17–27 there is a healthy dose of popular involvement, and the confirmation of the people is plainly evident in their cry *yĕḥî hammelek* (10:24). Third, subsuming 11:1–11 under the rubric of "testing" misconstrues the dynamic at work in the narrative. It is not so much concerned with

---

[66] Ishida, *Royal Dynasties,* 48–50.

[67] Soggin, "Charisma und Institution im Königtum Sauls," 57. Cf. Boecker, who takes the motif of the search for the tallest to represent a totally unreflective means of selection which allows little room for any divine role (*Die Beurteilung der Anfänge des Königtums,* 47).

[68] Edelman, "Saul's Rescue of Jabesh Gilead," 197.

[69] See especially Mettinger, *King and Messiah,* 112–13.

Saul establishing his credentials as it is with Saul vindicating his reputation against those few who whispered that no salvation could possibly come from these quarters (10:27). The note that Saul "held his peace" (literally, "he played dumb," *wayhî kĕmaḥărîš*, v. 27) sets up the next narrative not as a testing but rather as a "getting even" for such vile insinuations. Finally, most commentators take the reference in 11:14 to refer to "renewing" (*nĕḥaddēš*) the kingdom, a tacit acknowledgment that Saul was already recognized fully as king upon the people's endorsement in 10:24. It is not likely, therefore, that the text was ordered according to any idealized pattern of divine designation, testing, and popular ratification.

The present form of 9:1–11:15 seems to move in a different direction from that suggested by Edelman. It is often assumed that 10:16 concludes with the theme of the messianic secret so as to prepare the way for what follows in the selection by lots. However, it is insufficient to speak simply of a "messianic secret" as though Saul was the only one aware of anything prior to the selection by lots. The scene in which he demonstrates his prophetic ecstasy is clearly depicted to be a public demonstration. Saul does not fall into this ecstasy in some imagined splendid isolation. Nor is he surrounded solely by a small band of prophets who are sworn to silence. The text of 10:11 surrounds Saul with a myriad of close acquaintances who see very clearly what is transpiring and who wonder aloud what it all means. It is no secret that something is happening to Saul, but it is not yet quite clear what it is. Saul's uncle may not yet know about the kingdom. Nevertheless, the reader is certainly invited to assume that he knows fully about what happened in Gibeah.

When moving to the episode in 10:17–27 it is tempting to focus on the lot procedure, since the earlier form of the story was bound up in the issue of how Saul was designated. For the reader of the narrative in its present context, however, the issue of how Saul is selected has already been established by the preceding narrative. This redundancy draws the reader's attention away from the process of lots itself, and the focus of the text shifts to the other major theme present—the search for Saul. The reader's attention is riveted by the phrase in v. 21, "But when they sought him, he could not be found" (*waybaqšuhû wĕlō' nimṣā'*). The phrase echoes the statement in 10:16 that "the donkeys had been found" (*nimṣĕ'û hā'ătōnôt*) and recalls the theme of the search for the donkeys which set the stage for Saul's anointing and prophetic outburst. In 9:1–10:16 it was Saul who had searched but could not find (9:3–4). Now the action is reversed and Saul himself becomes the object of a new search in which there is likewise no finding. In both cases, however, it is God who searches out and finds. The reader of the "search for the donkeys" knows that with God there is no hiding, especially if the one who is hiding towers head and shoulders over everyone else. The focus of 10:17–27 is thus drawn away from the issue of designation and is fixed once again on the theme of "searching" and "finding." Whereas the last search concluded in Saul's public demonstration of the prophetic sign, here the search ends in that to which the sign pointed—Saul's elevation to the kingship.

The one who searched without finding now becomes the one who himself is found in a search. The sign achieves its goal. Rather surprisingly, however, the scene ends with Saul's overwhelming silence. "He was like one who was dumb." The silence is perhaps not so surprising, however, given Saul's silence at the conclusion of the previous scene when pressed by his uncle concerning what Samuel had said. Each scene ends in Saul's alarming silence, which prepares the reader for what is to follow. As mentioned above, the function of 11:1–15 in the present context is to vindicate Saul's reputation in the face of the challenge issued by the *běnê bělîyaʿal*. Not only does he vindicate his reputation, but he also demonstrates his commitment to justice by issuing a decree of clemency (11:13). The sign not only found its full fruition. Now Saul's kingship is reaffirmed. Whereas the first and second scenes had concluded with Saul's ominous silence, the third scene brings the cycle to resolution by concluding with the note that "Saul and all the Israelites rejoiced greatly" (*wayyiśmaḥ šām šāʾûl wěkol-ʾanšê yiśrāʾēl ʿad-měʾōd,* v. 15). Finally Saul does not restrain himself as he freely joins the people in their concluding jubilation.

From this perspective the unit 9:1–11:15 is not held together by a theoretical pattern of divine designation, test, and public affirmation. Rather it is given its coherence through the pursuance of the motifs of "finding and losing" as well as that of "silence and joyful release." The structural frame is provided by the movement from the sign to its fulfillment and reaffirmation. The issues of charisma, though still quite present in the final form of the text, are dissolved somewhat into the overarching plot structure.

As the result of this analysis of 1 Sam 9:1–11:15, it becomes even more problematic to single out a specific form of charisma as characteristic of Saul's kingship and of kingship in northern Israel. The charismatic impulses conveyed in the texts are made to serve the narrative flow of the story and are intended to reflect on the divine empowerment of kingship as such, not on the specific kingship of Saul. The royal charisma as demonstrated by Saul establishes the king as the one who is "signed, sealed, and delivered" by God. The focus of 9:1–10:16 is on the "sign" which such charisma forms. The royal charisma is itself significant because it signifies—that is, it points to—that transcendent moral order which lies beyond the limited confines of its own institutional existence. The charismatic endowment as characterized by 10:17–27 focuses on the king as the one "sealed" by God's own action. The king is the one hiding among the baggage, sought and found by God; the one whose charismatic endowment sticks out like a pair of legs on a giant of a man trying to hide his qualifications. God's seal is placed upon this one, and he is turned over to the people for their finding. He is the most obvious person found in the least likely place. Signed and sealed. The theme of delivery concludes the charismatic endowment in 11:1–15. The haunting question is met with screaming silence in 10:27, "How can this man save us?" (*mah-yōšī ʿēnû zeh*). The promise of 11:9 stubbornly resists answering the question, and leaves the matter in total ambiguity. "You will have deliverance" (*tihyeh-lākem tĕšûʿâ*). But the question remains: Could *this* man deliver? The resolution comes only in 11:13. No, this man cannot deliver. But God can! "Today the Lord has brought deliverance to Israel" (*hayyôm ʿāśâ-YHWH tĕšûʿâ bĕyiśrāʾēl*). The king was Israel's deliverer in warfare. But most often the Old Testament expresses this notion by making the king himself the object of God's own deliverance. It is the king himself who, in his role as symbol of the body politic, is endowed with the promised blessing of Yahweh's deliverance.[70] The people are delivered because their king is himself the particular object of Yahweh's own deliverance. The king is "signed, sealed, and delivered."

---

[70] E.g., 2 Sam 8:6, 14; Ps 20:7, 10; 144:10.

He is empowered with God's own spirit to bring deliverance to the people.

These three types of charisma, reflected in the stories of Saul's elevation, have approximate corollaries in the stories of David's own rise—that associated with anointing in 1 Sam 16:1–13 (David the shepherd), that focusing on divine providence in 16:14–23 (David the musician), and that of the savior in 17:19–58 (David the giant-killer). An analysis of these texts will have to await another occasion. The discussion of kingship must not conclude, however, without a consideration of the role of the people in ascribing charismatic designation to the royal subject.

Charisma and Popular Acclamation

The distinction between "charismatic" and "institutional" impulses relating to kingship has been reasserted in several recent attempts to distinguish between the role of the deity and that of the people in legitimating Israel's kings. Z. Weisman draws a distinction between two specific forms of royal anointing, one that he labels "prophetic-charismatic" and the other which, for lack of a better term, he refers to as "historical." The first, he argues, served as a form of private divine designation during which the king was charismatically endowed as God's select candidate and which expressed the king's divine legitimation. The second, following on a possible initiatory period of testing, was a public ritual investing the king with full legal authority and symbolizing the king's popular legitimation.[71] This distinction between two stages in the kingship ritual, the first relating to charismatic divine designation and the second to popular affirmation, separated from one another by a period of trial, was already proposed by Georg Fohrer in his analysis of the proposed "treaty" between the king and the people drawn up at the time of the king's coronation, and has subsequently been articulated in studies

[71] Z. Weisman, "The Prophetic Pattern of Anointing Kings in Ancient Israel," in *Monarchies and Socio-Religious Traditions in the Ancient Near East* (ed. T. Mikasa; Wiesbaden: Otto Harrassowitz, 1984) 21–26. See also idem, "Anointing as a Motif in the Making of the Charismatic King," *Bib* 57 (1976) 378–98.

by Jakob Grønbeck and B. Halpern.[72] The intent of all these studies is to stress the centrality of the people in ratifying, affirming, and even electing the royal candidate, who has up to this point been graced with divine nomination, and all reflect Alt's strict distinction between divine selection and popular acclamation of the king.[73] The role of the people is emphasized to the point that Halpern can say that, though God may designate the royal nominee, only the people could make him king. The process involving the election or confirmation by the people is assumed to have included a process of hard-nosed negotiation sealed with a treaty, which Halpern refers to as the "constitution" of the monarchy.[74]

It is extremely difficult, however, to ascribe to the general populace the sort of power and authority in king making that these studies suggest. In discussing the supposed standard treaty drawn up between king and people as a result of initial negotiation, Fohrer is continually forced to "assume" that treaties exist where there is no textual evidence. The only treaties reportedly drawn up were between David and the elders of Israel (2 Sam 5:3), possibly an aborted effort between

---

[72] Georg Fohrer, "Der Vertrag zwischen König und Volk in Israel," *ZAW* 71 (1959) 1–22; Jakob H. Grønbeck, *Die Geschichte vom Aufstieg Davids (1 Sam. 15–2. Sam. 5): Tradition und Komposition* (Copenhagen: Prostant Apud Munksgaard, 1971) 177; Halpern, *Constitution of the Monarchy,* 49, 66, 103; see also Edelman, "Saul's Rescue of Jabesh-Gilead," 197–98, who follows Halpern.

[73] L. Muntingh has suggested, on the basis of evidence from Ebla, that the Northwest Semitic style of kingship was originally electoral ("The Conception of Ancient Syro-Palestinian Kingship in the Light of Contemporary Royal Archives with Special Reference to the Recent Discoveries at Tell Mardikh (Ebla) in Syria," in *Monarchies and Socio-Religious Traditions in the Ancient Near East* (ed. T. Mikasa; Wiesbaden: Otto Harrassowitz, 1984) 1–10. However, his evidence only allows for four such elected kings at Ebla ruling for a total of twenty-eight years before the fifth established hereditary succession. Such a limited span can hardly serve as the basis for a comprehensive theory concerning a unique Northwest Semitic form of kingship.

See especially Alt, "Das Königtum in den Reichen Israel und Juda," 118. Here he clearly distinguishes between charismatic equipment through Yahweh and the secondary confirmation of the people. Elsewhere, however, Alt includes popular confirmation as a part of charismatic endowment (p. 121).

[74] Halpern, *Constitution of the Monarchy in Israel,* 185, 221–35. Mettinger, though not distinguishing between two stages in the kingship process, also envisions a process of negotiation between the royal candidate and the popular assembly which gathers to ratify his nomination, and speaks of a balance between divine designation and popular acclamation (*King and Messiah,* 112, 149–50).

Rehoboam and the elders of Israel (1 Kgs 12:1-6), and between Joash
and the people of the land (2 Kgs 11:17). However, nothing suggests
that either David or Rehoboam was required by custom to draw
up treaties with the elders of Judah (cf. 2 Sam 2:4). Rather than reflecting a theoretical and standard contractual relationship between king
and people, the episodes of David and Rehoboam securing a treaty
with the elders of Israel may relate to the custom of a king forming
a treaty arrangement with a foreign population.[75] As for the treaty
between Joash and the people of the land, it is possible that the treaty
was required to reconstitute the dynasty following the interregnum
of Athaliah. In any event, it is precisely here that there is a distinction drawn between the *'ēdût*, which Jehoiada presented to the king
(2 Kgs 11:12) and was likely the official document attesting to the
royal power and prerogatives, and the treaty, which was only subsequently drawn up (11:17). Whatever function the treaty had, it
clearly was made only subsequent to the king's official installation
and in no way was a prerequisite for it.

The primary difficulty of discussing the role of the people in "king
making" is the silence of the texts concerning popular involvement,
particularly in Israel. Only Omri's military coup is reported to have
been accompanied by the general support of the populace, but even
here the information is contradictory. The note that "all Israel made
Omri . . . king" (1 Kgs 16:16) is flatly contradicted by the note in
v. 21 that at best he was supported by half of the people. The other
military coups, those by Zimri (1 Kgs 16:9-10), Jehu (2 Kgs 9:1-10:31),
and Pekah (2 Kgs 15:25), make no reference to the general support
of the populace. Besides being backed by the military, or factions
within it, Jehu's coup was also effected with the active involvement
of ideological splinter groups such as the fanatical Rechabites (2 Kgs
10:15-16). The military putsch led by Pekah was executed with the
support of "fifty Gileadites" in what was perhaps a politically
motivated coup to install an anti-Assyrian government. In no case,
however, are we given clear information concerning the popular
dynamics at work in their rise to power. The reports concerning
the other coups are even less clear. The coups of Baasha (1 Kgs 15:27),

---

[75] So the people of Jabesh offer to establish a treaty relationship with Nahash
the Ammonite (1 Sam 11:1).

Shallum (2 Kgs 15:10), Menahem (15:14–16), and Hoshea (15:30) specifically refer neither to military nor to popular involvement, although it seems obvious that such putsches must have had the support of disenchanted and disaffected circles somewhere, whether in the military, at the court, or in outlying areas. Baasha's coup may have involved a regional dispute, since he was reported to have come from the house of Issachar. Menahem's may also have involved regional conflicts, since he came from the older capital of Tirzah and apparently met open resistance by certain cities.[76] The coup launched by Hoshea, however, clearly resulted from international intrigue and was instigated by pro-Assyrian circles, as indicated by Tiglath-Pileser's own report of the matter: "They overthrew their king Pekah and I placed Hoshea as king over them" (*ANET*, 284). In no case is it clear, however, what role was played by the general population: rather than resulting from widespread popular movements the texts suggest that the revolts issued from regional squabbling, foreign meddling, or sporadic and isolated instances of simple vicious power politics.

The involvement of the people in Judean politics is more apparent, but precisely here it is difficult to determine which information may be due to the theological bias of the redactor. Although Adonijah claims to have had the popular support of "all Israel" (1 Kgs 2:15), his attempt to seize the throne was evidently supported only by the oligarchy, including the royal family (excluding Solomon and David), Joab, and Abiathar (1:7–10). The redactor reports that "all the people" were also involved in Solomon's rival coronation (1:39b–40), but here again Solomon was apparently backed principally by competing members of the oligarchy, including Zadok, Nathan, the royal private guard, and David himself (1:32–39a). Similarly, Joash's installation upon the throne was due principally to the support of the Jerusalem priesthood in league with the military (2 Kgs 11:2–12). To the "people of the land" (vv. 14, 18–20) is attributed the actual act of "making Joash king" (*wayyamlīkû 'ōtô*, v. 12),[77] but their role in king making appears to be more ritualized than actual. The substantive involve-

---

[76] The text is extremely difficult, however. For a discussion, see T. R. Hobbs, *2 Kings* (Waco: Word, 1985) 196–97.

[77] But cf. LXX *ebasileusen*, which continues the singular, attributing the act to Jehoiada.

ment of the "people of the land" in king making becomes much more pronounced in the cases of Azariah (2 Kgs 14:21),[78] Josiah (21:24), and Jehoahaz (23:30). In all cases but the last the "people of the land" clearly intervened to restore a normalized succession in the wake of a plot originating within the very circles of the royal court itself. By the time of Josiah's death it appears that the "people of the land" were the primary power brokers of Judean politics. However, since their involvement in placing Joash on the throne was really more ritual than actual, caution is warranted against attributing to them more of a role than they actually may have played. As with the case of Joash, they may have been representing the forces of the priesthood and/or military over against certain members within the royal entourage itself.

How important was popular involvement for the success either of Adonijah, Solomon, Joash, or those who were placed on the throne by "the people of the land"? An instructive record is provided by the Prism B text of Esarhaddon (*ANET,* 289–90), in which Esarhaddon reports on his own fight for the Assyrian throne in the face of severe opposition by other members of the royal family. If the text is at all believable and does not simply reflect propagandistic rhetoric, Esarhaddon's right to succession was first established by oracular means and then reaffirmed by a solemn oath ceremony, which included the presence not only of the royal family but also of "the people of Assyria, young and old." When subsequently the brothers disputed the succession and a battle over the throne ensued, the "people of Assyria" apparently maintained their commitment to Esarhaddon, whether out of respect for their oath, out of deference to his military threat, or out of naked self-interest. Nevertheless, though Esarhaddon takes pains to comment on the support of the general populace that he received upon approaching the Tigris,[79] the impression is that they were "hedging their bets," remaining uncommitted until it became apparent because of massive defections from the opposing military forces that the attempted usurpation by the "brothers" was doomed. Esarhaddon himself implies that his victory

[78] Referred to here as "the people of Judah."

[79] Cf. David being greeted by the populace upon his return from exile (2 Sam 19:14–43). In both cases crossing the river is a major symbolic moment, perhaps mythically symbolizing the king's victory over the forces of chaos.

was due to his being divinely supported by Ishtar, but with no small thanks also to his overwhelming "battle array." The support of the populace is added almost as an afterthought, and the act of their "kissing the feet" of Esarhaddon implies more their capitulation to his claims than their active involvement in securing the throne for him or their engaging in a process of hard-nosed negotiation.

It can reasonably be surmised that Esarhaddon's brothers also claimed divine backing as well as the full support of the people, and had one of them secured the succession we would be reading instead about how Ishtar had led his troops in battle against the usurper Esarhaddon. It does not require a degenerate cynic to suspect that the claim both to divine succor and to popular support was not only required but also expected of any king who would ascend to the throne. The first was symbolically established on the battlefield. The second was symbolically established in the temple, when the action of "making P.N. king" was attributed to the populace.

It is impossible to establish the extent to which the succession to the throne was predicated on prior divine designation. Even in cases where divine designation is indicated, such as is the case for Esarhaddon, it was apparently neither decisive nor binding. It is likewise impossible to establish that the general populace had the decisive role in the matter, since the evidence suggests that, as may be expected, they held back their commitments until it became clear which faction would claim victory. It is therefore highly unlikely that a rigid pattern of divine or charismatic nomination and popular endorsement characterized the standard process of king making in Israel. Kings were made on the battlefield as well as in the trenches of political infighting and court intrigue. Whichever claimant to the throne gained access to the loyalty of priestly circles had an advantage in terms of securing favorable oracles pertaining to divine designation. However, it was also crucial to have the backing of the military; and if one had the latter one could easily manipulate the former. Once the throne was secured, legitimation was established in a number of ways. First, popular support was ritualized by attributing to the population the very act of king making. Second, the granting of throne names established the notion of divine selection.[80] Third, the iconography of the court and temple continually reinforced in the popular mind the connection between deity and monarchy.[81] Fourth, the publication of polemical material, written and oral, provided a defense for the king's "legitimate" succession.[82] And most importantly, the ideology of kingship itself, which revolved around the king's role as dispenser of justice and thereby ensurer of social and cosmic order, fostered a mentality that bolstered the popular predisposition to grant legitimation and central authority to the king.

The divine and the human, the charismatic and the institutional, were inseparably bound together in the attribution of legitimation and authority to the Israelite monarch. Though the cynic would say that authority was gained by force of arms and manipulation of the priesthood, and though the populace itself was undoubtedly painfully aware of the power politics involved in the process, kingship in Israel cannot be dismissed as a cancerous infection of Israel's religious soul. Nor can issues of divine designation and popular or official affirmation be sorted out as though they were clearly evident, easily distinguished, and evenly applied. Royal legitimation in its entirety was based on charismatic authorization, as manifest both in the belief that the king was divinely selected and the belief, equally unrelated to empirical evidence, that the king was "made king" by the people themselves. The charismatic principle was applicable to kingship since, as stated above, in its idealized conceptualization kingship was anchored deeply in the popularly held centering principle of cosmic justice and order.

[80] Ahlström, "Solomon, the Chosen One," 102–3; N. Wyatt, "'Jedidiah' and Cognate Forms as a Title of Royal Legitimation," *Bib* 66 (1985) 112–25.

[81] On the ideological nature of iconography, see Martin Metzger, "Der Thron als Manifestation der Herrschermacht in der Ikonographie des Vorderen Orients und im Alten Testament," in *Charisma und Institution* (ed. T. Rendtorff; Gütersloh: Gerd Mohn, 1985) 250–96.

[82] See especially Keith W. Whitelam, "The Defence of David," *JSOT* 29 (1984) 61–87.

5

The Prophetic Word:
Stretching the Mythic Consciousness

The Problem: Weber on the Prophets

NO FIGURE from the pages of the Old Testament has served more as illustrative of the popular charismatic hero than has the prophet. The images of Elijah single-handedly confronting the treacherous Ahab and Jezebel and of Amos railing against Jeroboam in the royal sanctuary at Bethel have inspired images of what it means to be truly "charismatic." As is well known and frequently rehearsed, scholarship of this century has often rallied to the thesis popularized in the last century that Israelite prophecy represented the zenith of Old Testament religion. The tendency of Protestant scholarship to regard the prophets as individual and isolated exemplars of confessional integrity ("I alone am left!" [1 Kgs 19:14]), as retrograde reformers fighting the corrupt church of their day, has unmistakably shaped our view of the prophets.[1]

As though propelled by the enormous extremity of this position, however, the converse notion was also spawned and promoted: Israel's prophets were not charismatically charged, isolated geniuses but rather institutional figures anchored deeply within Israel's cult. The studies of S. Mowinckel, A. Haldar, A. R. Johnson, and their followers

[1] For an early critique from a sociohistorical perspective, see Peter L. Berger, "Charisma and Religious Innovation: The Social Location of Israelite Prophecy," *ASR* 28 (1963) 940–50. Note also the response by James G. Williams, "The Social Location of Israelite Prophecy," *JAAR* 37 (1969) 153–65.

located prophecy precisely within the temple walls,[2] though the debate has continued as to which if any of the "classical" or "canonical" prophets might themselves have been members of such professional temple guilds. A distinction is commonly drawn today between such "cult prophets," whose primary responsibility was directed toward individuals and small groups within the cultic community in their function of "social maintenance," and at least certain of the "canonical prophets," whose irreversible judgments were directed against Israel in its entirety.[3] The purpose of this chapter is not to review the problem of "cultic prophecy" but rather to consider recent studies pertaining to the broader social location of intermediation and to draw conclusions concerning the interplay of the "charismatic" and "institutional" dynamics of Israelite prophecy.[4]

Confusion concerning whether or not the prophets were charismatic leaders is typified by the conflicting evaluations offered by Weber himself. From the perspective of his three ideal types of leadership, Weber clearly considered the prophets to be exemplary bearers of pure charisma. Unlike the priest, who laid claim to authority by virtue of his service in a sacred tradition, the prophets' claim was based on personal revelation and charisma. They did not receive their mission from human agency but rather seized it by force of personality.[5] From the perspective of his more programmatic thesis concerning the relationship of a biblical ethos and the modern capitalistic ethos, however, Weber focused on the prophets' rationality. Their ethos was not ecstatic but rather was post-ecstatic and rational.[6] Thus, they would reflect Weber's "legal/rational" form of authority rather than his "charismatic" form.

---

[2] S. Mowinckel, *Psalmenstudien III*, 4–29, reprinted as "Cult and Prophecy," in *Prophecy in Israel: Search for an Identity* (ed. D. L. Petersen; Philadelphia: Fortress, 1987) 74–98; A. Haldar, *Associations of Cult Prophets among the Ancient Semites* (Uppsala: Almqvist & Wiksell, 1945); A. R. Johnson, *The Cultic Prophet in Ancient Israel* (Cardiff: University of Wales, 1962).

[3] See, e.g., Jörg Jeremias, *Kultprophetie und Gerichtsverkündigung in der späten Königszeit Israels* (Neukirchen-Vluyn: Neukirchener Verlag, 1970).

[4] For a brief survey of six basic studies, see John S. Kselman, "The Social World of the Israelite Prophets: A Review Article," *RelSRev* 11 (1985) 120–29.

[5] Max Weber, *The Sociology of Religion* (Boston: Beacon Press, 1963) 46.

[6] Bernhard Lang, "Max Weber und Israels Propheten: Eine kritische Stellungnahme," *ZRG* 36 (1984) 157, 163.

Weber's attitude toward Old Testament prophecy was thus torn between two basic but conflicting instincts. His concern to show that religious ideas are not simply the reflex of social forces but rather themselves *drive* such forces led him to emphasize the freedom of the prophet over against any social group. The prophet was the isolated charismatic individual representing God alone. Weber's desire to anchor capitalism's legal/rational principles in the Judeo-Christian tradition, however, drove him in the opposite direction. In the popular views of those such as Wellhausen, the prophets became the proto-exponents of rational-ethical religion. Having transcended ecstatic irrationality, they became forerunners of Western rationality. Weber's vacillation as to whether the prophet is fundamentally driven by "charismatic"–thus in Weber's own system "irrational"–power or rather by "rational" force attests once again to the difficulty in distinguishing neatly between the ideal types. A closer consideration of the prophetic social function, informed by current social-scientific studies, will seek to illustrate the interworking of "charismatic" and "institutional" dynamics in prophetic experience.

The Origins of Israelite Prophecy

The once-popular notion that prophecy, at least in its "classical" form, was a uniquely Israelite phenomenon is generally regarded as untenable today, especially with the attention being given to the ancient Near Eastern antecedents of prophecy in Egypt, Mari, Assyria, and elsewhere.[7] Israelite prophecy must be regarded as a subtype of a broader pattern of intermediation in the Levant, albeit a type shaped by the particular characteristics of Israel's socio-economic environment. Prophecy was not invented by the Israelites, nor is the picture we are presented of Israelite prophecy wholly discontinuous with that depicted in the numerous oracle texts from Babylon and Assyria (*ANET,* 449–51, 604–6), Hamath (*ANET,* 655–56), Moab (*ANET,* 320–21), and especially from Mari (*ANET,* 623–26, 629–32).

---

[7] For a brief review of the literature, see Helmer Ringgren, "Prophecy in the ancient Near East," in *Israel's Prophetic Tradition: Essays in Honour of Peter R. Ackroyd* (ed. R. Coggins et al.; Cambridge: Cambridge University Press, 1982) 1–11.

If prophecy appears not to have been unique to Israel, there nonetheless has been a continuing desire to regard Israelite prophecy as coterminous with Israel's national existence and especially with the establishment of the monarchy. Siegfried Herrmann regarded the monarchy as an essential prerequisite for the existence of prophecy, especially as a fertile point of friction. Prophecy existed only insofar as it served as "charismatic king maker" and could oppose royal policies. Without the instability of royal intrigue there would be no social function for prophecy.[8] Similar attempts to locate the prophets' social function primarily in their opposition to the "presumed world of the kings"[9] recognize the fact that nearly all of the recorded prophetic oracles mentioned above (Mari, neo-Assyrian, etc.) address themselves to the king.

What such attempts do not adequately consider, however, is that the function of such oracles is predominantly that of "social maintenance" rather than social disruption.[10] Where there are warnings addressed to the king, they serve the purpose of directing him to a certain course of action so as to ensure his safety in the face of anticipated dangers or plots against his life.[11] Further, the fact that nearly all such oracles are addressed to the king must be qualified by the equally clear fact that the oracles in question were preserved in royal archives or royal inscriptions. We can only *expect* that such archives would primarily contain materials pertaining to the king. Thus, the mere fact that the king is their focus of attention cannot be taken as evidence that such oracles were not also dispensed to individuals outside the royal court. We simply lack the documentary evidence for the broader use of such oracles.

---

[8] Siegfried Herrmann, *Ursprung und Funktion der Prophetie im alten Israel* (Opladen: Westdeutscher, 1976) 22, 41. See also F. M. Cross's contention that classical prophecy is coterminous with the monarchy ("New Directions in the Study of Apocalyptic," in *Apocalypticism* (ed. R. Funk; New York: Herder & Herder, 1969) 161; and James L. Crenshaw, *Prophetic Conflict: Its Effect upon Israelite Religion* (New York: Walter de Gruyter, 1971) 105.

[9] Walter Brueggemann, *The Prophetic Imagination* (Philadelphia: Fortress, 1978) 65–67; see also idem, "The Prophet as a Destabilizing Presence," in *The Pastor as Prophet* (ed. E. E. Shelp and R. H. Sunderland; New York: Pilgrim, 1985) 49–77.

[10] E.g., the oracles from Ishtar of Arbela addressed to Esarhaddon (*ANET*, 449–50).

[11] The oracles of the gods Annunitum and Belet-ekallim to Zimri-Lim, warning him to surround himself with a bodyguard (*ANET*, 630, m) or to refrain from a particular campaign (*ANET*, 631, p).

The evidence from the Old Testament itself suggests that, while the royal court was the primary patron of such oracular activity, such oracles were accessible also to individuals in the broader community, particularly on a fee basis. Finally, there is no reason to doubt that prophetic "types" (seers, diviners, etc.) predated Israel's monarchy. The references to Abraham, Aaron, Miriam, and Moses as prophets (Gen 20:7; Exod 7:1; 15:20; Hos 12:13) are questionable and likely reflect later theological reinterpretation. The reference to Deborah as a prophet (Judg 4:4), however, is more difficult to explain away, as is the story of Samuel functioning as a "seer" (1 Sam 9:9). Such texts, as well as the reference to guilds of prophets functioning in close relationship to local sanctuaries (1 Sam 10:5–10), allude to the existence of intermediaries in the premonarchical period and illustrate the fact that prophecy was not a function of the monarchy but rather was a function of the needs of the community as such for the mediation of transcognitive information—that is, information not immediately available to humans by normal cognitive means.[12] The sudden appearance of prophets such as Gad (1 Sam 22:5; 2 Sam 24:11–18), Nathan (2 Sam 7:2–17; 12:1–15), and Ahijah (1 Kgs 11:29–39) can hardly be taken to reflect an institution that fell *de novo* into Israel's existence. As Gerald Sheppard noted, the simple overlapping of monarchy and prophecy in Israel does not at all explain their interdependence sociologically.[13] Because of its ideological centrality in the social structure and because of its control of revenue, the court was naturally the chief patron of prophetic intermediation. Such intermediation was not limited to court circles, however, and the function of intermediation as such resulted from the universal desire and need that social groups have for information accessible only by transcognitive means.

Prophecy did not originate in Israel, nor was it connected organically with Israel's monarchy. It has often been presumed, however, that prophecy in Israel took a different form from what it did in

[12] A valuable definition of the role of prophetic intermediation is given by Martin J. Buss, "The Social Psychology of Prophecy," in *Prophecy: Essays Presented to Georg Fohrer* (ed. J. A. Emerton; New York: Walter de Gruyter, 1980) 6.

[13] Gerald T. Sheppard, "True and False Prophecy within Scripture," in *Canon, Theology and Old Testament Interpretation: Essays in Honor of Brevard S. Childs* (ed. G. M. Tucker et al.; Philadelphia: Fortress, 1988) 274–75.

the broader Canaanite or Mesopotamian context. Some have argued that genuine forms of Israelite prophecy were set apart from the prophecy of Israel's Canaanite environment by the absence of "ecstatic" elements – prophecy in Canaan being exercised by groups of such ecstatics. This thesis, however, forces an unwarranted distinction between "authentic" Israelite prophecy (i.e., individual and nonecstatic) and "bogus" forms of canaanized prophetic experience, which, though evidenced in Israel itself, were not authentically Israelite.[14] Below we will consider ecstasy as it relates to stereotypical prophetic behavior. It is enough at this point to insist that no supposed "lack of ecstasy" set Israelite prophecy off from that of its neighbors. If Israelite prophecy seems to have taken a different form from that of its neighbors, then it is only because "classical" prophecy – that is, the "canonical" prophets – do not always fit the pattern. The question then is not whether or not prophecy in Israel shared common patterns with its neighbors. The question becomes, rather, whether or not the canonical prophets were in fact "prophets" at all, and that question will be addressed directly.

Prophecy and Divination

The term "prophet" itself is an artificial label derived from the Greek *prophētēs* and imposed upon various forms of Israelite intermediation. In actual fact there were no "prophets" in Israel. There were various forms of intermediaries divided roughly into two categories: those who mediated transcognitive information by means of revelations through dreams, visions, or auditions, among which were the *nābî'* (translated "prophet") as well as the *ḥōzeh* and *rō'eh* (the "seer"); and those who mediated such information by means of the analysis of omina and physical data (i.e., divination), such as the *kōhēn* ("priest"), who divined principally by means of Urim and Thummim. In addition there were other specialists who were eventually relegated

---

[14] For a discussion of the issue, see J. R. Porter, "The Origins of Prophecy in Israel," in *Israel's Prophetic Tradition: Essays in Honour of Peter R. Ackroyd* (ed. R. Coggins et al.; Cambridge: Cambridge University Press, 1982) 13–20.

more or less to the boundaries of Israelite intermediation,[15] such as the *qōsēm* (general term for "omina expert"), the *mĕʿônēn* ("soothsayer"), the *mĕnaḥēš* ("augerer"), the *mĕkaššēp* ("sorcerer"), as well as the person possessed by an *'ôb* ("necromancer") or by a *yiddeʿōnî* ("medium").

It ought not be assumed, however, that the two types of mediaries, the prophetic and the divinatory, were fundamentally distinct or that they understood themselves to be at odds with one another. It is quite common for societies that allow for the mediation of transcognitive information to acknowledge the use of a variety of such methods. Although every society may have its preferred method, there is generally a tolerance shown for other forms which comple-ment one another. Such tolerance is clearly demonstrated by 1 Sam 28:6, which lists the primary methods of transcognitive mediation (dreams, Urim, prophets), which failed Saul in his attempt to secure information concerning the pending battle with the Philistines. The "prophetic" or "mediumistic" type secures such information by receiv-ing communication by immaterial means, through the god or through the dead,[16] whereas the "divinatory" type secures information by careful analysis of material and physical evidence and omens by applying traditional and highly refined codes of interpretation.[17] However, since the deity was thought to be directly involved in the physical evidence or the omen (e.g., the condition of the liver, the pattern of the arrows, the fall of the lots), there is no qualitative distinction to be made between the two types. In both cases the con-cern is to determine how the course of human events aligns with the pattern of events as generated in the sphere of the divine. In many

[15] The Deuteronomic program in particular was biased in favor of the former type of mediation and proscribed against the latter type because of its connection with powers and means lying outside the normal sphere of Yahweh's interest with the world. On this issue, see the recent study by Thomas W. Overholt, *Channels of Prophecy: The Social Dynamics of Prophetic Activity* (Minneapolis: Fortress, 1989) esp. chap. 5, "Prophecy and Divination" (pp. 117–47). The fact that such cultic players continued throughout the period of the monarchy, Deuteronomic sensitivities aside, is evidenced by Jer 27:9.

[16] Recalling the fluidity between being a "god" and being "dead" (1 Sam 28:13), one ought not be surprised that the two would fall together in this way.

[17] For a discussion of Assyrian liver inspection and a catalogue of divinatory protases, see Ivan Starr, *Queries to the Sun God: Divination and Politics in Sargonid Assyria* (Helsinki: Helsinki University, 1990).

societies the various roles are not clearly distinguished, and in fact the same person may exercise several different methods.[18]

Because of its use of tangible material, however, the divinatory method was often preferred to the prophetic method. This preference is demonstrated at Mari, for example, where prophetic oracles were "put to the iron test" of divination in order to validate their accuracy. The typical pattern is as follows: a prophetic figure would go into a trance or otherwise receive an oracle from a deity, often while visiting a sanctuary, which he or she would report to the temple staff. The temple director responsible for such matters would send a letter to the king containing not only a report of the oracle itself but also the "hair and fringe" of the prophet, which evidently were used in a divination ritual to determine the validity of the oracle.[19] In the most illustrative letter the priestess Inibshina reports to Zimri-Lim, her father, that a certain prophetess named Sharrakiya received an oracle relating to assured victory over Zimri-Lim's enemies. At the conclusion of her oracle Sharrakiya states: "I hereby give you my hair and fringe. Let them declare (me) free (of legal claims)." Her hair and fringe were sent on to Zimri-Lim with his daughter's ad-monition that he "[have] an omen taken so that he may act in accordance with his omens" (*ANET,* 632w). This text demonstrates the twofold purpose of the divinatory ritual performed on the hair and fringe. First, it confirmed or disconfirmed the prophetic oracle; second, it served as a legal device by means of which the prophet could claim immunity from possible subsequent prosecution.

These texts illustrate a close interrelationship of prophetic and divinatory forms of mediation but also demonstrate that prophecy was perceived as less reliable than more standard forms of divina-

---

[18] See the references to "prophets" operating through means of "divination": Mic 3:6, 11; Jer 14:14. On the relation of the two forms of intermediation, see Overholt, *Channels of Prophecy,* 132. For comparative evidence suggesting that "priests" may seek to augment their status by assuming "charismatic" qualities and vice versa, see T. O. Beidelman, "Nuer Priests and Prophets: Charisma, Authority, and Power among the Nuer," in *The Translation of Culture: Essays to E. E. Evans-Pritchard* (ed. T. O. Beidelman; London: Tavistock, 1971) 399–400.

[19] *ANET,* 630 m, n; 631 p. Not always were the hair and fringe sent. On occasion the king would simply be encouraged to take the action he deemed appropriate (*ANET,* 624 e, g). On other occasions the temple director might himself or herself attest to the trustworthiness of the prophet, thereby assuming personal responsibility (*ANET,* 623 a).

tion. Prophecy functioned as a sort of "early warning system," which was then verified by more standardized forms of divination available to the central cultic officials.

Was there a similar relationship between prophecy and divination in Israelite practice, with divination serving as a "backup system" for the more uncontrollable prophecy? Some have noted the lack of any reference to submitting prophecy to divinatory rituals in the neo-Assyrian prophetic texts and have suggested that by the time of classical Israelite prophecy (eighth century B.C.E.) prophecy gradually had come to replace divination as the preferred means of intermediation in the ancient Near East, or at least operated as its equal. This theory is then applied to Israelite intermediation so as to heighten the status of prophecy over against divination. Such a conclusion is unwarranted by the evidence available, however. The primary text, a simple listing of oracles directed to Esarhaddon (*ANET,* 605), is of a different genre from the letter/reports to Zimri-Lim referred to above and cannot therefore be compared. In fact, the neo-Assyrian text does not elaborate on the process at all, so there is no way to make a determination one way or the other as to how its oracles were evaluated or authenticated. It seems likely that the situation clearly attested at Mari serves well as a general paradigm for practice throughout the ancient Near East, including Israel. That prophecy was in some fundamental way under the jurisdiction of the temple staff (Amos 7:10–13; Jer 20:1–2; 29:26) hints at the sort of relationship between prophecy and divination reflected in the Mari texts. Prophecy functioned as an "early warning system," which was then put to the test by standard "backup systems" available to cultic officials.

Prophecy, Intermediation, and the "Classical" Prophets

One of the chief difficulties of discussing prophecy in the Old Testament is the problem of classification. Above we spoke of various forms of prophets and diviners, arguing that the distinction between them was more fluid than is generally allowed. Nevertheless, the fact that such distinctions were made means that Israelite society was aware of diversified role expectations. There are two problems that arise when scholars attempt to classify the various types. The first relates to the *system* of classification, and the second relates to the issue of the continuity of "pre-classical" and "classical" forms of prophecy.

The problem of classification system arises because of the confusion of terms used for "prophets" in the Old Testament. The most popular classification system, however, ignores such terms and focuses on the location where the prophets appear: they are commonly grouped as "court" prophets, "temple" prophets, members of prophetic "guilds," and "free" prophets.[20] Court prophets, such as Nathan and Gad, functioned at the royal court; "temple" prophets, who eventually transmuted into the temple singers of the postexilic period, provided oracles to those "seeking" Yahweh at cultic occasions; prophetic guilds wandered freely from sanctuary to sanctuary offering their services; and "free" prophets, in which category at least the most daring of the "classical" prophets are generally placed, exercised their vocation as isolated individuals unencumbered by institutional links.

The advantage to this classification system is that it often reflects actual practices as suggested by the biblical narratives themselves. The disadvantages are threefold: First, the temptation is to make a facile alignment of specific messages with these various groups, so that the "court" prophets offer advice, the "temple" prophets are simple purveyors of peace, and the individual prophets are doomsayers. Second, such a classification system draws an unwarranted distinction between "court" and "temple" and indeed between temple and secular prophecy. The Mari texts evidence the fact that individual "lay" prophets had access to the temple during which they would receive and convey oracles, much as Amos might have functioned. The story recorded in 1 Kings 22 reports that the four hundred royal prophets actually did their prophesying at the city gate rather than in the temple or in the palace. Third, though the texts place prophets in these various settings, they make no conscious distinction between them. "Individual" prophets related to the king in the same manner

[20] See, e.g., Bernhard Lang, "Israels Propheten im Licht von Sundéns Rollenpsychologie," *ArRel* 14 (1980) 20; Hans Walter Wolff, "Prophets and Institutions in the Old Testament," *CurTM* 13 (1986) 6–7.

as did Samuel, Nathan, or Gad.[21] Isaiah, though closely associated with the temple (Isa 6:1–8; 2 Kgs 19:14–28), not only functioned as a royal advisor but offered words of assurance as well as oracles of doom. Jeremiah too exercised his vocation in the temple (Jer 7:1–2; 19:14) while serving as a royal advisor (Jer 21:1–2; 22:1–2) offering bleak oracles of judgment.

An alternative classification system is used by those who categorize the prophets according to role-specific labels, which the text itself uses for such classification purposes: *nābîʾ*, *rōʾeh, ḥōzeh, ʾîš ʾĕlōhîm*. The advantage of this system is that it takes its cue from the text's own classification system. The disadvantage is that attempts to align the various titles with specific social locations have led to chaos and frustration, since behind the titles stands a complicated historical growth process as a result of which social locations collided, diverged, and consolidated. Particularly problematic is what social function the *nābîʾ* exercised, since this is the primary title used for Old Testament prophets. It is often argued that *nābîʾ* originally designated a Canaanite-type ecstatic and only later came to be applied to Israelite prophets,[22] or alternately that the *nābîʾ* was a characteristically northern (i.e., Israelite) prophet as opposed to the type of prophet characteristic of Judah.[23] The *rōʾeh* and *ḥōzeh*, on the other hand, are variously regarded as authentically Israelite prophetic types[24] or as characteristically Judean or urban types of prophets.[25]

Though such labels as *rōʾeh, ḥōzeh*, and *nābîʾ* probably once related to specific roles within the broader category of Israelite intermediation, the differences are irretrievable for the modern investigator. The difficulty is demonstrated by 1 Sam 9:9, which relates that "the one who is now called a prophet (*nābîʾ*) was formerly called a seer (*rōʾeh*)." Already at this relatively early date the role distinctions had

[21] Compare Ahijah (1 Kgs 11:29–39) with Nathan (2 Sam 7:1–17).

[22] Mowinckel, "Cult and Prophecy," 79, 83; Simon B. Parker, "Possession Trance and Prophecy in Pre-Exilic Israel," *VT* 28 (1978) 274–75; Bruce Vawter, "Were the Prophets *nabiʾs?*" *Bib* 66 (1985) 206–20.

[23] David L. Petersen, *The Roles of Israel's Prophets* (Sheffield: JSOT Press, 1981) 63.

[24] Mowinckel, "Cult and Prophecy," 79. The theory of the Israelite origins of the *ḥōzeh*, however, is countered by the reference to "seers" (*ḥzyn*) in the Aramaic Zakir inscription of the eighth century (*ANET*, 655). See James F. Ross, "Prophecy in Hamath, Israel, and Mari," *HTR* 63 (1970) 1–28.

[25] Petersen, *Roles of Israel's Prophets*, 39–44 (on the *rōʾeh*), 56–87 (on the *ḥōzeh*).

been forgotten and the term *rō'eh* had fallen out of popular use. A similar leveling of distinctions is suggested by the story of Amos's confrontation with Amaziah (Amos 7:10–17). Amaziah (innocently?) calls Amos a *ḥōzeh*, to which Amos replies that he is *not a nābî'*, as though the two terms were, for all practical purposes, indistinguishable.

All that can be said with some amount of certainty is that at an earlier date there seems to have been more role differentiation within Israelite intermediation. This role differentiation was gradually lost, and the term *nābî'*, whatever its original social location, came increasingly to be applied across the board to Israelite prophetic intermediation. Such fine distinctions appear not to have been as important for Semitic societies as they are for modern researchers, who wish to impose their own drive for order upon the texts. Like prophecy in the wider environment, biblical prophecy is not a homogeneous phenomenon, and it was characterized by a considerable amount of fluidity among the chief types of actors.[26] This fluidity must be kept in mind as we seek to determine the social underpinnings of recognition and authentication.

The most bedeviling problem with regard to the classification of the prophets is the relationship between the so-called classical or canonical prophets and the broader prophetic phenomenon. Briefly stated, when one compares the early prophetic figures regularly appearing in the Deuteronomistic History with the highly baroque oracles as well as the prophetic style of Isaiah or Jeremiah, one gains the impression that, somewhere between the two, prophecy made a quantum leap into a new world. Early prophecy seems to be characterized by ecstasy (Saul and the prophets), magic (Elijah and Elisha), orientation to the king, and a crude and brief formal style, all driven by the *spirit* of Yahweh. The "classical" prophets, on the other hand, seem to be focused on elaborate and reasoned articulation of Yahweh's *word* addressed to the public.[27] The chasm between

[26] In support of such fluidity, see T. R. Hobbs, "The Search for Prophetic Consciousness: Comments on Method," *BTB* 15 (1985) 136–40; Porter, "Origins of Prophecy," 17–18; Ringgren, "Prophecy in the ancient Near East," 11.

[27] For a discussion of the problem, see Robert R. Wilson, "Early Israelite Prophecy," *Int* 32 (1978) 3–16. For a possible reason behind the shift from royal-oriented to public-oriented prophecy, see John S. Holladay, Jr., "Assyrian Statecraft and the Prophets of Israel," *HTR* 63 (1970) 29–51.

the two forms is so startling on the surface that the question has been raised whether the classical prophets were in fact prophets at all. While some would prefer the label "revolutionaries"[28] or "political propagandists,"[29] a more radical proposal would regard them as "poets," "intellectuals," or "ideologues." In this light, Jeremiah was no more a prophet than he was a priest or a prince. It was only later that the developing tradition attributed to these poets the honorary title "prophet."[30]

Though the present literary style of the prophetic books does clearly represent a significant baroque expansion of traditional ancient Near Eastern prophetic style, R. Wilson is certainly correct in insisting on the continuity of the canonical prophets with their vocational forebears.[31] The baroque expansion of prophetic oracles may in fact be evidenced in the wider Near Eastern environment. In a letter sent by Adad-shumusur to Assurbanipal, a reference is made to "reliable oracles" received from the gods Shamash and Adad, establishing the king's reign firmly over the land. Then follows this baroque hymnic expansion:

Old men dance, young men sing;
Women and maidens are gl[ad (and) ma]ke merry.
Wives they take, deck with ear-[ri]ngs;
Beget sons and daughters—the offspring are instructed.
Whom his crime had condemned to death,
    the king my lord has let live;
[who] was held prisoner many [ye]ars, is set free;
[wh]o were sick many days, have recovered.
The hungry have been sated; the lice-infested have been anointed;
    the naked have been clad in garments.

                                                                (ANET, 627)

---

[28] Martin A. Cohen, "The Prophets as Revolutionaries: A Sociopolitical Analysis," *BARev* 5 (1979) 12–19.

[29] Jesper Høgenhaven, "Prophecy and Propaganda: Aspects of Political and Religious Reasoning in Israel and the Ancient Near East," *SJOT* 1 (1989) 125–41.

[30] A. Graeme Auld, "Prophets and Prophecy in Jeremiah and Kings," *ZAW* 96 (1984) 72, 82; idem, "Prophets Through the Looking Glass: Between Writings and Moses," *JSOT* 27 (1983) 7–9; Robert Carroll, "Poets Not Prophets: A Response to "Prophets through the Looking-Glass," *JSOT* 27 (1983) 25, 27–28.

[31] Wilson, "Early Israelite Prophecy," 7–8.

It is unclear whether these words reproduce the oracle itself or record a baroque hymnic expansion added by Adad-shumusur himself. Nevertheless, the text clearly establishes a connection between oracular activity and a baroque literary style characteristic of the canonical prophets, thereby making their style not wholly discontinuous with Near Eastern antecedents.

There is therefore no reason to argue that poetry was unrelated to prophecy and that the canonical prophets, using a baroque poetic style, were by definition not prophets. Vawter's observation seems most pertinent: though it is difficult to determine how the prophets would have understood their vocation, they certainly would not have thought of themselves as poets, simply because there was no such vocational designation in Israelite society.[32] They may have been reluctant to use a specific professional label for their vocation, but they did not hesitate to refer to their *activity* as "prophesying" (so Amos 7:14-15). The classical prophets certainly understood themselves to be standing in a prophetic tradition reaching back throughout Israel's history. Hosea, for example, understood the *nĕbî'îm* to have been agents of Yahweh's judgment against his people (Hos 6:5),[33] a function with which he must easily have related his own work. When Micah satirized popular expectations concerning who would be a good "preacher" (*maṭṭîp*) for the people (2:6, 11) he used a word for his own activity (*hiṭṭîp*) that is clearly connected with prophetic activity (Amos 7:16; Ezek 20:46; 21:2). When Micah attacked the prophets (3:5-7), he was not attacking the institution as such but those who had debased it by shaping their message to the price tag. When the elders regarded Jeremiah as standing in the succession of prophets such as Micah (Jer 26:16-19), they were not attributing a status to either Micah or Jeremiah that would have surprised them.[34] Similarly, when Isaiah criticized the prophets, it was because they had betrayed their responsibility in leading the people. Instead of

---

[32] Vawter, "Were the Prophets *nabi's?*" 207.

[33] Hosea's references to prophets in 4:5 and 9:7-8 are more difficult to evaluate: 4:5 may be a gloss, since the unit otherwise is limited to priests (see *BHS* and Hans Walter Wolff, *Hosea: A Commentary on the Book of the Prophet Hosea* [Hermeneia; Philadelphia: Fortress, 1974] 70-71). The negative reference in 9:7 may report popular sentiments or may be satire or irony. Certainly the reference in 9:8 is positive, as are 12:10, 13.

[34] Contra Vawter, "Were the Prophets *nabi's?*" 214.

being the head that leads, they had become the tail that is wagged by the self-important people in society (Isa 9:15).[35] In brief, the fact that the classical prophets criticize "the prophets" does not force us to the conclusion that they would have refused the title or would not have understood their own vocation as that of "prophesying." It requires an extremely skeptical mind to deny the title "prophet" to the canonical prophets.[36] Even the earliest among them were not simply opposed to the prophetic vocation. There is sufficient evidence to establish that they clearly considered themselves to be standing solidly within a long prophetic tradition.

The Social Location and Function of Israelite Prophecy

In spite of the fluidity that existed between "prophetic" and "divinatory" types of intermediation as well as the difficulties involved in classifying the various actors, it is assumed here that there was a broad social role in Israelite society that was sufficiently stabilized as to designate it, for lack of a better term, prophetic intermediation. If, as we have argued, there was not only synchronic continuity between the various forms but also diachronic continuity between the earlier and later types, the difficulty becomes that of determining the social location and function of this broad role. Whereas Petersen speaks of the various *roles* played by the discrete types,[37] the concern here is to consider the social function of prophetic experience taken as a whole, thereby risking a degree of generalization for the sake of coherence.

[35] On the negative connotation of being the "tail" in relation to the "head," see Deut 28:13, 44.

[36] So R. Carroll's evaluation of Jeremiah, who, he argues, was promoted as a "prophet" only at a much later date (*Jeremiah* [Philadelphia: Westminster, 1986] esp. 55–64).

[37] Petersen, *Roles of Israel's Prophets*. Hobbs rightly criticizes the rigidity and high degree of detail of Petersen's social grid upon which he plots his various types (Hobbs, "Search for Prophetic Consciousness," 136–40). Buss correctly reminds us that the playing of a role is not only one of "role-taking" but also one of "role-making" ("Social Psychology of Prophecy," 4).

Role Actions of Prophetic Intermediation

From the perspective of modern Western societies, with their highly stratified social structures and precisely defined task-specific occupations, the role of the prophetic intermediary presents us with a confusing mix of activities. We will consider these various activities and seek to determine, first, whether or not the activity was integral to the broader vocation or whether it was only tangentially related, and, second, how the various activities related to the overall social location of the prophet.

Clearly, one central social role played by the prophet in Israelite society was that of the clairvoyant who, for a fee, could foresee future events or events that were unfolding in the present. The centrality of this role action is already clearly attested in the first recorded appearances of prophecy in Israel – Saul's encounter with the "man of God" or "seer" (*rō'eh*) Samuel (1 Sam 9:6ff.). Saul expected that this seer would be able to instruct him which road to take in order to find the lost asses he had been seeking. Even before being queried about the asses, however, the seer reported to Saul that they had already been found (9:20). He then went on to fulfill Saul's expectations about being told which road to take – on his way to becoming Israel's king (10:1-8). Unfortunately, the story does not relate the process by which the answer to the query was revealed to the seer. Though divination cannot be ruled out, and though some take the title "seer" to relate to visionary experience, 9:15 suggests an auditory experience (*YHWH gālâ 'et-'ōzen šĕmû'ēl*).

A similar instance of clairvoyance is illustrated by the story of Micaiah ben Imlah and the four hundred prophets of Israel (1 Kings 22). As was customary, the king of Israel requested an oracle prior to a planned military campaign in order to determine the success of the venture. The way the inquiry is phrased, "Shall I go . . . or shall I refrain?" (v. 6), suggests that a divinatory process was conducted. This process could have been conducted in one of two ways: either an omen was read that selected one of two possible answers ("this" rather than "that"); or the omen would stipulate positive or negative ("Yes, go up" or "No, do not go up"). What is somewhat confusing about the narrative is that elsewhere such "binary" oracles are conducted by priests rather than prophets (1 Sam 14:36-37, 41-42;

23:11–12). Further, Micaiah's response suggests not simply a divinatory process but a visionary experience ("I saw [*rā'îtî*] all Israel scattered . . . ," 22:17). Finally, Micaiah's argument concerning his vision of the heavenly council suggests that the means of securing the oracle was not mechanical, since otherwise the statement that one of the "spirits" would go and "be a lying spirit in the mouth of all his prophets" (v. 22) would be meaningless. Perhaps what we see here is the combination of divinatory and prophetic practices similar to those alluded to above.

The last example of prophetic clairvoyance we will mention is that demonstrated by the prophet when inquired of concerning the outcome of illness. When Abijah, the son of Jeroboam, fell ill, Jeroboam sent his wife to Ahijah, who could foresee the fate of the child (1 Kgs 14:1–18). Likewise, the ailing Ben-hadad of Syria sent Hazael to Elisha to learn of his fate (2 Kgs 8:7–10), just as the injured Ahaziah sent to Baalzebub of Ekron to determine whether he would recover from injuries (2 Kgs 1:2–4). None of these texts suggests that the prophet used mechanical means to effect the inquiry, however; and we should assume that the prophet normally secured the oracle by means of visionary or auditory experience.

Closely related to the texts in which the prophet is approached about the outcome of disease or injury are texts in which the prophet functions as a "healer." It may seem odd to us that it was the prophet who functioned as the doctor in Israelite society. In point of fact, there was in Israel no medical practice as we know it. However, two narratives clearly illustrate the role of the prophet as healer. In the first, Naaman comes to Elisha to be cured of leprosy (2 Kgs 5:1–14). In the second, Isaiah administers a fig poultice to heal the deathly ill Hezekiah (2 Kgs 20:7). In this category of the prophet as "healer" we ought also to include the narratives of the resuscitation of the widow's son, attributed both to Elijah (1 Kgs 17:17–24) and to Elisha (2 Kgs 4:18–37), as well as the curious note concerning the amazing power of Elisha's bones to revive the dead (2 Kgs 13:20–21).

Was such "healing" really an identifiable part of the prophetic role, or was the association simply accidental? That "healing" and "being a prophet" were in fact closely connected is illustrated by the response of the widow to Elijah's healing of her son: "*Now* I know that you are a man of God" (*'îš 'ĕlōhîm*, 1 Kgs 17:24), a technical term referring to the prophetic vocation. The connection of healing with prophecy is illustrated also by the story of Jesus' healing of the man born blind (John 9). After being healed by Jesus, the man is queried by the Pharisees: "What do you say about him? It was your eyes he opened." The man's answer, stated as though one would have to be blind himself not to know: "He is a prophet!" (v. 17). That the Israelite prophet was something of a "medicine man" ought not be surprising, given the common phenomenon of the shaman, who combines healing powers with divinatory and prophetic functions.[38] It is only our relatively recent "enlightened" sensitivity to what we consider to be the imprudent coalescence of medicine, magic, and religion that causes us to bristle at the notion. Throughout the major part of human social organization, it has been considered only natural that the prophet and the doctor should be overlapping roles, as appears to have been the case in Israel.

To be able to heal the sick, however, implied that the prophet also performed the social function of praying for the sick. The role of "healer" therefore slides over into that of "intercessor." The association of the role of intercession with the prophetic vocation has certainly not gone unchallenged.[39] Nevertheless, without denying that intercession was not *limited* to the prophet it seems almost certain that intercession was understood to be associated more directly with the prophet than with any other person. It was the prophet in Israel who, more than anyone else, was understood to be the community's chief intercessor. Granted that the allusion to Abraham as a prophet in Gen 20:7 is hardly defensible historically, it nevertheless attests to the connection between healing, intercession, and the prophetic office as popularly understood by the community. Abimelech, who is judged by God to be "a dead man," is commanded to restore Abraham's wife with these words: "for he is a prophet, and he will pray for you and you shall live" (cf. v. 17). The central role that Moses

---

[38] On the sociological connection of "shamans," "prophets," and other intermediaries, see Thomas W. Overholt, *Prophecy in Cross-Cultural Perspective: A Sourcebook for Biblical Researchers* (Atlanta: Scholars Press, 1986) esp. 7–10. The case studies presented by Overholt demonstrate the interconnection of prophetic and healing aspects of the prophetic role.

[39] Samuel E. Balentine, "Jeremiah, Prophet of Prayer," *RevExp* 78 (1981) 331–44; idem, "The Prophet as Intercessor: A Reassessment," *JBL* 103 (1984) 161–73.

plays in interceding for the people (Num 11:2; 21:7; Deut 9:20, 26) may likely lie behind the tradition that he was a prophet (Hos 12:13).[40] The prophetic function of intercession is attested also by Amos's response to the initial divine threats against Israel in the vision reports (Amos 7:2–3, 5–6), as well as requests made to Jeremiah that he might not simply "inquire" of the Lord but would in fact "intercede" for the people (Jer 37:3; 42:2, 4). Only by understanding the signal importance of the prophet's role as the community's chief intercessor can we appreciate the bitterness of Isaiah's dilemma, who was called as prophet to make his people's "heart fat," "ears heavy," and "eyes shut," thus guaranteeing their destruction (Isa 6:10), or Jeremiah's pain at being disallowed by God to perform his intercessory role for a time (Jer 7:16; 14:11; 15:1–2).

The Social Function of "Doom" Prophecy

Clairvoyant, healer, chief intercessor: Insofar as the prophets performed these roles, they obviously served "social maintenance" functions, that is, served in the capacity of maintaining social cohesion and balance. The premier problem concerning the social location of the prophetic role is what to do with the "other side" of prophecy, the side that advocated disruption, destruction, and an end to the present social configurations. One possible solution is to equate the prophetic social role in its entirety with this "social disruptive" function, and to argue that the "social maintenance" aspects were either an anomaly or else a perversion of genuine prophecy.[41] This conclusion seems to be suggested by Jeremiah's response to Hananiah in which he gives a brief synopsis of prophetic tradition:

> The prophets who preceded you and me from ancient times prophesied war, famine, and pestilence against many countries and great kingdoms. As for the prophet who prophesies peace, when the word of that prophet comes true, then it will be known that the LORD has truly sent the prophet. (Jer 28:8–9)

[40] To Moses is also attributed the communal lament, Psalm 90, attesting to the role he served in the corporate memory as Israel's chief intercessor.

[41] E.g., Walter Brueggemann, *The Creative Word: Canon as a Model for Biblical Education* (Philadelphia: Fortress, 1982); idem, "Prophet as a Destabilizing Presence," 51, 69.

There is no doubt that Jeremiah's perception is not wholly false. Prophets probably *did* proclaim such messages. The question is against whom did they proclaim them. Jeremiah is likely alluding here to the function served by earlier prophets in the context of "war prophecy," in which favorable oracles of victory would be accompanied by pronouncements of destruction directed against the "many countries and great kingdoms" with whom the Israelite armies were about to engage in battle. Jeremiah is applying a new hermeneutic to a historical fact, thereby turning what was primarily a social maintenance function (war prophecy) into one of social disruption. His hermeneutical application reeks of polemical interest and cannot be accepted as an accurate assessment of what constituted the commonly perceived prophetic social function.

A second possible solution is to argue that prophets played both sides of the field, some serving social maintenance functions and others social disruptive functions. This solution is commonly articulated today by those who locate various forms of prophetic activity either at the "center" or at the "periphery" of society. "Central prophecy" is taken to maintain social cohesion by supporting the society's chief deities and by being exercised through centrally located social structures. "Peripheral prophecy," on the other hand, is viewed as providing an entrée for marginalized groups into alternative power structures or for upgrading their status through association with former or foreign deities exercising power through peripheral social structures.[42] Such a distinction has the tremendous advantage of recognizing the broader aspects of prophetic social function and is extremely helpful for understanding the diversity of Israel's prophetic experience. However, as Overholt has observed, it can as easily be argued that peripheral possession itself contributes to social stability insofar as it provides the intermediary and his or her support group an acceptable means to vent frustration and an avenue to achieve part of their social program.[43] One cannot simply align "central" and "peripheral" prophecy respectively with social maintenance and social disruptive functions. Furthermore, whether a

---

[42] Robert R. Wilson, *Prophecy and Society in Ancient Israel* (Philadelphia: Fortress, 1980); Petersen, *Roles of Israel's Prophets.*

[43] Overholt, *Prophecy in Cross-Cultural Perspective,* 17.

group is "central" or "peripheral" is often relative to the observer or group, and prophetic figures often seem to cross back and forth across such imagined boundaries.[44]

The problem of prophetic social location comes to its crisis point over the function played by the prophets, including most of the canonical prophets, who issued unconditional judgments of doom against their own people. Were such prophets the "true" prophets who articulated God's disruptive will against the easy consensus of *shalom* articulated by the "false" prophets? Or were they "peripheral" prophets who represented a specific social location at the margins of polite society? The question has to do with how such oracles of doom would have been perceived by the community as well as by the broader prophetic tradition. The answer to this question is closely related to a yet unmentioned social role that the prophet played: "dispenser of curses and blessings."

If to the prophet was attributed the power to heal, the corollary must also be asked: Was the power to inflict wounds or disaster through the act of cursing also attributed to him or her? The best illustration of such a social function is unfortunately compromised because the figure is that of a non-Israelite prophet, Balaam, who is hired by Balak, king of Moab, to hurl a curse upon the people of Israel (Numbers 22–24). Does Balaam represent a social role that was characteristic of Israel's environment but utterly foreign to Israelite practice? Or does he, even though a foreigner, play a role that would have been totally intelligible to the Israelite audience hearing the story? Any answer can be only speculative. However, given the evidence concerning the real fear of "curses" which existed in Israelite society (e.g., Exod 21:17; 22:28; Lev 19:14) the question concerning the existence of "professional cursers" must be asked. Though it appears that anyone could hurl a curse, it seems most likely that certain persons were thought to possess a particularly strong power that could result in a higher frequency of effective curses. Not

---

[44] Wilson himself allows for such movement back and forth. Isaiah, he suggests, began as a central prophet; he moved to the periphery under Ahaz and back to the center again under Hezekiah (*Prophecy and Society,* 273–74). Cf. Overholt's observations concerning the Native American shamans Wavoka (*Prophecy in Cross-Cultural Perspective,* 18) and Handsome Lake ("Prophecy: The Problem of Cross-Cultural Comparison," in *Anthropological Perspectives on Old Testament Prophecy* [ed. R. C. Culley and T. W. Overholt; Chico, CA: Scholars Press, 1982] 67).

surprisingly, it is prophetic figures who often are portrayed as functioning in this role. So Elijah curses Ahab (1 Kgs 21:19–22) and Jezebel (v. 23), and Elisha hurls a particularly "grisly" curse upon a band of obnoxious boys (2 Kgs 2:24). Similarly, Elisha brings a curse of blindness down upon the entire Syrian army (2 Kgs 6:18), just as Amos threatens the life of Jeroboam with the sword (Amos 7:11). Such stories, as fanciful as they are, illustrate what must have been perceived to be a commonly recognized social function performed particularly well by prophets by virtue of their inordinate power over sickness and well-being.[45]

This social role provides the answer to one of the most perplexing problems regarding the role of the prophets: Were their symbolic actions and oracles of utter doom thought to be cases of "sympathetic magic" by which they effected what they proclaimed? Or were their actions and oracles of doom intended to effect an appropriate response in their audience and thus bring about repentance and restoration? Did the prophets of unconditional doom desire "blood and destruction," or did they desire "repentance"? In other words, were these oracles and actions a function of the ultimate social disruption, or were they the logical consequence of social maintenance functions? The answer lies in how the prophets were perceived by society as experts in the art of cursing.

Though prophets were popularly thought to be the community experts in cursing, the community also knew that such curses were not inevitably the last word. Curses were not thought to be automatically and inexorably effective.[46] An illustrative text is Lev 19:14, which stipulates that "You shall not curse (*qillēl;* cf. NRSV "revile") the deaf or put a stumbling block before the blind. . . ." Why would "cursing the deaf" be such a grave offense? Simply because they would, under normal circumstances, be utterly incapable of effecting any countermeasures to ward off the curse, just as the blind would be helpless in the case of someone sabotaging their path with a stumbling block. The obvious implication is that it was socially permissible to curse the hearing! The text implies that, under normal circum-

---

[45] Cf. the encouragement "not to be afraid" in Deut 18:22, which makes sense only if the prophet is a threatening type who might normally induce dread.

[46] So David can hope that the curse hurled against him by Shimei might be turned into good (2 Sam 16:12).

stances, a curse would be spoken aloud so as to be clearly heard by the person.[47] Furthermore, the victim of the curse could then take the necessary measures to ward off the curse or to mitigate its effects.[48]

The ability to mitigate such curses or, in the case of prophetic oracles, the announced doom was already alluded to in the case of the Mari prophetic texts in which the king would be encouraged to have the usual battery of divinations conducted in order to determine whether or not the oracle held up under scrutiny. Or he would be encouraged to take measures to ensure his safety in the face of such possible threats to his well-being. In other words, the function of such prophecies was to provoke an appropriate response from the king in order to mitigate the perceived threat. Such mitigating actions might take a variety of forms. David mitigated the oracle announcing his death by means of repentance (2 Sam 12:7–13), and similarly Hezekiah mitigated a similar oracle with sincere lamentation (2 Kgs 20:1–6). Jer 36:20–26 possibly records another attempt to mitigate the effects of announced judgment: King Jehoiakim burned Jeremiah's prophetic scroll column by column as it was read to him.

Prophetic oracles of unconditional doom were likely understood by the king and all concerned to be a function of the prophet's role of "dispenser of curses." As such they were understood to be remediable and served to prompt the persons affected to take the necessary action to ward off the otherwise certain catastrophic effects. It is not only conceivable but highly likely that the king was surrounded by the same sort of divinatory apparatus that was customary throughout the ancient Near East. One can imagine that, as soon as an oracle was directed his way, the king would mobilize his technical experts in order to clarify the matter, determine the validity of the oracle, and implement the appropriate procedures to counter the threat.

This proposed reconstruction answers the question concerning the function of the prophetic actions and oracles of doom. Such actions and oracles were not simply "street theater" intended for didactic purposes.[49] As curses, they were potentially effective and disastrous,

[47] Again, cf. Shimei's rather persistent efforts directed against David (2 Sam 16:5–13).

[48] Thus Yahweh can promise, "The one who curses you I will curse" (Gen 12:3).

[49] Bernhard Lang, *Monotheism and the Prophetic Minority: An Essay in Biblical History and Sociology* (Sheffield: Almond, 1983) 81–88; idem, "Street Theater, Raising

particularly because they were hurled by those known for their super-
abundant power in such matters. However, they were also not considered to be irremediable acts of sympathetic magic that effected
the judgment acted out or articulated. Instead, they were understood
to function precisely as curses were thought to function: the targeted
person was expected to take appropriate action or risk suffering the
consequences.[50]

The social function of such "prophets of unconditional doom" was
that of effecting an appropriate response from their audience—and
in their estimation the only appropriate response was repentance.
Were the "prophets of doom" thought to effect an irretrievable future
of destruction, then surely Micah would have been remembered as
a failure since his oracle that "Jerusalem shall become a heap of ruins"
(Mic 3:12) was utterly disconfirmed. However, Micah was recalled
in tradition not as a dismal failure but rather as a raging success!
He accomplished that which his social role and function determined
was primary, namely, the repentance and conversion of Hezekiah
(Jer 26:16-19).[51] Carroll is correct when he insists that the prophet's
goal was not "accurate prediction" but rather persuading the community to change.[52]

This social function takes a humorous and satirical form in the
Jonah novella. Here was a prophet who *must* have known his social
role—that of effecting repentance (4:2). Yet it was precisely this role
which made Jonah despair of life, since he knew that if he flung his
curse effectively ("Yet forty days and Nineveh shall be destroyed,"
3:4) he would in all likelihood be successful, Nineveh would repent,
and his party would be over. Many scholars misunderstand the irony
of the story because they misunderstand the function of "doom
prophecy." They argue that the function of "doom prophecy" was

the Dead, and the Zoroastrian Connection in Ezekiel's Prophecy," in *Ezekiel and
His Book: Textual and Literary Criticism and their Interrelation* (ed. J. Lust; Leuven:
Leuven University Press, 1986) 297–316.

[50] For a fuller treatment of the issue, see Georg Fohrer, *Die symbolischen Handlungen
der Propheten* (2nd ed.; Zurich: Zwingli, 1968), with whom I am in general agreement.

[51] Contra Wesley J. Fuerst, who argues that Micah was vindicated because, as a
"doom" prophet, he met the criterion of true prophecy set by Jer 28:9 ("A Study
of Prophetic Disagreement," *TBT* 20 [1982] 20–25).

[52] Robert P. Carroll, *When Prophecy Failed: Reactions and Responses to Failure in
the Old Testament Prophetic Traditions* (London: SCM, 1979) 33, 67.

to effect the judgment pronounced, no questions asked. Accordingly they insist that Jonah, as a doom prophet, was afraid of failure since he was afraid God might respond to the people's conversion. Such an interpretation simply misses the irony of the story. Jonah was not afraid of failing. Jonah was afraid of *succeeding!* He was afraid that what he full well knew to be the social function of the prophet would have its intended effect: the people would hear his curse; they would take the appropriate action to remedy its effects; and God would respond to their actions. He succeeded in his task and he rued his plight.

If it is the case that the social function of such prophetic oracles was to prompt the appropriate effect in the lives of the hearers, then there obviously can be no facile alignment of "doom prophecy" with social disruption. Such prophets were not interested simply in radical dislocation. But neither were they interested in maintaining a smooth consensus. Rather than calling people "back to the future," their program at one and the same time called the people "ahead" to that which articulated the sacred myth of the "past." Hosea invited the people to encounter God once again in the wilderness (Hos 2:14–23). Jeremiah envisioned a "new covenant" that articulated the myth of the old one (Jer 31:31–34): the focus on Torah, the inscription on their hearts (Deut 6:6; 30:14), the covenant formula "I their God, they my people." But the new myth took new shape and transcended the limitations of the old. Whereas the old depended on human achievement, on parents teaching their children (Deut 6:7–9; 11:18–21), the new would be so innately impressed upon the human heart that instruction would be a superfluous vestige of the past. Deutero-Isaiah similarly summoned the people into a "new" future which transcended the "former things" (42:9; 43:18–19), into a new myth which was but the ultimate revelation of that old myth told from the very beginning (40:21). Protology, history, and eschatology coalesce in kaleidoscopic patterns, using the articulated myth of the past to remythologize the future for a people who had lost their mythic orientation (51:9–11).

The function of the prophet was that of "de-mythologizing" the past by "re-mythologizing" the future. To speak of them as simple "social maintainers" or "social disrupters" trivializes their mission. If one wishes to use the term "charismatic" of the prophets, then it is best used in the sense of their ability to articulate the "mythic consciousness" of their people.[53] They were not proto-Protestants standing alone against all oppressive structures. Nor were they simple janitors whose job was to maintain Israel's ivory ediface. Their job was to extrapolate out the truth of the old myth in order to overcome its limitations and to reshape it into a new myth that would articulate God's graciousness in the midst of the people.

The Social Validation of Prophecy

The question concerning the social location and function of Israelite prophecy must also address two fundamental issues: In what was it that such prophecy was thought to ground its authority, and by what means was it evaluated and authenticated? The tension between the "psychological" and "sociological" dynamics of prophetic validation are most clearly and painfully evident in struggling with these two issues. When considered as psychological "personalities," the prophets seem to draw their power from some wellspring of charisma which sets them over against any process of social empowerment or validation. It is not only prophets themselves who assume that their power is grounded in "divine appointment." The community itself attributes such divine empowerment to the prophet. However, if there has been any single insight which recent attention to sociological dynamics has taught us, it is that *charisma, insofar as such an abstract concept exists, is itself a function of the social group*. The prophet is "charismatic" insofar as she or he exhibits the ability to articulate the community's mythic consciousness, or to awaken the community's disposition toward the centering principles of cosmic justice and order.[54] It is the community rather than the individual which is the nexus of charismatic power. Thus, we ought not speak

[53] See the definition of charisma given by A. R. Willner and D. Willner: The charismatic presence of a leader refers to his or her ability to "draw upon and manipulate the body of myth in a given culture and the actions and values associated with these myths." One is charismatic in that he or she is able to evoke and associate him- or herself with the sacred symbols of the culture ("The Rise and Role of Charismatic Leaders," *The Annals of the American Academy of Political and Social Science* 358 [March, 1965] 77, 84).

[54] E. Shils, "Charisma, Order, and Status," *ASR* 30 (1965) 201. See chapter 3 above.

so much about "charisma" as about the "attribution of charisma."[55]

Prophetic empowerment is derived in sociological terms from the disposition and the need of the community itself to empower such persons. Prophets are persons with electrical cords attached to their bodies. The question is: Where is the wall outlet located into which they plug themselves in? The outlet is located squarely in the community itself. Prophets derive their energy, in this sense, from the stored but diffused energy residing in the social group. Prophets serve to do what the community is of itself incapable of doing: they harness and focus this energy and redirect it back into the community so as to empower the community itself.

The corollary of this observation is that it is also the social group that attributes validation to the prophet. Though the prophet would likely claim divine inspiration, and though the community would attribute divine inspiration to the prophet, it was in fact the willingness of the community to make such an attribution that was the basis for the prophet's social validation.[56] The claim to such divine inspiration was in actuality a claim to social validation, and the community would likely not be inclined to grant such validation to anyone who did not claim it on the basis of divine appointment.[57]

The social validation of prophecy in Israel came to its own crisis point in texts relating to prophetic conflict. How was it that the community could differentiate between competing messages, thereby validating one and disqualifying the other? The biblical text itself struggles with the issue, proposing a wide range of conflicting criteria:

[55] See the recent attempts to distinguish between "pure" charisma and "manufactured" charisma by Ronald M. Glassman ("Manufactured Charisma and Legitimacy") and Joseph Bensman and Michael Givant ("Charisma and Modernity: The Use and Abuse of a Concept") in *Charisma, History, and Social Structure* (ed. R. M. Glassman and W. H. Swatos; New York: Greenwood, 1986). In the sense that charisma derives from and is legitimated by coherence to a society's specific conventions (see below), *all* charisma is a socially manufactured phenomenon.

[56] It is quite beside the point to argue, as does Douglas Stuart, that the prophet knows he is right and the others are wrong because he knows what God has told him ("The Old Testament Prophets' Self Understanding of their Prophecy," *Themelios* 6 [1980] 10).

[57] An anomaly to this pattern is the case of Yali, the cargo-cult prophet, to whom was attributed such a status in spite of his not actively claiming it. See the case study in Thomas W. Overholt, "Commanding the Prophets: Amos and the Problem of Prophetic Authority," *CBQ* 41 (1979) 530–31.

success in prediction (Deut 18:22; 1 Kgs 22:28); adherence to an orthodox or tradition-bound position (Deut 13:1–5; Jer 28:8); mode of reception (Jer 23:28); life-style (Jer 23:14). The modern debate has been intensified by the conclusion drawn by Georg Quell and endorsed by James L. Crenshaw that in fact there were no adequate criteria to allow the community to distinguish between true and false prophets, and that it was precisely this fatal flaw which led to prophecy's eventual demise.[58]

Others, however, have objected to this capitulation to pessimism and have searched valiantly for that criterion above all others which would promise a way out of the dilemma. Carroll and Simon J. De Vries have argued that the test of fulfillment was, or at least *ought* to have been, the adequate criterion legitimating true prophecy—except that precisely the disconfirmation of such predictions proved prophecy's undoing.[59] De Vries, however, confused the issue somewhat by suggesting at the same time that adherence to theological orthodoxy—namely, to "the radical theonomy of Yahwistic faith"—was the *sine qua non* of authentic prophecy.[60] James A. Rimbach also applied the criterion of confessional orthodoxy, the true prophet being the one who "called to repentance."[61] Obviously this criterion could be applicable only in some forms of prophecy, and cannot be applied to prophecy as such. Thomas B. Dozeman suggested that the prophet's life-style, the "way" in which he walked, was the key to discerning true from false prophecy.[62]

In addition to a simple recitation of the Old Testament's own criteria, some recent attempts to decipher the riddle have applied new, if not exotic, criteria. The most popular solution has been to see true prophecy as a matter of being able to apply the right her-

---

[58] G. Quell, *Wahre und falsche Propheten: Versuch einer Interpretation* (Gütersloh: C. Bertelsmann, 1952); Crenshaw, *Prophetic Conflict.*

[59] Carroll, *When Prophecy Failed,* esp. 186–202; S. J. De Vries, *Prophet Against Prophet: The Role of the Micaiah Narrative (I Kings 22) in the Development of Early Prophetic Tradition* (Grand Rapids: William B. Eerdmans, 1978) 144.

[60] De Vries, *Prophet Against Prophet,* 147.

[61] J. A. Rimbach, "Prophets In Conflict—Who Speaks for God?" *CurTM* 9 (1982) 174–77.

[62] T. B. Dozeman, "The Way of the Man of God from Judah: True and False Prophecy in the Pre-Deuteronomistic Legend of 1 Kings 13," *CBQ* 44 (1982) 392–93.

meneutic to the present historical situation,[63] to see the "wholeness" of the present moment and to engage in open-ended praxis rather than mere "logos."[64] Others have taken recourse in the final canonical shape of the text as the ultimate determinant of true prophecy,[65] although such a criterion would obviously have been meaningless for the "precanonical" community struggling with the issue.

Burke O. Long has pointed out that most such efforts have focused on message- or person-oriented criteria and have overlooked the fact that such prophetic conflict is a normal function of social groups, needing therefore to be understood in terms of its social dynamics. Long insists, in my opinion correctly, that prophetic conflict is built into the social order precisely because claims of supernatural warrant and even successful mediation are not enough to guarantee success and social status. Authority is not predicated simply on meeting set criteria, but rather is built and maintained by creating a network of client and peer relationships. Prophetic conflict has less to do with ideological and theological differences than with social and political dynamics.[66]

The question then is not what single criterion "proves" the true prophet to be true and the false to be false. Rather the question is what constellation of criteria is significant in the process of social confirmation and affirmation—that is, in building and maintaining such client and peer relationships. There are two aspects to this issue. First, prophets are evaluated according to culturally specific social conventions and traditions to which they are expected by their potential support group to conform. Such criteria are gradually compiled and modified over time, based on the community's own evaluation of previous intermediaries whom it considers in retrospect to have

[63] Eva Osswald, *Falsche Prophetie im Alten Testament* (Tübingen: J. C. B. Mohr, 1962) 21–23, 28–29; James A. Sanders, "Hermeneutics in True and False Prophecy," in *Canon and Authority: Essays in Old Testament Religion and Theology* (ed. G. W. Coats and B. O. Long; Philadelphia: Fortress, 1977) 21–41.

[64] Henri Mottu, "Jeremiah vs. Hananiah: Ideology and Truth in Old Testament Prophecy," in *The Bible and Liberation: Political and Social Hermeneutics* (ed. N. K. Gottwald; Maryknoll, NY: Orbis, 1983) 244, 247–48.

[65] Brevard S. Childs, *Old Testament Theology in a Canonical Context* (Philadelphia: Fortress, 1985) 134–39; Sheppard, "True and False Prophecy within Scripture," 271.

[66] Burke O. Long, "Social Dimensions of Prophetic Conflict," in *Anthropological Perspectives on Old Testament Prophecy* (ed. R. C. Culley and T. W. Overholt; Chico, CA: Scholars Press, 1982) 37, 43.

been effective.[67] In other words, the prophet must be performing a "recognizable" role as defined by the social group itself. Included among these role expectations would be the prophet's own claim to divine inspiration, though Long's caution is to be heeded at this point: the recitation of a call narrative would never have been sufficient in itself to have elicited acceptance, and prophets seldom take recourse in them when needing to defend their status.[68] Often accompanying the prophet's claim to divine inspiration is the claim that such appointment by the deity was not actively sought out but was forced upon the prophet against his or her will.[69] Societies often respond by pressuring the candidate to accept such divine appointment, in spite of the candidate's own fears or reluctance.[70] Many societies also expect its prophets to have a recognizable form of training or apprenticeship[71] as well as the acknowledgment of an established diviner or peer group.[72] The community learns to identify certain forms of speech patterns with what it regards as legitimate prophecy[73] and measures the prophet's message against certain canons of received tradition.[74]

It is not only the prophet's claims and message that must be congruent with social conventions and expectations. Prophetic actions must also fall within the general pattern of role expectations. Within this category fall those behavior characteristics often collectively

[67] Porter, "Origins of Prophecy in Israel," 24. On the general issue, see Overholt, "Commanding the Prophets," 532; idem, *Prophecy in Cross-Cultural Perspective*, 12–16.

[68] B. O. Long, "Prophetic Authority as Social Reality," in *Canon and Authority: Essays in Old Testament Religion and Theology* (ed. G. W. Coats and B. O. Long; Philadelphia: Fortress, 1977) 3–20.

[69] Norman Habel, "The Form and Significance of the Call Narratives," *ZAW* 77 (1965) 297–323.

[70] Wilson, *Prophecy and Society,* 49–50.

[71] Lang, "Israels Propheten," 21–23; idem, *Monotheism and the Prophetic Minority,* esp. 92–102.

[72] Martin J. Buss, "An Anthropological Perspective upon Prophetic Call Narratives," in *Anthropological Perspectives on Old Testament Prophecy* (ed. R. C. Culley and T. W. Overholt; Chico, CA: Scholars Press, 1982) 12.

[73] Claus Westermann, *Basic Forms of Prophetic Speech* (Philadelphia: Westminster, 1967).

[74] See Overholt's discussion concerning the message of Handsome Lake, which, though it contained new ideas such as heaven and hell, was accepted because it was compatible with the old system ("Prophecy: The Problem of Cross-Cultural Comparison," 67–68).

referred to as "ecstasy." Though ecstasy has often been regarded as tangential to Israelite prophecy if not antithetical to it,[75] Wilson has demonstrated that possession behavior, which always follows stereotypical and culturally specific patterns, includes a much broader pattern of behavior than the uncontrollable or unconscious behavior with which it is often associated. Wilson thus speaks of "controlled" possession behavior, which is learned by the prophet and which takes specific forms that the community can recognize as such.[76] The community expects of its prophets that they will exhibit certain patterned behavior which we might regard as "ecstatic" or "deviant."[77] Such expectations allow the community to continue to ascribe "charisma" to the prophet even if it refuses to subscribe to a particular program which the prophet advocates.[78] Closely related to ecstatic behavior are actions considered to be symbolic acts or acts of power.[79] Whether or not such acts follow a certain "repertoire,"[80] the very *action* itself takes certain forms which can be recognized as "prophetic drama" by those observing the "performance," and the performance is itself evaluated by the "audience" in terms of its overall effectiveness.[81]

The prophet must meet socially established role expectations as to what constitutes a prophet, and his or her performance is evaluated in terms of its relative consonance or nonconsonance with the social

[75] Mowinckel, "Cult and Prophecy," 79–88; Herrmann, *Ursprung und Funktion der Prophetie*, 41; more recently Parker, "Possession Trance and Prophecy," 281–84; Petersen, *Roles of Israel's Prophets*, 25–30.

[76] Robert R. Wilson, "Prophecy and Ecstasy: A Reexamination," *JBL* 98 (1979) 321–37.

[77] Long, "Prophetic Authority as Social Reality," 18. So Overholt refers to "normalized deviant behavior" (*Prophecy in Cross-Cultural Perspective*, 11).

[78] I disagree with Reinhard Bendix, who argues that charisma calls for unconditional obedience ("Reflections on Charismatic Leadership," in *Charisma, History, and Social Structure* [ed. R. M. Glassman and W. H. Swatos, Jr.; New York: Greenwood, 1986] 25).

[79] Thomas W. Overholt, "Seeing is Believing: The Social Setting of Prophetic Acts of Power," *JSOT* 23 (1982) 3–31.

[80] So Fohrer, *Symbolischen Handlungen*, esp. 20–74; cf. the critique of such a repertoire by Lang, "Street Theater," 305.

[81] Overholt makes a very important observation concerning the role of "trickery" in such performances, drawing on the case of Qaselid, the shaman among the Kwakiutl Indians of British Columbia. The audience is aware that the performer engages in tricks and fakery, but evaluates the performance on the basis of how well he performs the tricks (*Prophecy in Cross-Cultural Perspective*, 54–55).

structure and social values.[82] However, does this conformation to social expectations mean that the prophet simply shows and tells the people what they expect to hear, preaching to them of "wine and strong drink" (Mic 2:11). Quite the opposite. Part of the identifying role characteristic of prophecy is that prophets are also *expected* to tread the brink of what is tolerable. One aspect of their role is to *stretch the community's mythic consciousness to its breaking point.* Of course, if they stretch the community's consciousness too far or depart too widely from recognizable role expectations, they run the risk of simply causing role confusion,[83] are credited with the role of the "demented person," or fall victim to "witchcraft" accusations.[84] There are cultural boundaries beyond which the prophetic role simply cannot be understood or will not be tolerated. But these boundaries are never clear in any society, and prophets are therefore granted immunity to walk the edge and even occasionally to cross into the blurry buffer zone separating the tolerable from the intolerable—so long as the elastic thread of the community's mythic consciousness is not snapped in the process.

The interplay of "charismatic" and "institutional" dynamics in Israelite prophecy is therefore much more subtle than is often assumed by those who line up "cultic prophets" against "free prophets" or "central prophets" against "peripheral prophets." The "disruptive" function of the prophet is not something that stands over against antithetical social configurations but rather is closely related to those configurations themselves. The prophet represents not a shattering of the social consensus from the outside in, but rather a stretching of that consensus to its limits from the inside out. The elements of charisma and institution are so interrelated in the person and social function of the prophet that they cannot be distilled out or isolated.

[82] Ronald M. Glassman, "Charisma and Social Structure—The Success or Failure of Charismatic Leadership," in *Charisma, History, and Social Structure* (ed. R. M. Glassman and W. H. Swatos, Jr.; New York: Greenwood, 1986) 196; cf. Anthony Phillips's remarks concerning Amos's articulation of well-recognized social and ethical principles known to all his hearers ("Prophecy and Law," in *Israel's Prophetic Tradition: Essays in Honour of Peter R. Ackroyd* (ed. R. Coggins et al.; Cambridge: Cambridge University Press, 1982] 220, 222).

[83] See Petersen's remarks concerning "role dissensus" and "role conflict" (*Roles of Israel's Prophets,* 93–96).

[84] Wilson, *Prophecy and Society,* 32–33, 36–37, 56, 74–75.

Again we see that any understanding of how authority "works" which imagines that one may distinguish neatly between traditional, legal/ rational, and charismatic forms of empowerment is motivated more by prior social or theological commitments than by a reasoned consideration of the issues involved.

In his essay on the "prophetic" dynamic of the pastoral office S. M. Hauerwas criticizes the common distinction made between the "nurturing" (i.e., priestly) and the prophetic aspects of ministry, insisting as has this study that the prophetic function is to keep the community true to the story (the "mythic consciousness") that determines its character as a community of faith. He therefore argues that there is no conflict between "pastoral" and "prophetic" tasks, since the pastor is prophetic by definition of the office.[85] Hauerwas's essay is an attempt to overcome the tension between "charismatic empowerment" and "office," and to that extent I am fully in support of his interests. It is unclear, however, whether Hauerwas is able to overcome the split between the prophetic and the priestly or whether he simply removes the pastor from the priestly side and positions her or him squarely on the prophetic side. What does Hauerwas imply, for example, when he agrees with John H. Yoder's contention that the priest "manages nature" while the prophet "interprets history"?[86] The implication that the priest is a manager or a clerk while the prophet is a hermeneutician or a theologian leaves the chasm between office and charisma potentially wide open, as intent as Hauerwas may have been on overcoming the difficulty. Having addressed the issue of the interplay of charisma and office with regard to the prophet, we must now take up the issue raised by Yoder, Hauerwas, and others, and explore the social location and function of the priest.

[85] S. M. Hauerwas, "The Pastor as Prophet: Ethical Reflections on an Improbable Mission," in *The Pastor as Prophet* (ed. E. E. Shelp and R. H. Sunderland; New York: Pilgrim, 1985) 27–48.

[86] Ibid., 39; see John H. Yoder, *Preface to Theology: Christology and Theological Method* (Elkhart, IN: Goshen Biblical Seminary, 1982) 246–47.

6

The Priest:
Charisma by the Book

THE PREVIOUS CHAPTER on prophetic identity concluded with the comment made by John H. Yoder and echoed by S. M. Hauerwas that the priest managed the interpretation of nature whereas the prophet interpreted historical events unique to Israel's self-consciousness. The corollary to this thesis is that whereas the prophet was essential to Israel's self-identity the priest was superfluous: Israel could have been Israel without the priestly function.[1]

Such a tendency to promote the prophet to the visionary center of biblical faith and to demote the priest to clerk or bureaucrat has long been recognized as an unfortunate part of the Reformation's legacy, with its romantic fascination with the freedom of the "word" over against the captivity of "law" and legalistic clericalism. As has often been acknowledged today, such an ideological perspective, especially in Protestant scholarship, undergirded a negative valuation of Israel's legal/priestly traditions, a valuation epitomized in the work of Wellhausen and others who thought that these traditions epitomized a degenerate form of religious expression.

It is true, however, that whereas the prophet was associated with the "word" (*dābār*) or "vision" (*ḥāzôn*) in Israel's social life, the priest was responsible for "instruction" (*tôrâ;* see Jer 18:18). This distinction between prophetic *dābār* and priestly *tôrâ,* which reflect fundamental social realities, is the key to understanding charismatic

---

[1] John H. Yoder, *Preface to Theology: Christology and Theological Method* (Elkhart, IN: Goshen Biblical Seminary, 1982) 247.

and institutional impulses within the priesthood. The purpose of this chapter is to explore issues pertaining to the priest's association with *tôrâ* in order to understand the social function and location of the priest; the means of priestly diagnosis; the nature of temple, cult, and sacrifice; and the relationship of nature and creation to history. The result will once again be to test the adequacy of any thesis that pits unbounded charisma over against priestly managerial clericalism.

The Priesthood as Professional Guild

Exploring the social role and location of the priesthood is complicated by the fact that the biblical materials do not provide a careful definition of the office. Though there are descriptions of assorted priestly activities, especially sacrifice (Leviticus 1–7), nowhere do the texts provide an intentionally detailed description of the priestly institution as such. Various traditions clearly present radically different assessments of the office, but there is vigorous debate as to whether these diverse portraits are due to diachronic issues relating to dramatic changes in Israelite priesthood over the centuries or to synchronic issues relating to the office being evaluated from a variety of distinct sociocultural perspectives.

Undoubtedly both diachronic and synchronic issues must be considered. For example, in the priestly material in Leviticus and Numbers the priest is regarded primarily as an agent of sacrifice and atonement rituals and the arbiter of community purity. Elsewhere, however, the priest is associated with the administration of justice (Exod 22:7–13; Deut 17:8–13; 19:16–17; 2 Chr 19:8–11), the issuance of war oracles in conjunction with the ark of the covenant serving as war palladium (Judg 20:18–28; 1 Sam 4:4–9; 14:36–37; 23:1–12; Num 10:35–36), and the communication of "blessings" in the form of priestly salvific oracles (Num 6:22–27).[2] In addition, the priests have a primarily "teaching" function, responsible for the public rehearsal of Israel's legal tradition.

[2] See the classic study by Joachim Begrich, "Das priesterliche Heilsorakel," *ZAW* 52 (1934) 81–92.

How can one account for this kaleidoscopic portrait of priestly functions? This wide assortment of tasks is often attributed diachronically to a series of fundamental shifts in the priestly office over the centuries. Several major studies of the development of priesthood, for example, have suggested that Israelite priests were originally oracular agents whose oracles were procured through various means such as the manipulation of Urim and Thummim and possibly by the inspection of livers of sacrificial animals. According to this common reconstruction, over the centuries the priests came increasingly to have a juridical role, especially under the reforms of Jehoshaphat, as a result of which their sphere of competency shifted to that of being tradents and preservers of Israel's legal traditions. As the distinction between priests and Levites became sharper during the late monarchy, hitting a crisis point when Josiah shut down the outlying country sanctuaries, and as the teaching and juridical function was shifted increasingly to the Levitical circles, the priests gradually became specialists in sacrifice, particularly those involving expiatory blood rites, the hallmark of the postexilic temple cult.[3] Thus, the priestly office is assumed to have experienced a rather marked transformation from oracular consultant to legal tradent to sacrificial specialist.

An alternative reconstruction is one that places emphasis on synchronic perspectives. Common to such reconstructions is an unwillingness to hammer wedges between the oracular, teaching, and sacrificial functions of priesthood. Such a reconstruction stresses the continuity throughout time in both the form of the priestly office and the functions that were exercised by Israel's priests. Israel's oldest prophetic traditions already attest to the fact that Torah and sacrifice (*zebaḥ*) early coexisted under priestly auspices (Hos 8:12–13). The complaint leveled against the priests by Hosea, that they "feed on the sin [i.e., the *ḥaṭṭā't* or 'sin offering'] of my people" (Hos 4:8) is the most pointed evidence possible that already in the preexilic period the priesthood had long been responsible for expiatory sacrifices and

---

[3] On histories of Israelite priesthood that stress the diachronic development of the office, see Aelred Cody, *A History of Old Testament Priesthood* (Rome: Pontifical Biblical Institute, 1969); Leopold Sabourin, S.J., *Priesthood: A Comparative Study* (Leiden: E. J. Brill, 1973).

disproves the theory that such expiatory sacrifices were primarily a postexilic cult phenomenon.[4]

A major problem confronting anyone wishing to determine the social location and function of Israelite priesthood focuses on the relationship of the priestly guild to the circle of Levites. It is beyond this study to solve such a complex issue, but it does severely impact our discussion and so must be discussed even if only briefly.

Theories regarding the relationship of priests to Levites are divided into two basic camps: those which insist that the Levites always formed a distinct professional guild with their own areas of competency, and those which maintain that the Levites as a professional guild distinct from priests did not exist until relatively late in Israel's history, perhaps not until the postexilic reconstruction of Israel's cult, and that there is therefore no fundamental distinction between Levite and priest until that time. The former position, which is more or less that of the priestly tradition itself, insists that from the very beginning the Levites comprised a nonsacrificial and subordinate temple office which positioned itself over against the office of the priesthood.[5] Others allow that the Levites, as one priestly family among others, shared full priestly activities, including sacrifice, although they maintained their unique focus on instruction and proclamation of divine law as opposed to other priestly families which were more heavily invested in sacrifice.[6]

A more extreme version of this "early Levite" hypothesis is that proposed by a number of recent studies that present the Levites as a militarized group of persons who, having renounced their families, took up the sword for Yahweh and for Moses or the Mosaic tradition. This group of Levites, which is variously designated as Moses'

---

[4] Cf. Hos 8:11 as well as the formula of expiation recited in Isa 6:7, "Your guilt is taken away and your sin forgiven." The reference in 2 Kgs 12:16 to revenue gained from guilt offerings and sin offerings also supports the existence of expiatory sacrifices in the preexilic cult.

[5] See Raymond Abba, who calls attention to similar classes of Assyrian temple officials ("Priests and Levites in Deuteronomy," *VT* 27 [1977] 257–67; see also idem, "Priests and Levites in Ezekiel," *VT* 28 [1978] 1–9).

[6] Hans-Joachim Kraus, *Worship in Israel: A Cultic History of the Old Testament* (Richmond: John Knox, 1966) 97–101; Alfred Jepsen, "Mose und die Leviten: Ein Beitrag zur Frühgeschichte Israels und zur Sammlung des alttestamentlichen Schrifttums," *VT* 31 (1981) 318–23.

"armed gang"[7] or as an intertribal military police, exponents of a "religio-militaristic Yahwism,"[8] was the bearer of the genuinely Israelite amphictyonic traditions focusing on morality and teaching, in conscious and bitter opposition to the priests, who were bearers of canaanized forms of religion focused on sacrifice and cult ritual.[9] Hermann Schulz has suggested that this basic social conflict between an urban-priestly model focusing on cultic ritual and a tribal-village-Levitical model focusing on social ethos is characteristic of the broader ancient Near Eastern society and long predated the advent of Israel's own institutions, setting the context for the rise of similar competing groups in Israel's religious institutions.[10]

Any thesis that posits a clear distinction between priestly and Levitical circles must face the fact, however, that the early epic sources as well as the prophets are absolutely silent concerning the existence of a discrete social group of Levites clearly distinguished from the priests.[11] The only references to the Levites as a group of subordinate clerics are late, and even where Levites are known, they are not at all distinguished from the priests (Jer 33:18, 21–22; Mal 2:4–9; 3:3). Of course the Levites figure prominently into the scheme of Ezekiel's reconstruction (Ezek 43:19; 44:10–16; 45:5; 48:11–13), but the tendentious nature of these texts is widely recognized. Furthermore, wherever lists of officials are provided (2 Sam 20:23–26; 1 Kgs 4:1–19; Isa 3:1–3; Jer 27:9; Zeph 3:3–4) Levites are conspicuously absent.

[7] Götz Schmitt, "Der Ursprung des Levitentums," *ZAW* 94 (1982) 585–87.

[8] Hermann Schulz, *Leviten im vorstaatlichen Israel und im Mittleren Osten* (Munich: Kaiser, 1987) 33–35. On the militaristic aspects of the Levitical tasks, see John R. Spencer, "The Tasks of the Levites: *šmr* and *ṣb*," *ZAW* 96 (1984) 267–71.

[9] The primary study on this topic is A. H. J. Gunneweg, *Leviten und Priester: Hauptlinien der Traditionsbildung und Geschichte des israelitisch-jüdischen Kultpersonals* (Göttingen: Vandenhoeck & Ruprecht, 1965) esp. 220–25. Sabourin, too, posits a primary conflict between Levitical groups, representing the old Yahweh amphictyony, and other groups, such as the Aaronites, who represent canaanized forms of worship, except that he allows that the Levites fully exercised priestly functions (*Priesthood,* 105–9).

[10] Schulz, *Leviten im vorstaatlichen Israel,* 95–97, 178–79.

[11] Though this silence on the part of early pentateuchal sources might be attributable to the simple ignorance of temple "outsiders," as suggested by Menahem Haran (*Temples and Temple-Service in Ancient Israel: An Inquiry into the Character of Cult Phenomena and the Historical Setting of the Priestly School* [Oxford: Clarendon, 1978] 93–95), such can hardly be the case with the prophets, who were not unknowledgeable about temple politics.

In Deuteronomy priests and Levites seem to be equated and the two terms thought to be interchangeable, though the issue is hotly disputed. One crucial passage is Deut 18:1-8, which discusses Levitical rights within the Jerusalem sanctuary. The expression in v. 1 (*lakkōhănîm halĕwîyîm kol-šēbeṭ lēwî*), which juxtaposes priests and Levites, is variously translated as "the Levitical priests (*and*) all the tribe of Levi" or as "the Levitical priests, (*that is,*) all the tribe of Levi." The former translation is adopted by those who insist that the priests were a subgroup of the larger group of Levites, the rest of whom were subordinate temple officials.[12] The latter translation is proposed by those who maintain that Deuteronomy knows of no distinction between priests and Levites and that all Levites were eligible to be priests.

This latter understanding best represents the syntax of the Hebrew of v. 1 and in fact reflects what has been the classical position since the studies of Wellhausen, which runs as follows. Early in Israel's history there was no limitation of the priesthood to any one family among the "Levites." In Israel's premonarchic cult a single guild of temple specialists emerged, known as Levites. Though members of this guild comprised a pool of "preferred" priestly specialists, priests were not exclusively locked into strict hereditary families, and anyone could serve as a priest.[13] Being a "Levite" was basically a matter of joining the professional "guild." Under David and the early monarchy certain priestly families gradually consolidated their authority within certain sanctuaries, with the Zadokites[14] and Abiatharites sharing duties in the lucrative and prestigious royal sanctuary in Jerusalem. Under Solomon, however, the Zadokites achieved a

[12] E.g., Abba, "Priests and Levites in Deuteronomy," 262–63.

[13] The oft-cited test case for this reconstruction is the story in Judges 17 of Micah's appointment of his son as family priest and his eventual designation of a more legitimate Levitical priest.

[14] A secondary but equally volatile issue concerns Zadok's origins. Was he a priest of the former Jebusite cult of Salem, assumed into David's court as a political gesture? (So, e.g., H. H. Rowley, "Zadok and Nehushtan," *JBL* 58 [1939] 113–41; and C. Hauer, "Who was Zadok?" *JBL* 82 [1963] 89–94). Or was he already associated with David from an earlier time, perhaps even at Hebron (so F. M. Cross, *Canaanite Myth and Hebrew Epic: Essays in the History of the Religion of Israel* [Cambridge, MA: Harvard University Press, 1973] 208–15; and Haran, *Temples and Temple-Service in Ancient Israel,* 88) or Kabzeel (Saul Olyan, "Zadok's Origins and the Tribal Politics of David," *JBL* 101 [1982] 177–93)?

monopoly in the royal sanctuary; the Abiatharites were exiled to their hometown of Anathoth; and country sanctuaries were staffed by an odd assortment of Levitical and non-Levitical priests. According to this common assessment, Deuteronomy knows no distinction between priests and Levites, but does reflect the crisis precipitated when Josiah shut down the outlying sanctuaries. Since all legitimate priests were considered technically to be Levites, and since all Levites had full rights to serve in the Jerusalem sanctuary, there is an attempt in Deuteronomy at power sharing in the temple. But this program failed, and there continued to be a power struggle between Zadokite priests and priests from other families. Ezekiel, himself a Zadokite, envisioned in his postexilic cultic restoration that only Zadokite priests should maintain their status in the second temple, with all non-Zadokite priests demoted to the status of "mere" Levites because of their unfaithfulness (Ezek 44:10–16).[15] The actual postexilic restoration, canonized in the Priestly program, found Ezekiel's proposal unmanageable or unrealistic, and a deal was struck by which certain non-Zadokite Levitical groups once again were permitted to share power with the Zadokites, a deal sealed by the genealogical fiction that both groups of priests—Zadokite and non-Zadokite—could now trace their ancestry back to Aaron, who for the first time became the postexilic eponymous figure for Israel's priesthood.[16]

Though we cannot be dogmatic on the issue, we must resist any effort to pit Levite over against priest, especially in such a way that assigns Israel's Torah tradition to the Levite, thereby playing it off against priestly ritual and sacrifice. To siphon the proclamation of Torah off from the priest and to hand it over to the Levite is to ignore

---

[15] Debate focuses on the disputed meaning of the phrase *halēwîyîm 'ăšer rāḥăqû mē'ālay* (v. 10). Most take it to be all inclusive ("the Levites, [all of] whom removed themselves from me"), while others understand it to be a specification of certain Levites ("those [specific] Levites who removed themselves from me"). The former reading is definitely supported by the parallel statement in 48:11, which directly counterposes the Zadokite priests and the Levites as a whole.

[16] The position adopted for the most part by H. H. Rowley, *Worship in Ancient Israel: Its Forms and Meaning* (London: SPCK, 1967) 95–101; Cody, *History of Old Testament Priesthood*, 131–72; Sabourin, *Priesthood*, 105–35. A similar position is adopted by Haran, *Temples and Temple-Service*, 63–111. According to Haran, all Levites were originally priests. It was only with P, which Haran dates prior to 722, that a distinction was made between Aaronides (southern Levites) and "mere" Levites (northern Levites).

the fact that the prophetic material universally understands Torah to be the primary symbolic expression of priestly activity.[17] Whether proclamation of such Torah relates to the priest's oracular dispensing of blessings or instruction concerning clean and unclean, holy and profane; whether it relates to the priest's judicial competency or his leadership in catechetical rites of admission to the sanctuary; or whether it designates the priest as the bearer of Israel's non-negotiable story,[18] the priest is clearly the arbiter of Torah, and Torah is not opposed to other priestly activities such as sacrifice.

The Ideological and Socioeconomic Structures of Priesthood

As in nearly all human societies, the Israelite priesthood appears to have been a privileged guild, the members of which were granted considerable compensation and material security in exchange for their professional competence. The security of participation in the rights of guild membership could be jeopardized by a number of factors, including various physical injuries or defects, occasional periods of uncleanness, or the abuse of a strict code of behavior (Lev 21:1–22:9), which could disqualify one from exercising priestly rights. Apart from such occasional or unusual cases, however, there appears to have been little censure exercised for individual cases of malfeasance or malpractice,[19] so that the priest enjoyed a secure tenure based increasingly on patrimony and the political support of royal patronage, as is illustrated by Solomon's support of the Zadokites at the expense of the Elide line.

The socioeconomic position of the priesthood is suggested by the

---

[17] See Hos 4:1–6; 8:11–13; Mic 3:11; Isa 2:3; 51:4; Zeph 3:4; Jer 2:8; 18:18; Ezek 7:26; 22:26; 44:23–24; Mal 2:6–7.

[18] Walter Brueggemann, for example, defines Torah as the community's "root consensus," which lies beyond defense, doubt, or debate (*The Creative Word: Canon as a Model for Biblical Education* [Philadelphia: Fortress, 1982] 20–21, 35).

[19] Consider the cases of the sons of Eli (1 Sam 2:12–36) and of Aaron himself (Exod 32:1–24), the two classic cases of priestly malfeasance. The stories are obviously shaped by political interest, but nevertheless show that, apart from occasional references to apostasy (Zeph 1:4–6), when royal authority exercised political censure (2 Kgs 10:18–27; 23:5, 20), such abuse of the office was difficult to sanction.

very term used of their "ordination," expressed in Hebrew by the phrase "filling the hand." This expression may refer to the gesture of vesting the ordinand in the symbolic clothing of the office, suggested by Exod 29:1–9, which concludes such vesting with the phrase "You shall then ordain ("fill the hand of," *ûmillē'tā yad*) of Aaron and his sons." It may likewise refer to the ordination ritual of "placing in the hand"[20] of the ordinand the "wave offering" (*tĕnûpâ*), which was then burned as a "fire offering" ('*iššâ*). More probably, however, the term relates to the priestly claim to the "priest's portion" (*tĕrûmâ*) of certain sacrifices, comprised of the animal's breast and right thigh, which went to the sacrificing priest for his and his family's personal consumption as compensation for his oversight of the ceremony.[21] A major portion of grain offerings also was given to the officiating priest as his "due" (*ḥōq*; Lev 2:1–10; 6:14–16). This "priestly portion," which was considered "most holy" (*qōdeš qŏdāšîm*) from the priestly perspective, was protected in priestly legislation by stiff fines if encroached upon (Lev 22:10–16).

Particularly important in this regard was the priestly claim to the portion of the "sin offering" (*ḥaṭṭā't*; Lev 5:13; 6:24–30) and the "guilt offering" ('*āšām*; Lev 7:1–7), often associated with atonement rituals. Under the influence of critical Protestant scholarship it was once popular to assume that such a solemn focus on sin, guilt, and atonement was characteristic of the postexilic cult, in contrast to the preexilic cult, which was thought to be marked by a more festive and celebrative mood. This evolutionary position has long been challenged, however, and it is clear not only that all sacrifice carried within it the germ of the idea of atonement[22] but also that the sin and guilt offerings themselves were a fundamental part of Israel's preexilic cult.[23] Hosea's critique of the priestly office largely presup-

[20] Exod 29:22–25. Note, however, that the term used in v. 24 for "hand" is not *yād* but *kap*.

[21] The priestly claim to the *tĕrûmâ* is closely associated with the priest's ordination in Exod 29:26–28; cf. Lev 10:12–15 and, for a slightly different and possibly earlier tradition, Deut 18:3–4.

[22] Kraus, *Worship in Israel*, 116.

[23] For a fundamental study of the problem, see R. J. Thompson, *Penitence and Sacrifice in Early Israel Outside the Levitical Law: An Examination of the Fellowship Theory of Early Israelite Sacrifice* (Leiden: E. J. Brill, 1963). 2 Kgs 12:16 supports the antiquity of such offerings and further suggests that the "priest's portion," rather than being paid in kind, may have been converted into some form of currency.

poses that the priest was most popularly conceived of as gaining his primary revenue from conducting such atonement rituals. They are accused of "feeding on the sin" of the people (Hos 4:8–10) and of proliferating "altars for sinning" (8:11), obvious references to their major source of revenue and privilege. The reference in Isa 61:6 to Israel, collectively envisioned as priests of the Lord, "who shall eat (*'ākal;* contra NRSV "enjoy") the wealth of the nations," also alludes to this fundamental aspect of priestly identity. The fact that Ezekiel's envisioned temple had kitchens for boiling the sacrifices for priestly consumption (Ezek 46:24) is hardly an invention of the postexilic cult.

Such involvement in atonement rituals was not only one of the chief sources of revenue for the priesthood; it was also the basis for the priesthood's own ideological self-understanding. The payment of the priestly portion of the *ḥaṭṭā't* was the largess granted to the priest for the danger incurred by him in "bearing the sin" of the offender and thereby purging the sancta of the contaminating effects of the offender's sin.[24] Since the eating of the *ḥaṭṭā't* was not itself part of the atonement ritual, the priest ought not be thought of as a "sin eater" and all that that implies. Nevertheless, at least according to priestly ideology the priest did exercise a crucial social function, fraught with danger from contact with the combined powers of the uncontrollably numinous and of deadly contamination. He was the equivalent of the modern nuclear reactor supervisor who must channel the tremendous energy of the reactor while at the same time facing potential death in preventing radioactive contamination, core meltdown, and nuclear catastrophe, and who must supervise the decontamination of the environment in the case of disaster, which in cultic terms was an everyday occurrence.

A further and essential aspect of this priestly ideology was the notion that the Levitical priesthood was, in some significant way, different from all other members of the community. This difference was conceived of as its members having been "consecrated" (*qiddēš*) and therefore "separated" from the normal community and its environment, which was "common" (*ḥōl*). Furthermore, this separation was symbolized in Deuteronomic language by the ideology that

---

[24] On the "purgative" nature of atonement, see especially several articles by Jacob Milgrom, collected in *Studies in Cultic Theology and Terminology* (Leiden: E. J. Brill, 1983) esp. 70–84 and 237–39.

they had no regular inheritance or portion in common with everyone else. The Lord alone was their portion (Deut 18:1–5), and they were completely dependent on temple revenue. A later and more theologically reflective ideology, which was applied to the Levites in distinction to the priests, understood them to be a substitute for the rest of the people. They were conceived of as the equivalent of the "sacrificed firstborn," offered up to God for the sake of the larger family (Num 3:11–13, 44–45; 8:14–19). Though priestly ideology applies this "substitutionary" language strictly to the Levites, it is likely that the notion of a substitutionary group, sacrificially set apart for the sake of the larger community, lies deeper in the tradition, going back to a time when the distinction between priest and Levite was not as clearly defined.[25]

In addition to these chief means of revenue and the ideology that sustained them, there were other obvious sources of revenue which supported the priest's social position. The temple cult and its personnel were supported especially by regular tithes of produce and livestock, especially those associated with the major agricultural pilgrimage festivals (Exod 23:19; 34:19–23; Lev 23:37–38; Num 18:21–32; Deut 14:28–29; 16:10–17). Temple revenue was also generated by periodic nongraduated census taxes (Exod 30:11–16);[26] by private gifts, vows, dedications, and redemptions (Exod 28:38; 35:20–29; Lev 27:1–34; Deut 23:21); by booty secured through warfare (Num 31:28–30, 54); and by judicially imposed fines and forfeitures (Lev 5:16; Num 5:8; Deut 22:9).[27] As elsewhere in the ancient Near East, the temple in Jerusalem was not only the religious but also the economic and "banking" center of the nation, holding large estates of land as well as herds of livestock used in the sacrificial cult. Because

[25] Though the priests undoubtedly comprised the core of the literate in Israelite society, Sabourin's proposal that what made the group distinctive was their "above average intelligence" is to be rejected (*Priesthood*, 6).

[26] The temple staff may well have been exempt from these taxes (Num 1:47–49), which is only logical if the revenue was going to the temple in any event.

[27] One's patrimony, which was normally inviolable, was forfeited to the throne in certain capital cases involving offenses against the king. So Naboth's vineyard (1 Kgs 21:1–16) was not confiscated simply in a manner characteristic of Canaanite kings, as is often assumed, but rather by means of the normal process whereby the property of an offender charged with treason (Naboth "cursed God and the king") was confiscated by the throne.

the major sanctuaries were undoubtedly royal sanctuaries, there was no clear distinction between these temple holdings and the holdings of the royal court, and all such property was likely under the supervision either of the chief steward, who was "over the house" (*'al habbāyit*), or of the "royal governor" (*śar hā'îr*), the king's administrative assistant.[28]

The priesthood, therefore, enjoyed marked stability based on its economic resources, material holdings, and favors granted through royal patronage. Overlaying these material and political considerations was a sophisticated ideology that not only promoted the priesthood as divinely selected and set apart for the realm of the "holy" but also reinforced the social position of favored families by granting them full power to make atonement for private and corporate sin, thereby maintaining the equilibrium (*šālôm*) of the community.

The priesthood was also given institutional stability through a bureaucratic structure characteristic of national ecclesiastical cults throughout the ancient Near East.[29] The temple staff was under the direction of the "chief priest" (*kōhēn hārō'š*), who in turn was assisted by a "second priest" (*kōhēn mišneh*).[30] The interesting references to Ira as "priest to David" (*kōhēn lĕdāwid*, 2 Sam 20:26) and to Zabud as "priest and king's friend" under Solomon (*kōhēn rē'eh hammelek*, 1 Kgs 4:5) suggests, however, that the king exercised control over temple matters through two different channels, including one that

[28] The classic study of royal officials is Tryggve N. D. Mettinger, *Solomonic State Officials: A Study of the Civil Government Officials of the Israelite Monarchy* (Lund: Gleerup, 1971) esp. 79, 89. See also R. M. Good, "The Israelite Royal Steward in the Light of Ugaritic *'l bt*," *RB* 86 (1979) 580–82. On temple holdings, see Jacob Milgrom, *Cult and Conscience: The ASHAM and the Priestly Doctrine of Repentance* (Leiden: E. J. Brill, 1976) 51–60. Haran makes an important distinction between temples and freestanding altars (*Temples and Temple Service*, 15–16).

[29] For the use of this term in relation to the development of cultic organizations, see Chris Hauer, Jr., "David and the Levites," *JSOT* 23 (1982) 33–54. Whether Hauer is correct in arguing that, prior to David, Israel's cult was "shamanistic" is questionable.

[30] 2 Kgs 25:18; contrast 23:4, where the title *kōhēn haggādôl* is used. The latter title is seldom used in preexilic texts, and came to be the technical term for the head of the theocratic community in the postexilic reconstruction. The lists of officials under David and Solomon include the names of these chief priests; under David the duties were shared by Zadok and Abiathar (2 Sam 8:17 [correcting the MT]), and under Solomon the chief priest was Azariah (1 Kgs 4:2).

owed allegiance more directly and personally to the king himself. It is not unreasonable to assume that the king may have played these two channels of authority off against each other as political needs suggested. The book of Jeremiah alludes twice to a priestly chief officer (*pāqîd nāgîd*, Jer 20:1; 29:26–27), who apparently was a sub-ordinate official whose duty was to supervise the temple prophets and give guidance to the king concerning the legitimacy of prophetic oracles.[31] In addition, the priests certainly must have regulated internal matters through counsel directed from the "elders of the priests" (Jer 19:1). The king was himself the figurative head of the temple staff, much as the president of the United States is the commander-in-chief of the armed forces even though he likely holds no formal rank and may not have had professional military experi-ence. The king's status as head of the temple cult was expressed by the ideology that he was a special type of priest, a "priest forever after the order of Melchizedek," the "priest-king" of Salem (Ps 110:4; Gen 14:18). Considerable debate has focused on the king's role in the cultic life of Israel, which may have extended to his central role in the performance of national cultic dramas and leadership in the primary agricultural festivals. At the least he offered sacrifice and engaged in other priestly actions, even if only on an irregular basis, led the community in communal rites of penitence and thanksgiv-ing, and could exercise royal authority in restructuring temple arrangements and appointing personnel.[32] Solomon consolidated his power in part by giving full temple authority to the Zadokite dynasty at the expense of the Elides, and instituted far-ranging cultic reforms, including the very building of the temple itself as well as the installation of foreign-inspired cult objects (1 Kgs 2:26–27; 5:1–8:66; 11:4–8). Jeroboam similarly implemented a national cult at Bethel and Dan, installing a clergy consistent with his own political aims (1 Kgs 12:26–33). The actions of Jehoash, Ahaz, and Hezekiah demonstrate that the king had final control of temple revenue (2 Kgs 12:4–16; 16:8; 18:15–16), and Ahaz himself oversaw an "updating"

---

[31] See the discussion of the relation of divinatory and prophetic mediation in chapter 5 above. Amaziah the priest exercised such authority over Amos at the royal sanctuary at Bethel (Amos 7:10–13).

[32] For a review of the problem, see Cody, *History of Old Testament Priesthood*, 98–107.

of the temple furnishings expressive of political commitments to Assyria (16:10–16), as did his grandson Manasseh (21:3–9). The two most thoroughgoing cultic reform movements were those instituted by Hezekiah (18:1–4) and Josiah (23:4–25), both demonstrating the control the king exercised over cultic appointments and personnel.

With the priesthood enjoying such a relatively secure economic base intimately tied into state and royal revenue, with such thoroughly institutionalized channels of authority and accountability, and with so sophisticated an ideological program, it is not surprising that the distinction would often be made between "charismatically" inspired individual prophets on one hand and "institutionally" grounded office-holding priests on the other.[33] The intent here is not to challenge the obvious fact that the priesthood had strong institutional support structures. The concern, rather, is to question the validity of locating priestly authority in a type of formalized leadership, characterized by Weber's "legal/rational" form, in conscious opposition to the "charismatic" form exercised by other members of the community, particularly that of the prophets. Consideration of this issue must give attention first to the chief areas of professional competency exercised by the priests and second to the ideology with which the priesthood was apparently closely allied, that of "creation theology."

The Social Role of the Priest

The emergence of distinctively contemporary forms of ministry exercised by twentieth-century members of the clergy, forms that vary considerably from those of former centuries, is evidence that social roles do not stay frozen over long periods of time. The Israelite clergy experienced similar shifts in the ways in which their areas of professional competency were understood and exercised. However, it is unwarranted to presume that a shift from oracular agent to specialist in Torah and finally to sacrificial expert on the part of the Old Testament priest was any more dramatic or required any more fundamental a shift in basic self-awareness than has the shift in con-

---

[33] E.g., Sabourin, *Priesthood,* 101, 136.

temporary ministry from guardian of the sacraments and the creeds to *"Seelsorger"* and finally to "community enabler." Such shifts in competency and self-awareness naturally take place but are not necessarily the result of radical redirection or of conscious ideological reprogramming. Such shifts come slowly and are nearly always understood to be consonant with primary identity-conveying ideological structures, not in open revolt against them.

As stated above, therefore, it is best to resist the evolutionistic notion that overstates the discontinuity between the oracle dispenser, the Torah giver, and the blood manipulator—the three chief areas of priestly competency. The common tendency to take the simple order of priestly activity as stated in Deut 33:8-10 (oracles via Urim and Thummim, v. 8; Torah instruction, v. 10a; and sacrifice, v. 10b), and to presuppose that this order is chronological, representing an evolutionary development of Israelite priesthood, misconstrues the much more obvious conclusion to be drawn from the text—namely, that these three areas of competency were exercised simultaneously and were not seen as contradictory to one another. There may have been shifts over the centuries in priestly social function, particularly as a result of the crisis of exile and the reconstruction of the postexilic cult. But such shifts are not to be overly stressed nor understood as fundamental changes in the ideological base of priestly self-awareness.

Undoubtedly, one of the primary tasks of the priest in Israel, as throughout the ancient Near East, was to provide extracognitive information from the divine realm to the royal court/temple complex. Such information was solicited specifically in crisis situations, such as when the court was considering military maneuvers (1 Sam 23:1-14) and legal judgments (Exod 22:8-11), but such priestly oracles were certainly sought in many daily situations. In the preceding chapter we considered the interesting fact that priests in the ancient Near East were associated with forms of divination, the physical manipulation of material objects such as livers and arrows,[34] which apparently were held in somewhat higher regard than were prophetic oracles received through intuitive media (dream, vision,

---

[34] Ezek 21:21-22 knows of the Babylonian practice of shaking arrows, consulting teraphim, inspecting livers, and using lots.

audition). How priests in Israelite society gained their oracles is largely unknown, but the early use of Urim and Thummim certainly suggests that Israelite priests, like their ancient Near Eastern counterparts, also were experts in the lore of divination through the manipulation of physical objects. The preference given to such forms of divination over prophecy throughout the ancient Near Eastern accounts for the fact that in Israel, as at Mari, the priesthood was considered the controlling agency for screening the less controllable forms of prophetic activity.

The "religiously correct" official polemic, which was stamped by Deuteronomic theology, inveighed heavily against "unorthodox" forms of divination in Israel. Nevertheless, lists of officials such as those provided in Isa 3:1-3 and Jer 27:9 clearly depict the reality: "divination" was not unknown in Israelite society.[35] Both lists are interesting because, in spite of their comprehensiveness, neither mentions the priest among its officials. However, Isaiah does mention the diviner (*qōsēm*), the magician (*ḥăkam ḥărāšîm*), and the charmer (*nĕbôn lāḥaš*), and Jeremiah refers to the diviner (*qōsēm*), the soothsayer (*'ōnēn*), and the sorcerer (*kaššāp*). Though such terms may be strictly derogatory labels, they occur with such frequency as to suggest that Israelite society was replete with a variety of forms of divination. The priesthood itself may have been connected with such forms, which would explain the absence of the title "priest" in these lists.[36]

When the earliest traditions reflect upon the social location and function of priests, they do not confine them solely to conjuring oracles by means of Urim and Thummim or other forms of divination. Above all else, the priest is understood to be responsible for

[35] J. J. M. Roberts warns against the naïve notion that divination in the ancient Near East sought simply to manipulate God through magic whereas Israel sharply avoided such forms ("Divine Freedom and Cultic Manipulation in Israel and Mesopotamia," in *Unity and Diversity: Essays in the History, Literature, and Religion of the Ancient Near East* [ed. Hans Goedicke and J. J. M. Roberts; Baltimore: Johns Hopkins University Press, 1975] 182, 185).

[36] Exod 22:18; Judg 9:37; Deut 18:10; 1 Sam 28:7; 2 Kgs 17:17; 21:6; 2 Chr 33:6; Isa 2:6; 47:9, 12; Ezek 13:20-23; Mic 5:12; Zech 10:2; Mal 3:5. The term "divination" (*qesem*) is a somewhat broader term that sometimes is used of prophetic activity, such as in Jer 14:14; 29:8; Ezek 13:6, 9; 22:28; Mic 3:6-7, 11. This occasional blurring of the distinction between divination and prophecy may account for the interesting fact that Pashhur the priest is credited with "prophesying" in Jer 20:6.

Torah in the same way the prophet is responsible for the word and the sage for wisdom. Although Torah in broader terms is a possession unique to Israel as a whole (Deut 4:7-8) and is a mark of Israel's true wisdom (Jer 8:8), such Torah was understood to be specifically under the protection and administration of Israel's priesthood. When the priesthood was censured by Israel's prophetic voice for its malfeasance, the critique focused on the failure of the priesthood to pursue its responsibilities in guarding Israel's Torah tradition.[37] Deut 31:24-26 symbolizes the fact that the priesthood was the bearer of Torah by instructing that a copy of the Torah be placed in the temple precincts, precisely where one such copy was "discovered" during the Josianic reforms (2 Kgs 22:8-10).

The priesthood was not simply the archivist of Torah, however. It was above all responsible for "teaching" Torah. What such "teaching" included, however, is extremely vague. Mic 3:11 associates the priest who "teaches" (*hôrâ*) Torah with the "head" (*rō'š*) who "judges" and with the prophet who "divines."[38] The term *hôrâ*, "to teach" (literally, "cast, throw; point toward") is alternately connected with the act of "casting" lots, such as Urim and Thummim, for purposes of divination, or of "pointing" or directing a person in a correct direction.[39] The realm of this "Torah competency" related directly to the priest's responsibility for the administration of justice, whether through "pointing the direction" by means of the application of precedent judgments (Deut 17:8-11; Ezek 44:24) or through "casting" instruments of divination in the administration of oath or curse rituals (Exod 22:8-11; Num 5:11-31). When the priest abrogated his responsibility for Torah, therefore, Hosea could complain of the wholesale disintegration of the social moral fabric: there was lying, murder, stealing, and adultery—a total breakdown of faithfulness (*'ĕmet*), kindness (*ḥesed*), and knowledge of God (*da'at 'ĕlōhîm*, Hos

---

[37] Jer 2:8; Hos 4:1-6; 8:12; Mic 3:11; Zeph 3:4; Mal 2:6-7; Ezek 22:26.

[38] See the proposed emendation of Jer 5:31, *wĕhakkōhănîm yôrû*.

[39] The classical studies are those of Joachim Begrich "Das priesterliche Heilsorakel"; "Die priesterliche Tora," in *Werden und Wesen des Alten Testaments* (BZAW 66; ed. Paul Volz et al.; Berlin: Alfred Töpelmann, 1936) 63-88; and Gunnar Östborn, *TORA in the Old Testament: A Semantic Study* (Lund: Hakan Ohlssons Boktryckeri, 1945). For a more recent study, see P. J. Budd, "Priestly Instruction in Pre-Exilic Israel," *VT* 23 (1973) 1-14.

4:1–6). Torah and *mišpāṭ* (justice) were corollaries of each other (Isa 51:4).

In addition to formal oversight over judicial matters, the "teaching" responsibility of the priesthood possibly was extended to entail periodic public instruction or recitation of the Torah (Deut 31:9–13).[40] However, the reaction of Josiah upon the "discovery" of the Torah scroll (2 Kgs 22:11) and the sense that Ezra's reading of the Torah was a unique occurrence (Neh 8:1–8) both suggest that any such "periodic" reading was a rare occurrence at best. Such public instruction may have been limited to the priest serving as "catechist" during entrance rituals into the sanctuary. The teaching of Torah most certainly did relate to the priest's regular task of offering priestly "diagnoses" to separate the "holy" and the "common" as well as the "clean" and the "unclean" (Lev 10:10–11; Ezek 22:26; Hag 2:10–13). The concern for ritual purity, demonstrated in the Levitical laws regarding leprosy and bodily discharges (Leviticus 12–15), relates less to the priest's concern for the health of individuals than to the sanctity of the cult and the maintenance of a strict separation of distinct realms, symbolic of the manner in which Israel sought to frame its conceptual universe and maintain cherished patterns of order.[41] The priest was not a doctor who "cured" people but rather a diagnostician who "labeled" objects and events and "pronounced" them "clean, unclean, holy, profane." He did not *make* them so. He simply declared them to be what they already were, thereby assigning them to their appropriate category. But he also supervised the necessary rituals of reintegration into the worshiping community wherever such rituals took place.

This priestly concern for cultic sanctity also underlies the connection of the priesthood with sacrifice, involving as it did the animal's blood, understood to be the source of life and a powerful decontaminant useful in purging the sancta of uncleanness. Theories abound that attempt to explain the origin and primal function of sacrifice:[42]

[40] See William Holladay's reconstruction of the chronology of events in the book of Jeremiah, which he fixes around such a seven-year cycle of public readings (*Jeremiah 1* [Philadelphia: Fortress, 1986] 1–10).

[41] On the psychosocial dynamics of purity laws, see the classic study by Mary Douglas, *Purity and Danger: An Analysis of Concepts of Pollution and Taboo* (New York: Frederick A. Praeger, 1966).

[42] For reviews of classical theories understanding sacrifice as gift or communion,

it is variously understood as an attempt to establish communication between the realms of the holy and the common by sending a victim through the barrier,[43] as a cathartic act of ritualized violence to stem the tide of social upheaval,[44] as the attempt to unleash an apotropaic force to ward off disaster and maintain the status quo,[45] or as the restoration of misaligned categories and the reordering of social relations.[46] Rogerson's caveat regarding attempts to reconstruct an anthropological, structuralist, or theological understanding of sacrifice from Israel's narrative texts must caution against the rigid application of such attempts.[47] Sacrifice in Israel's cultic life was multivalent, comprised of apotropaic and purgative as well as communicative and generative dynamics. J. H. M. Beattie, for example, distinguishes between four primary types of sacrifice, depending on whether the sacrifice is understood to be conjunctive or disjunctive, personal or impersonal, and Paul Rigby isolates three primal types of sacrifice: the foundational, the communal, and the expiatory.[48]

It is not possible to resolve issues pertaining to "original" significations of sacrifice or to discuss the various specific types of sacrifice practiced in the Israelite cult. It is important, however, to focus on those sacrifices pertaining to atonement and expiation, since they reflect most directly on the priest's social function in Israelite society concerning the maintenance of ordered categories.

---

see Rolf Rendtorff, *Studien zur Geschichte des Opfers im alten Israel* (Neukirchen-Vluyn: Neukirchener Verlag, 1967) 253–59; Raymond Abba, "The Origin and Significance of Hebrew Sacrifice," *BTB* 7 (1977) 124–30.

[43] Henri Hubert and Marcel Mauss, *Sacrifice: Its Nature and Function* (1898; London: Cohen & West, 1964) esp. 95–102.

[44] René Girard, *Violence and the Sacred* (Baltimore: Johns Hopkins University Press, 1977) 2–10.

[45] Victor Turner, "Sacrifice as Quintessential Process: Prophylaxis or Abandonment?" *HR* 16 (1976–77) 214–15.

[46] Douglas Davies, "An Interpretation of Sacrifice in Leviticus," *ZAW* 89 (1977) 396.

[47] J. W. Rogerson, "Sacrifice in the Old Testament: Problems of Method and Approach," in *Sacrifice* (ed. M. F. C. Bourdillon and Meyer Fortes; London: Academic, 1980) 56–58.

[48] J. H. M. Beattie, "On Understanding Sacrifice," in *Sacrifice* (ed. M. F. C. Bourdillon and Meyer Fortes; London: Academic, 1980) 38–42; Paul Rigby, "A Structural Analysis of Israelite Sacrifice and Its Other Institutions," *EgT* 11 (1980) esp. 312–43.

The Priest, Atonement, and Expiation _____

Priestly involvement in rituals of atonement and expiation did not represent a late baroque expansion of clerical duties into the legalistic realm of a pedantic fascination or phobia regarding purity. It was instead the logical and necessary corollary of the priestly responsibility for Torah. The priest's concern for the moral and ethical integrity of the social order necessitated a means of remedying that order when threatened or ruptured, and the atonement ritual, focusing on the *ḥaṭṭā't* and *'āšām* sacrifices, provided that means.

The term *kippēr* ("atone") seems to carry as its primary meaning the notion of "wiping off,"[49] thus indicating the purgative notion underlying the application of blood involved in the ritual. Baruch Levine has confused several categories, suggesting that the blood was sometimes purgative (i.e., ridding the sancta of contamination already contracted) and sometimes prophylactic (i.e., warding off contamination not yet contracted). His theory of the prophylactic nature of atonement is flawed from the start, since he relates it to the apotropaic notion that sacrifice could ward off Yahweh's wrath, thereby confusing God's wrath with contamination from sin.[50] Jacob Milgrom has been most insistent on understanding the blood of the atonement ritual strictly as a detergent or disinfectant which decontaminates (*ḥiṭṭē', piel*) the infectious residue of sin (*ḥaṭṭā't*), which adheres like an aerial miasma to the sancta.[51]

Not every offense was open to this "remedy," however. The damage done to social and cosmic order by intentional offenses was repaired by means of normal judicial punishments and fines. Those offenses committed "unknowingly" or "without intent," particularly when

[49] It is also argued that the primary meaning is that of "covering over." On this discussion, see Bernd Janowski, *Sühne als Heilsgeschehen: Studien zur Sühnetheologie der Priesterschrift und zur Wurzel KPR im Alten Orient und im Alten Testament* (Neukirchen-Vluyn: Neukirchener Verlag, 1982) 100. Janowski argues that the term can be derived directly neither from Akkadian *kappāru* (wipe off) nor from the Arabic KFR (cover), since each allows for both meanings. The Akkadian *kuppāru* in fact already was a technical term meaning "cultically to purify."

[50] Baruch A. Levine, *In the Presence of the Lord: A Study of Cult and Some Cultic Terms in Ancient Israel* (Leiden: E. J. Brill, 1974) 69–74.

[51] Milgrom, *Studies in Cultic Theology and Terminology*, 75–84, 237–39.

accompanied by "repentance,"[52] were remedied by the ritual of atonement whereby the priest applied the disinfecting blood to the sancta thereby removing the contaminating uncleanness that resulted from the offense or action.

The *ḥaṭṭā'ṭ* (sin offering) and the *'āšām* (guilt offering) may originally have involved different rituals or remedied different sorts of offenses,[53] though it is impossible to reconstruct their origins. Furthermore, there were two distinct *ḥaṭṭā'ṭ* sacrifices: one conducted on behalf of the laity, a portion of which was eaten by the priest; and one conducted on behalf of the clergy itself, the whole of which was immolated and disposed of outside the "camp."[54] In either case, however, the primary object of the atoning ritual was the sancta, which was purged of contamination.

If the sancta was the "primary" object of the benefits of the atonement ritual, however, where did that leave the individual on whose behalf atonement was made? In his analysis of this question, Levine proposed two contradictory solutions: on the one hand he traced the two *ḥaṭṭā'ṭ* sacrifices mentioned above to these two poles—the sancta and the individual. The *ḥaṭṭā'ṭ* of the priest, Levine suggested, was a riddance rite purging the sancta of contamination. The *ḥaṭṭā'ṭ* of the people, however, was an expiatory rite, freeing the people of offense and preparing them for worship.[55] One rite purged impurity and the other rite expiated sin. On the other hand, Levine suggested that atonement concerns itself in a mechanical and automatic manner strictly with purgation of contamination. Only as an *indirect* result, and because of divine action, does God consequently grant the

---

[52] On "repentance" (*hitwaddâ*) as the priestly mechanism converting advertent sins into inadvertencies, thus qualifying them for atonement, see Milgrom, *Studies in Cultic Theology and Terminology*, 47–66. Though Milgrom is correct in relating repentance and atonement, it is doubtful that many "intentional" sins ever qualified for atonement, with or without "repentance." The texts cited by him (Lev 5:1–4; 16:21; 26:40; Num 5:6–7) are illustrative not of advertent sins but rather of unknown or unintended sins, or of general community confessions.

[53] Num 5:7–8 and 2 Kgs 12:16 suggest that the *'āšām* involved the transference of money or compensation to the victim (Rowley, *Worship in Ancient Israel*, 129–31; Rendtorff, *Studien zur Geschichte des Opfers*, 233).

[54] On these distinct types, see Levine, *In the Presence of the Lord*, 26–27; Milgrom, *Studies in Cultic Theology and Terminology*, 70–74; Janowski, *Sühne als Heilsgeschehen*, 222–34.

[55] Levine, *In the Presence of the Lord*, 27.

individual forgiveness of sin. Decontamination of sancta is the immediate and automatic result of atonement. Expiation of the individual is a mediate and consequent act requiring divine intent.[56] Not only are these two proposals contradictory; what is more important, they both hammer a wedge between "impurity" and "sin/ guilt," which is highly questionable. Reacting against Levine, Milgrom was even more extreme in insisting that atonement did not relate in the least to the expiation of individual guilt. His focus was so strictly on decontamination of sancta that there is little benefit left for the individual on whose behalf atonement was made.[57]

Both Levine and Milgrom, in different ways, force "purification" and "expiation" so far apart that they can have little to do with each other. The end result is to blow apart any connection between the ethical and the ritual aspects of priestly concern so as to reduce priests strictly to "exterminators" who were more interested in disinfecting the altar than in remedying the brokenness of the social order. Although neither Milgrom nor Levine would support such a position, this gross disjunction of purity and ethics easily leads to the logical concluson that the priests were so entirely preoccupied with protecting their space from contamination that they had little time or use for the fine points of justice and righteousness.

A necessary protest against this forced rending apart of purity and ethics was already sounded by Jacob Neusner in his insistence that impurity is nothing less than a metaphor for sin and that the details of holiness concern both ethical and ritual matters.[58] More recently, N. Kiuchi has also rightly protested against Milgrom's thesis that the purification of sancta is wholly unrelated to the expiation of sin. Kiuchi correctly insists that "sin" and "uncleanness" are not essentially different; thus there is no essential difference between purification and expiation. When the priest purified the sancta, he also, at the same time, bore the guilt associated with uncleanness.[59]

The Israelite worldview insisted that matters of ethics and cultic

[56] Ibid., 63–66.

[57] Milgrom, *Studies in Cultic Theology and Terminology,* 67–69.

[58] Jacob Neusner, *The Idea of Purity in Ancient Judaism* (Leiden: E. J. Brill, 1973) 21–25, 113.

[59] N. Kiuchi, *The Purification Offering in the Priestly Literature: Its Meaning and Function* (Sheffield: JSOT Press, 1987) 38–40, 65, 109.

purity were integrally related—indeed, were corollaries of one another. The priestly focus on Torah as concern for the solidarity of the social order did not degenerate into the legalistic pedantry of dilettantes absorbed in the deadly minutia of cultic purity. It is illegitimate to assume that a priestly concern for temple and magical ritual stood in opposition to a "prophetic" concern for ethics and the socioeconomic order of society. As Gary Anderson has demonstrated, the world of myth and ritual associated with the temple is not unrelated to the world of economic and social issues. It is precisely in the cult where the worlds of the mythic-ritual and the social-ethical merge.[60]

The Prophetic Assessment of the Priesthood _____

This conclusion is not to suggest, however, that the priesthood was not subject to corruption and abuse as well as to the abandonment of its highest values. Nor is it to suggest that the ideology which sustained the social status of the priesthood was entirely benevolent to the social order as a whole. Below we will discuss creation theology as it relates to the ideological structure of the priesthood. First, however, we must consider in a bit more detail what we can learn of the priesthood by listening to the voice of prophetic critique.

It has already been suggested that when the prophetic critique turns against the priest it generally concerns the priestly abrogation of specifically priestly responsibilities relating to the guarding of Torah. Whenever the prophet criticizes the priest, the complaint is not that he is acting just like a priest; rather the objection is that he has *ceased* acting like a priest. He has forsaken his duties relative to Torah.

The priesthood also suffers prophetic censure at several points because of issues relating to sacrifice. Two points must be made here, however. First, the critique of sacrifice does not relate to the nature of sacrifice itself, nor does it regard sacrifice as utterly tangential to the normal concern for Torah. As shown above, sacrifice falls under the priestly concern for Torah no less than does the priest's role in

---

[60] Gary A. Anderson, *Sacrifices and Offerings in Ancient Israel: Studies in their Social and Political Importance* (Atlanta: Scholars Press, 1987) 105–16.

the judicial sphere. Second, when the prophets level their sights on sacrifice, it is not the priest who is targeted but rather the lay member who is taking refuge in sacrifice, grossly misunderstanding its true intent. In Hos 8:12-13, for example, it is not the priest who comes under fire but rather the people's contradictory disdain for Torah yet their love for *zebaḥ*, that is, for gluttony. Amos attacks not the priest but rather the people for their love of offering *zebaḥ* and *tôdâ* at Bethel and Gilgal (Amos 4:4-5). Jeremiah questions the validity of incense, *'ōlâ*, and *zebaḥ* only because the people hide in the temple like bandits in a safe house and because they reject Torah (Jer 6:19-20; 7:8-11; 21-23). The prophetic critique of sacrifice was directed not against the institution of the priesthood nor even against sacrifice itself but rather against the popular abuse of sacrifice, an abuse based on a false dichotomy between Torah, justice, and faithfulness on one hand and sacrifice on the other.

Furthermore, the prophetic critique nearly everywhere centers its fire on specific sacrifices: the *zebaḥ* (feast sacrifice), the *minḥâ* (cereal offering), the *šelem* (peace offering), and the *'ōlâ* (immolation offering).[61] These are precisely the sacrifices associated principally with celebrative occasions when the people focused on God's benevolence and on the fact that the social and cosmic order was restored, whole, and intact. Such feasts marked times when the people were feeling confident and secure, placing unwarranted trust in God's good will. Amos's fiery critique begins with the phrase "I hate, I despise your festivals (*ḥaggêkem*), and I take no delight in your solemn assemblies (*'aṣṣērōtêkem*)." The use of "solemn" to define the second noun is misleading. Elsewhere the noun "assembly" (*'ăṣārâ*) is used in reference to the *feasts* of Maṣṣot and Booths (Lev 23:36; Num 29:35; Deut 16:8), indicating that the gatherings were not "solemn" in the sense of subdued and even penitent, but rather were "festive" days of vacation and celebration. Amos, as is typical of the prophetic critique in general, is lashing out against the inappropriateness of holding "celebrations" in desperate times that call for deep soul-searching. Amos is not challenging the entire system of sacrifice; he is grieved over the audacity and the lack of propriety shown in the popular misperception of what sort of religious mood the times require. There

---

[61] Amos 5:21-25; Hos 6:6; Mic 6:6-8; Isa 1:11-17; 66:3; Jer 6:19-20; 7:21-23.

is no critique here of the truly "solemn" sacrifices of penance, which one might easily imagine would have been entirely endorsed by Amos, given the sort of proper mood required by such desperate times. Amos is grieved that the people do not recognize what is at stake in the cosmos and in their history: this is not a time for "feasting" but rather for "fasting." The only prophetic critique of Israel's truly solemn sacrifices occurs in Isa 58:1–9; but here the prophet is challenging not the validity of sacrifice but rather of penitence that is entirely superficial. The people are pretending to grieve but are going about their violent "business as usual."

The prophetic critique is deeply anchored in the *assumed connection* between sacrifice and Torah. Sacrifice without justice and mercy is a mockery. Concern for ritual without an attendant concern for ethics is an aberration. The priests are culpable insofar as they, in neglecting Torah, have allowed such a horrid gulf to develop between the two. The prophets are critical not of the system of sacrifice but rather of the degenerate state into which it has fallen in popular usage.

It is commonly assumed that such a critique is generated by the charismatic prophetic spirit in conscious opposition to priestly institutional systems management. Therefore, whenever this critique surfaces in the Psalter—that is, in material related to Israel's temple worship itself—it is assumed that we must have a prophetic "incursion" into the realm of the cult. So it is common to speak of certain "prophetic" psalms, as though the ideas expressed in them were somehow in conscious violation of the theology of the cult itself. The sacrificial critique expressed in Pss 40:6; 50:8–15; 51:16–17; and 69:30–31 suffers under the misbegotten hermeneutical premise that the perspective of the prophet was in violent opposition to the perspective of the priest, and that these psalms cannot have reflected the conscious and generally accepted ideological foundation of sacrifice cherished *especially* by the priests. Such sentiments as reflected in these psalms are generally traced, therefore, to one of three different sources: first, to the prophetic rejection of the sacrificial system exterior to the cult;[62] second, to a more subtle prophetic critique internal to the cult exercised by "court prophets";[63] or, third, to a

---

[62] The well-known position of Wellhausen, Duhm, Hölscher, and others.

[63] Sigmund Mowinckel, *Psalmenstudien IV* (Amsterdam: P. Schippers, 1961) 8–36; idem, *The Psalms in Israel's Worship* (New York: Abingdon, 1967) 2:71.

process of "spiritualization" by which worship was transformed from an impersonal focus on sacrifice to a personal and private focus on personal piety.[64]

The so-called prophetic critique expressed in these psalms, I would insist, derives from none of these sources. The similar critique lodged by Samuel against Saul in 1 Sam 15:22, expressed as it is in the typical wisdom format of a "*ṭôb*-saying" (*hinnēh šěmōaʿ mizzebaḥ ṭôb lěhaqšîb mēḥēleb ʾêlîm*) betrays a crucial point: such awareness was common to Israel's, and indeed to the ancient Near East's, wisdom tradition.[65] Similar sentiments expressed in Prov 21:3, 27 and 15:8 support the contention that the social values expressed in the critique of sacrifice by the prophets and in the Psalter itself represent the common knowledge of Israel and the ancient Near East. Such a critique represents cherished values lying at the heart of the community's ethos and self-understanding. The prophet, when articulating these sentiments, was not generating new insights based on "anti-institutional prophetic charisma." Nor were such sentiments, when expressed in the psalms, evidence of some anticultic subterfuge meant to undermine priestly integrity. The priest knew the truth of the matter no less than did the prophet: the worlds of ritual and ethics cannot be wrenched apart. Rather than being imposed on the apostate cult from above by prophetic charisma, this truth "trickled up" from below as common knowledge and as a long-held and fundamental truth lying at the heart of Israel's religious and social structures. It provided the bedrock for the "mythic consciousness" of Israel's cultic institutions, and thus was expressive of the "charismatic" ideology undergirding Israel's priesthood.

[64] Already hinted at by Hermann Gunkel, *Einleitung in die Psalmen: Die Gattungen der religiösen Lyrik Israels* (Göttingen: Vandenhoeck & Ruprecht, 1933) 415–33; and fully developed by Hans-Jürgen Hermisson, *Sprache und Ritus im altisraelitischen Kult: Zur "Spiritualisierung" der Kultbegriffe im alten Testament* (Neukirchen-Vluyn: Neukirchener Verlag, 1965).

[65] On this issue, see esp. Leo Perdue, *Wisdom and Cult: A Critical Analysis of the Views of Cult in the Wisdom Literatures of Israel and the Ancient Near East* (Missoula, MT: Scholars Press, 1977) 118–19, 156–62.

History and Nature in Priestly Ideology _____

Finally, we return to the problem raised at the beginning of this chapter: namely, the thesis that the priest was an institutionalized manager of nature whereas the prophet was a charismatic hermeneutician interpreting history. The central issue revolves around the relationship between nature and history in Israel's worldview and is particularly problematic because the two, nature and history, are often seen as opposites expressive of competing worldviews and religious and social structures. On the one hand, there is the "authentically Israelite" understanding of reality, focusing as it does on God's saving deeds in history. On the other hand, there are the "pagan forms of Canaanite or ancient Near Eastern religion," thought to focus on the manipulation of recurrent patterns in nature. To the extent that the priest is seen as a manager of nature, therefore, the clear intent is to revert to a not-so-subtle form of Wellhausen's jaundiced view that the priest is the representative of a degenerate form of religion whereas the prophet is the bearer of authentic religion. The institutional nature manipulator loses again to the charismatic history interpreter.

Typical of this position is the work of Bernhard Anderson, who draws heavily upon the insight of Mircea Eliade that the "archaic mind" was trapped insecurely in a world beyond its control, frightened into attempts to manage it through nature-oriented rituals, afraid to "make history"—that is, to take up the burden of freedom and the terror of history.[66] Against this background, Anderson argues, the faith of Israel stands out as a unique phenomenon—a revolutionary development. Israel reacted against the prevailing nature religions, consciously demoting its own creation traditions and thereby embracing what others feared—historical drama, *Heilsgeschichte*.[67] As is well known, works such as those by Gerhard von Rad and Wolfhart Pannenberg made it a virtually incontestable point of doctrine that the faith of Israel focused on history, relegating the

[66] Mircea Eliade, *Cosmos and History: The Myth of the Eternal Return* (New York: Pantheon, 1954) esp. 35–57, 85–92.

[67] Bernhard W. Anderson, *Creation Versus Chaos: The Reinterpretation of Mythical Symbolism in the Bible* (1967; reprint, Philadelphia: Fortress, 1987) 22–30, 49–53.

world of nature and creation to the Canaanite mythmakers.[68] This problem is obviously far too encompassing to take up in any detail in this study. I wish only to make some general observations as they pertain to our study of the interplay of "institution" and "charisma" relating to the priesthood.

To say that the priests were "managers of nature" is correct insofar as there does appear to be a connection between Israel's creation traditions and its cultic life. Creation is a dominant theme in the psalms, especially in those which celebrate Yahweh's victory over the primal forces of chaos (e.g., Psalms 33, 74, 89, 104). The Enthronement Psalms (Psalms 24, 29, 47, and 93–100), celebrating the fact that God "has become king," enthroned upon the vanquished forces of Sea/River, played a central role in the cultic celebrations conducted in connection with the major agricultural pilgrimage festivals, especially the feast of Booths. Furthermore, the temple itself was understood to be a symbolic embodiment of cosmos, and Zion a localization of the sacral center of the universe, the true Eden.[69] In veiled language the psalmist could rhapsodize, "They feast on the abundance of your house, and you give them drink from the river of your delights/Eden (*'ădānêkā*, Ps 36:8 [Heb 36:9])." The narratives of creation in Genesis 1 and 2 were both inspired by and expressive of the mythic complex undergirding the temple and royal cult.[70]

However, the psalms were not fixated on the theme of creation to the exclusion of Israel's historical awareness. In Ps 44:1 the reference to Yahweh's deeds in "the days of old" (*bîmê qedem*, Heb 44:2) refers to Israel's historical traditions, as does the remark in 66:5 concerning the "terrible deeds" that God performed. The psalms frequently rehearse the "mighty acts of God" performed in Israel's history, indicating that Israel's cult was also sustained by a mythic complex relating to its historical traditions. This mythic complex is particularly

[68] Gerhard von Rad, "The Theological Problem of the Old Testament Doctrine of Creation," in *Creation in the Old Testament* (ed. B. W. Anderson; Philadelphia: Fortress, 1984) 53–58, 62 (first published in 1936); Wolfhart Pannenberg, *Basic Questions in Theology* (Philadelphia: Fortress, 1970) 1:17–22.

[69] Ps 78:69; Isa 51:3; Ezek 36:35; Joel 2:3. Cf. the same mythic identification of Tyre and Eden in Ezek 28:13–16 (Jon D. Levenson, *Sinai and Zion: An Entry into the Jewish Bible* [Chicago: Winston, 1985] 129–31).

[70] Anderson, *Creation versus Chaos,* 60–70.

fully developed in Pss 78:1–72;[71] 105:5–45; 106:7–46; but allusions
to it can be found throughout the Psalter (e.g., Pss 80:8–11; 135:8–12).
A fundamental cultic creedal formula of Yahweh's self-identification
in fact focused on Israel's historical awareness: "I am the Lord your
God, who brought you up out of the land of Egypt" (81:10). This
confession and the creedal formula that it is the Lord "who made
heaven and earth, the sea, and all that is in them" (146:6; cf. 124:8;
134:3) stood side by side.

A particularly interesting case is presented by Ps 77:11–20, where
cosmogonic and historical images merge and the two mythic complexes coalesce as the waters of chaos and the waters of the Reed
Sea flow into one another. The historical theme of the redemption
of Jacob, introduced in v. 15, yields to the cosmogonic language of
divine combat in vv. 16–18, only to resurface climactically in
vv. 19–20.

Such a coalescence of these two mythic traditions raises the question of how these complexes, history and creation, were related. Many
assume, and with some justification, that the two mythic complexes
were independent of each other and indeed reflected competing
worldviews—one possibly Israelite and one Canaanite—until relatively late in Israel's history, when they were fused by Deutero-Isaiah,
for whom God's creative and redemptive actions coalesce (e.g., Isa
51:9–10). Given the assumption that these two complexes represented
conflicting worldviews, the debate has often degenerated into an argument over which has priority. The more celebrated position is that
of Eliade, popularized by Thorlief Boman and others, that Hebrew
mentality was fundamentally different from non-Hebrew mentality.[72]
The one was linear, the other cyclical; the one focused on history,
the other on nature.

It is very telling, however, that whereas Eliade and Boman contrasted the Hebrew mind with the Greek mind, others have made
the same contrast between the Hebrew and the Canaanite or ancient
Near Eastern mind. In these oft-rehearsed scenarios one could
substitute the words "Greek" and "Canaanite" for each other and not

---

[71] Note that Ps 78:1 introduces a lengthy discourse on Israel's historical traditions
by referring to it as "Torah."
[72] Thorleif Boman, *Hebrew Thought Compared with Greek* (London: SCM, 1960).

miss one significant beat. Priority was naturally given to the Hebrew or biblical mind, with its focus on linear reality and history. Though it is still popular to insist on the uniqueness of the Hebrew or biblical mind, such an overstated position was early and vigorously discredited by James Barr.[73] There is an increasing consensus today that many twentieth-century scholars, particularly those associated with the "Biblical Theology movement," overstated the case for Israel's uniqueness. As such, the mythic complexes of "history" and "creation" cannot be attributed to discrete theological systems, the former Israelite and the latter Canaanite.

Having admitted this fact, there is still a tendency, even among scholars who accept that both traditions were integral to Israel's mythic universe, to determine which held priority of place. There is the persistent need to promote one side of the dialectic over the other. Echoing the extreme position of Eliade and Boman, and following the theological lead of von Rad and Pannenberg, most understand "creation" to be a subcategory of "history," or at least a complex that exists "in the service" of Israel's historical awareness.[74] More recently, however, there has been an important and concerted effort by scholars such as H. Schmid and Rolf Knierim to reverse the polarity. Creation, they argue, is the dominant pole, and Israel's historical liberation is determined by and is fundamentally a result of the prior commitment God has to the liberation of the world in creation. God is the liberator of Israel because God is first and foremost the liberator of the world.[75]

[73] James Barr, *Biblical Words for Time* (London: SCM, 1962); idem, "Revelation Through History in the Old Testament and in Modern Theology," *Int* 17 (1963) 193–205.

[74] In addition to the work of Anderson cited above, see Werner H. Schmidt, *Die Schöpfungsgeschichte der Priesterschrift* (Neukirchen-Vluyn: Neukirchener Verlag, 1964) 185, who typically argues that the priestly redactor "deals with nature as if it is history." Also the work of Odil Hannes Steck, *World and Environment* (Nashville: Abingdon, 1980) 75, 99, 124, who subsumes nature under history by referring repeatedly to the "event" character of creation.

[75] Rolf Knierim, "Cosmos and History in Israel's Theology," *HBT* 3 (1981) esp. 95–99; the more extensive work of H. H. Schmid is summarized in "Creation, Righteousness, and Salvation," in *Creation in the Old Testament* (ed. B. W. Anderson; Philadelphia: Fortress, 1984) 102–17. The same position has recently been laid out by Terence Fretheim, "Suffering God and Sovereign God in Exodus: A Collision of Images," *HBT* 11 (1989) 33.

It has always been tempting, sometimes irresistibly so, to divide reality into dialectical warring camps, a temptation that is being associated today with a "particularly male" view of reality. Whether "typically male" or not, it at least seems particularly romantic to develop lists of characteristics that might describe a "historical" perception of reality on the one hand and a "naturalistic" perception on the other. The list could be developed to look as follows:

NATURE	*HISTORY*
myth	narrative
cyclical mind	linear mind
spatial perspective	temporal perspective
abstraction	concretion
being	becoming
Platonic idea	Aristotelian event
eternity	eschatology
coherence	dynamism
psychology	logic
science, magic	ethics
priestly ritual	prophetic critique
cultic drama	historical action
institution	charisma

The dominant move in Old Testament theology today is toward such a dialectical understanding of Israel's traditions, symbolized by such polarities as "blessing and saving," "aesthetics and ethics," and "form and reform."[76] Such an approach is welcome and warranted as long as we resist the notion that reality is simply dualistic, characterized by antagonistic macroforces hammering away at one another. Such attempts to wrench apart history and nature invariably break down when it is assumed that either one has priority over the other.[77] From a psychological perspective it is erroneous to suggest

[76] For a review of the recent studies of C. Westermann, S. Terrien, and P. Hanson, see Walter Brueggemann, "A Convergence in Recent Old Testament Theologies," *JSOT* 18 (1980) 2–18.

[77] Even those such as Anderson and Knierim, who promote one pole of the dialectic over the other, also acknowledge that the two sides are really insolubly merged, a point also stressed by Richard J. Clifford, S.J., "The Hebrew Scriptures and the Theology of Creation," *TS* 46 (1985) 515, who speaks of creation and redemption as "God's seamless action."

that humans perceive reality either strictly linearly or cyclically, with a commitment either to "saving" or to "blessing," to "creation," or "redemption." The human soul demands both assurances: the assurance that the given structures of today do not have the final say, that there is "hope for the future"; as well as the assurance that I will not be confronted tomorrow by unfettered chaos, that the structures of the universe in place today will survive the dark night and greet me with the light of day.

Above all, the cultic and historical myths celebrated by Israel sought to quell the human spirit in the face of both the brokenness (sin) of history and the brokenness (chaos) of nature. Precisely this interplay between sin and chaos, between the guilt produced by the threat of history as well as the meaninglessness produced by the threat of nature, underlies the fact stressed above that priestly activity was directed both toward ritual and toward ethics, both toward purity (maintenance of created orders) and toward expiation (restoration of historical sequentiality). History and nature did not simply coexist in Israel's religious life by mutual and dogged toleration. They sang the same song and danced the same dance. They were like Siamese twins connected at the heart, their lungs nourished by the same blood and sucking in the same air. Where one tended toward the extreme it was corrected by the other,[78] not always gently but always faithfully.

It is tempting to assume that Israel's creation tradition was an ideological program designed and managed by the priests and other power brokers to keep the members of society chained to what the priests, in their own interest, articulated as the iron laws of nature and the cosmos. Though myths may have the power of persuasion, however, they do not appear to have the power of coercion, and when popular myths no longer embody a cherished worldview, or when they no longer satisfactorily answer the questions that social life raises, they break down.[79] Knierim has rightly objected to the implication by H.-J. Kraus that Israel's cult promoted the cosmos as so "undisturbable" and "inextinguishable" that it passed itself off

[78] Levenson, *Sinai and Zion*, 208–9.

[79] Robin W. Lovin and Frank E. Reynolds, "In the Beginning," in *Cosmogony and Ethical Order: New Studies in Comparative Ethics* (ed. R. W. Lovin and F. E. Reynolds; Chicago: University of Chicago Press, 1985) 24–25.

as the "presence of the perfect creation."[80] The creation tradition itself
knew that the simple *fact* of creation did not translate directly into
the absolute assurance of stability. The power of Chaos was at best
subdued and tamed. But just as one cannot domesticate a wolf, so
the Israelite knew that the power of Chaos lurked in the shadows
as a constant threat to human existence.[81] The creation myth functioned to provide Israel encouragement in the face of this threat,
not to subdue Israel in a specific form of systems management.

Charisma by the Book

The mythic consciousness of the priest, that is to say, the basis for
charismatic attribution, lay precisely in the priest's relationship to
Torah. What is meant by Torah here is not simply an attachment
to legalistic codes. Torah is a symbol for a comprehensive religious
perspective and worldview, one characterized by the truth that divine
revelation is given in the fixed, tangible, and concrete data of earthly
existence. God is incarnate in that which you can get your hands
on, that which you can sink your teeth into, that which you can
see and measure, prod, and poke. Whether the roll of Urim and
Thummim or the shape of a cow's liver, whether a traditional compilation of technical priestly lore or the broad and encompassing
canon of Israel's mythic story—the priest mediated God's self-
revelation with a "data base" that was hands-on. When Brueggemann
speaks of the non-negotiability of Israel's Torah, he is absolutely
correct in a way perhaps unintended: Urim and Thummim do not
lie. The individual prescriptions of priestly professional lore are there
in black and white. The myth of origins—national as well as natural—
is impressed on every child's mind. Israel's confessional canon, its
charter for life together, is not open for negotiation.

All of these manifestations of Torah certainly require interpretation, and to that extent the priest was every bit as much the

---

[80] Hans-Joachim Kraus, "Schöpfung und Weltvollendung," *EvT* 24 (1964) 467;
Knierim, "Cosmos and History in Israel's Theology," 103.

[81] See esp. Jon D. Levenson's critique of the position of Y. Kaufmann in *Creation
and the Persistence of Evil: The Jewish Drama of Divine Omnipotence* (San Francisco:
Harper & Row, 1988) 48–49.

"hermeneutician" as the prophet. But there is a givenness to the world of the priest, a givenness symbolized by Torah and characterized by an inductive rather than an intuitive approach to religious knowledge and experience. The prophetic Word was the evocative voice of intuition, but priestly Torah was the thoughtful voice of analysis. The fiery passion of the Word and the persistent reason of Torah complemented each other and corrected each other, but at the same time drew their strength from each other. On occasion these two perspectives, the inductive and the intuitive, the analytical and the impassioned, could clash violently with each other. But they were not children of estranged parents nor fundamentally at odds. They simply represented two different ways of perceiving the same truth: the priestly Torah and the prophetic Word represented two vantage points, both of which were required, from which to survey the broad horizon of divine grace.

When Jesus invited Thomas to "handle" him (John 20:27) he was inviting him into the world of Torah, the world in which priests "handle" or "grab hold of" (*tāpaś*) the law (Jer 2:8). He was summoning Thomas into the world where those who seek encounter with the divine plunge their fingers into the meat of the matter; a eucharistic world where we take the body into our mouths and chew on it. If there was a sense of security in this world of Torah—leading to forms of divination being given precedence over intuitive forms of prophetic revelation—it was not a self-satisfied confidence that declared itself to be beyond discussion. If not negotiable, everything is at least ultimately discussable. Ever reminded of the presence of creation's Chaos and history's Sin in its own myth, the world of Torah was fully aware of its limitations. The pen of the scribe fully grasped the pen-ultimate character of truth; it knew that just as the Sea had its limits so too did any pretensions that Torah was coterminous with truth. How else can one explain the fact that Israel's legal tradition was open to the future, open to transformation and modification? This was the world of the priest—one characterized as "charisma by the book."

7

Wisdom:
The Charisma of Order

_____

THE CONCEPTUAL FRAMEWORK for this study has been the impact of Max Weber's theories regarding authority and leadership on the interpretation of Old Testament institutions. The distinction he made between traditional, legal/rational, and charismatic leadership has formed the theoretical basis for several generations of scholarly interpretation. Though at one level Weber mitigated the effect of his theory by invoking notions of the "routinization" of charisma or of the transference of charismatic power into "office" charisma, succeeding generations have not been so cautious in nuancing their application of Weber's social analysis. The attempt of this study has been to collapse false dualisms that have arisen around the notions of "institution" and "charisma," and to understand the extent to which charisma is itself a fundamentally social phenomenon. The final chapter in this study seeks to consider the social matrices of authority underlying Israel's wisdom tradition, especially in relation to the interplay of traditional, legal/rational, and charismatic impulses at work in Israel's social self-consciousness.

One major difficulty immediately confronts any such attempt: the question of how wisdom is to be understood in relation to Weber's three ideal types. Is it to be aligned with one of the three types, in contrast to Torah and prophecy? Or does it instead manifest all three? On one hand, some would argue that wisdom, in contrast to Torah (a particularly legal/rational enterprise) and prophecy (an essentially charismatic phenomenon), is a traditional mode of expression, imparting as it does the wisdom "of the ages." Israel's indices of authority could thus be divided into three discrete modes: traditional (wisdom), legal/rational (Torah), and charismatic (prophecy). Brueggemann, for instance, understands Torah (*ethos*) as consensus, prophecy (*pathos*) as disruption, leaving wisdom (*logos*) to describe the process of discernment and discovery which articulates the dialectical conflict.[1] We have already cautioned against distinguishing between prophecy and Torah in such fashion, however. Furthermore, the fact that Brueggemann has to position wisdom on the sidelines as a spectator, where it can only watch and comment on the game that is being played out on the field by the two major players, suggests the limitations of such a synthesis, as helpful as it otherwise is.

On the other hand, it can equally be argued that all three "ideal" authority types are manifest in wisdom literature: In Israel's early history, as it was constituted as a confederation of tribal and family groups (Weber's "community"), wisdom was based on tradition. As Israel's social structures hardened into institutionalized offices (Weber's "society"), the locus of wisdom's authority shifted to that of legal/rational "schools" associated with the court and temple. To the extent that wisdom was understood to be a product of the inspired individual, it was expressive of "charismatic endowment." Viewed in this way, all three indices of authority lie behind Israel's wisdom tradition: traditional (clan/family), legal/rational (court/temple schools), and charismatic (the inspired individual). The difficulty, however, is that charisma is immediately seen to be an anomaly over against the other two types; inspiration is denied to family and institution; and an unwarranted evolutionary view of the development of wisdom is interjected into the picture, all of which will be discussed below.

Other methodological problems follow quickly upon this more comprehensive issue. What person or institution lies behind the production and dissemination of wisdom? Is it the "elder" of families and cities or the "scribe" of schools and royal/temple institutions? And what is the relationship of the "sage" to these two groups? Is there an ethos characteristic of wisdom, and if so is it that of a class

---

[1] Walter Brueggemann, *The Creative Word: Canon as a Model for Biblical Education* (Philadelphia: Fortress, 1982) 71, 75, 81.

(e.g., royal bureaucrats) or of popular culture as a whole? Finally, does the question of the index of wisdom's authority relate to any evolution that it underwent, evolving from a pan-sacralism to an enlightened secularism or from an a-theological pragmatism of self-interest to a self-consciously confessional theism? Such formidable questions are probably insoluble. However, since any discussion concerning the matrices of authority underlying Israel's proverbial wisdom must confront them, we shall nonetheless press the issue, once again to question whether charisma and institution dare be wrenched apart when seeking to understand the power and authority underlying Israel's proverbial wisdom.

Wisdom, Prophecy, and Law

There were clearly three indices of authority in ancient Israel, designated "law" (*tôrâ*), "word" (*dābār*), and "counsel" (*'ēṣâ*). Jer 18:18 associates these indices with the priest, the prophet, and the "sage" (*ḥākām*) respectively, and Ezek 7:26 attests a similar understanding, substituting the term "vision" (*ḥāzôn*) for "word" and the term "elder" (*zāqēn*) for "sage."[2] We dealt with the relation of prophetic "word" to priestly "Torah" in the previous chapter, and now must consider the relation of the third to the first two.

Such a distinction between these three indices is very helpful, but is fraught with the temptation to overgeneralize. A clear warning is sounded by Jer 8:8–9, which challenges any presumed neat arrangement:

> How can you say, "We are wise (*ḥākām*)
>   and the law (*tôrâ*) of the Lord is with us,"
> when, in fact, the false pen of the scribes (*sōpĕrîm*)
>   has made it into a lie.
> The wise shall be put to shame,
>   they shall be dismayed and taken;
> for they have despised the word (*dābār*) of the Lord,
>   and wisdom (*ḥokmâ*)—what is that to them? (Author's translation)

---

[2] The relationship between the *ḥākām* ("sage") and the *zāqēn* ("elder") in Israelite society is very complicated. On the role of the elder in society and his relationship to the royal administration, see Hanoch Reviv, *The Elders in Ancient Israel: A Study of a Biblical Institution* (Jerusalem: Magnes, 1989) esp. 88–109.

Who is it that is boasting, "We are wise"? Is it the sage? Or is it more likely the priest, who logically claims to possess Torah? But if the priest, then are the scribes who pervert the Torah "priestly scribes" or are they educated courtiers? And is it this same group that not only is "wise," and not only makes claims upon the "law," but also despises "word" and scorns "wisdom"? To complicate matters, whereas v. 10 refers to prophet and priest, it makes no reference to a class of sages, allowing the scribes in v. 7 to be understood as priestly scribes and the "wise" to be a general adjective appropriated by the prophets and the priests together. The three indices of authority are so interlaced in this text that one must caution against any facile arrangement that would gloss over their mutual interconnectedness.

Prophecy and Wisdom

In spite of such ambiguity, we must presume that underlying texts such as Jer 18:18 and Ezek 7:26 was a commonly accepted epistemological assumption: the type of knowledge gained by "counsel" or "wisdom" was essentially different from that gained by "Torah" or "prophecy." But different in what way? Was the counsel of wisdom antithetical to the word of prophecy? One recurring argument positions prophetic *dābār* and priestly *tôrâ* against wisdom's *'ēṣâ* in fundamental opposition. Walther Zimmerli's classical thesis insisted that wisdom, anchored as it was in creation theology, was simply the human voice of nonrevelatory anthropology, at best backed by the "authority of insight." The admonition of the wisdom teacher cannot be confused with the commanding voice of the lawgiver or prophet, "the controlling authority of the commanding Lord."[3] It was a matter of the timid human voice of wisdom against the powerful voice of God. G. von Rad's relegation of wisdom to the periphery of Israel's theology logically followed. The same argument is persuasively restated more recently with an eye toward social analysis. Wisdom, it is argued, represents the epistemology (read "ideology") of the monarchy, the "royal definers of reality," over against the pro-

[3] Walther Zimmerli, "Ort und Grenze der Weisheit im Rahmen der alttestamentlichen Theologie," in *Gottes Offenbarung: Gesammelte Aufsätze zum Alten Testament* (Munich: Kaiser, 1963) 302, 308.

phetic voice of God (read "theology") interceding on behalf of the oppressed;[4] or it represents the political pragmatism and rationality of court officials in conflict with the claims and demands of prophets.[5] Understood as such, wisdom stands in opposition to prophecy on both formal and substantive grounds: first, it is a human voice as opposed to the divine voice. Second, it represents human policies that are opposed to the will of God.

There has been a widespread reaction against any simple reduction of wisdom to a human ideological program. Many insist, as does this study, that the authority of wisdom cannot be reduced to human response. Wisdom understands its appeal to cosmic order as an appeal to the will of God itself. Indeed, the *'ēṣâ* of the counselor or sage can lay claim to being no less a divine word than the *dābār* of the prophet. The remark in 2 Sam 16:23, that receiving *'ēṣâ* from Ahithophel was "as if one consulted the *dābār* of God," attests to the high status and authority that wise counsel could attain. Knowledge of the world and of its processes was understood to be revealed knowledge, and the bedrock of Israel's epistemology was the "fear of the Lord."[6] Though not sufficiently nuanced, James L. Crenshaw stated it boldly long ago in an excursus on the relationship of *'ēṣâ* and *dābār*: "Between 'Thus saith the Lord' and 'Listen, my son, to your father's advice' there is no fundamental difference."[7] Though there are differences in the way wisdom and prophecy substantiate their claims, they do not reflect incompatible theological commitments. Any conflict in perspective may result from wisdom's *tendency* to affirm order as expressive in fixed social institutions,[8] a point we will pursue below.

[4] Walter Brueggemann, "The Epistemological Crisis of Israel's Two Histories (Jer 9:22-23)," in *Israelite Wisdom: Theological and Literary Essays in Honor of Samuel Terrien* (ed. J. G. Gammie et al.; New York: Union Theological Seminary, 1978) 85–105.

[5] Joseph Blenkinsopp, *Wisdom and Law in the Old Testament: The Ordering of Life in Israel and Early Judaism* (New York: Oxford University Press, 1983) 13.

[6] Philip J. Nel, *The Structure and Ethos of the Wisdom Admonitions in Proverbs* (New York: Walter de Gruyter, 1982) 91; Brian W. Kovacs, "Is There a Class-Ethic in Proverbs?" in *Essays in Old Testament Ethics* (ed. J. L. Crenshaw and J. T. Willis; New York: Ktav, 1974) 184–85.

[7] J. L. Crenshaw, *Prophetic Conflict: Its Effect upon Israelite Religion* (New York: Walter de Gruyter, 1971) 123.

[8] Donn F. Morgan, *Wisdom in the Old Testament Traditions* (Atlanta: John Knox, 1981) 65–66.

The debate on the interface between Israel's wisdom and prophetic traditions has been so extensive that even a review of the issue would take us far beyond what is possible here. Major studies by S. Terrien, H. W. Wolff, and J. W. Whedbee on the connection of Amos, Hosea, Micah, Isaiah, Jeremiah, and Habakkuk to the wisdom tradition are well known in the discussion.[9] All seek to make claims for the strong influence of Israel's wisdom tradition on its prophetic voice. The insoluble issue is whether one can assume that simple familiarity with wisdom themes and forms means that these prophets were themselves more or less directly connected with guilds of sages. In fact, can one speak legitimately even of the "conscious borrowing" of wisdom forms and themes by the prophets? Crenshaw and Roger Whybray have protested against the notion of "conscious borrowing" and have, correctly in my opinion, warned that such familiarity may simply indicate the unconscious absorption of widespread cultural values, of a pervasive intellectual tradition, and of concerns common to the human situation.[10]

Israel's prophets breathed deeply of this common ethos, filling their lungs with its values and perspectives on life. The notion that Israel's prophetic tradition did or even could stand in fundamental opposition to the values of Israel's wisdom is based on the unwarranted polarization of "royal" (i.e., Zion, priestly) and "prophetic" (i.e., Deuteronomic, Mosaic) modes of thought. There are prophetic texts that do indeed sound the alarm against the presumptuous claims of wisdom insofar as it is a human enterprise. Wisdom pales and perishes in view of God's own marvelous work. The wisdom of the wise is easily turned into foolishness by God, who is the source and

---

[9] S. Terrien, "Amos and Wisdom," in *Israel's Prophetic Heritage: Essays in Honor of James Muilenburg* (ed. B. W. Anderson and W. Harrelson; New York: Harper, 1962) 108–15; Hans Walter Wolff, *Amos' geistige Heimat* (WMANT 18; Neukirchen-Vluyn: Neukirchener Verlag, 1964); J. W. Whedbee, *Isaiah and Wisdom* (Nashville: Abingdon, 1971). For reviews of the issues, see Morgan, *Wisdom in the Old Testament Traditions*, 72–89; Raymond C. Van Leeuwen, "The Sage in the Prophetic Literature," in *The Sage in Israel and the Ancient Near East* (ed. J. G. Gammie and L. G. Perdue; Winona Lake, IN: Eisenbrauns, 1990) 295–306.

[10] James L. Crenshaw, "Studies in Ancient Israelite Wisdom: Prolegomenon," in *Studies in Ancient Israelite Wisdom* (ed. J. L. Crenshaw; New York: Ktav, 1976) 1–12; Roger N. Whybray, *The Intellectual Tradition in the Old Testament* (New York: Walter de Gruyter, 1974).

goal of all wisdom. Wisdom itself can become an idolatrous object of worship, and true worship is to be directed to the Lord of loyalty, justice, and righteousness. Indeed, wisdom can be perverted by human invention and can lead one astray in self-confidence in one's own sophistication, worldly wealth, and power.[11] However, these prophetic reservations express nothing that the wisdom tradition itself did not insist on as a corrective to its own temptation to self-importance. The most sustained prophetic attacks against wisdom and its "keepers" are those directed against foreign nations, such as Babylon (Isa 47:10), Tyre (Ezek 28:1–10; Zech 9:2), and Egypt (Isa 19:11–12). In these cases, as with the attack against the "wise" in Jer 10:6–10, the assault is not upon the values and epistemology of wisdom per se, but rather upon the presumptuous and false wisdom of foreign deities and their defenders. Even the solitary prophetic critique on the "scribes" in Jer 8:8–9, the text discussed above, is most definitely not an attack on the epistemological convictions of the wisdom tradition but is obviously criticizing the "lying" pen (*'ēṭ šeqer*) of the scribes. Elsewhere in Jeremiah scribes are mentioned with no censure at all. Jeremiah's colleague, Baruch, came from the ranks of the scribes, and Jeremiah's attack on these "scribes/sages," whoever they were, must have been selective. Further, to the extent that some scribes themselves were the focus of Jeremiah's attack, it was not because they represented Israel's wisdom/Torah tradition but rather because they were perverting and subverting its legitimate and authentic claims.[12] Jeremiah calls the sages back to their legitimate perspective, which recognizes the limitation of any human capacity or institution.[13]

Far from opposing the essential nature and claims of Israel's wisdom tradition, Jeremiah and Isaiah shared the view of wisdom itself that it is a divine gift of God which stands in close relationship with the principles of justice, righteousness, and salvation. They confess that wisdom embodies these very principles in which the earth and

---

[11] Isa 5:21; 29:14; 44:25; 47:10; Jer 9:12; 8:8f.; 9:23–24.

[12] Van Leeuwen correctly insists on this point ("The Sage in the Prophetic Literature," 300). Cf. the earlier remarks directed against the position of R. B. Y. Scott by John Mark Thompson, *The Form and Function of Proverbs in Ancient Israel* (Paris: Mouton, 1974) 101.

[13] Morgan, *Wisdom in the Old Testament Traditions*, 88–89.

the heavens are anchored from their creation (Isa 33:5–6; Jer 10:12; 51:15). The difference between prophetic modes of thought and those characteristic of wisdom has indeed to do with an epistemological distinction; but such a distinction was not the crisis point envisioned by some.[14] The *dābār* of the prophet was gained by means of an essentially intuitive revelatory experience (vision, audition), whereas the *ʿēṣâ* of the sage was the product of observation and induction drawing on concrete experiences of nature and the human condition. Below we will consider the relationship of these epistemological systems more fully; for now it must be insisted not only that these systems were not in conflict with one another but also that they were not wholly divorced from one another. To some extent the prophet's *dābār* was also induced from concrete experience (e.g., in mapping out current political movements), and the sage's *ʿēṣâ* was equally the product of revelatory imagination.[15]

Torah and Wisdom

Epistemologically, wisdom and Torah are very closely related. Both are primarily derived by means of the observation and analysis of concrete data—whether those of liver inspection, Urim and Thummim, professional knowledge of regulations relative to distinctions of clean/unclean or holy/profane, or the examination and systematization of orders and species of life or of patterns of nature and of human behavior. Conceptually, both priest and sage derive truth claims from the observation and manipulation of hard facts. As Blenkinsopp has suggested, wisdom and Torah were two great rivers that eventually flowed together.[16] This convergence was inevitable, given their common epistemological commitments.

Given this epistemological convergence, it is small wonder that the distinction between Torah and wisdom was easily blurred. The end result of this convergence was the nearly total coalescence of

[14] E.g., Brueggemann, "Epistemological Crisis." He suggests that the crisis was one of epistemology. Yet the crisis spelled out by Brueggemann has less to do with the "act of knowing" itself than with the "content" of that knowledge. Thus, it is not essentially an epistemological crisis but a crisis of competing confessions, regardless of the epistemological methods by which such confessions were gained.

[15] See below under "Nature, History, and the Question of Revelation."

[16] Blenkinsopp, *Wisdom and Law in the Old Testament*, 130.

Torah and wisdom in early Jewish Torah piety, especially that found
in Ben Sira, where the Torah of Moses is very nearly identified with
the preexistent wisdom of God by means of which the order of the
cosmos was established. In Ben Sira, wisdom, with its heavenly
origins, is equated with "the book of the covenant of the Most High
God," the law of Moses (Sir 24:23).[17] An earlier stage in this development is evidenced by Ezra the priest, the "scribe skilled in the law
of Moses" (Ezra 7:6). The use of the title "scribe" (*sōpēr*) to designate
Ezra's competency probably points to a development in second
temple Judaism in which the earlier office of scribe as royal official
has given way to the priestly office of the learned expositor (*Schriftgelehrte*) of an increasingly written religious tradition.[18]

Such "Torah piety" is evident already in Psalms 19 and 119, where
cosmogonic language (19:1–6; 119:89–91) yields to a hymn of praise
to God's Torah, through which come knowledge and understanding
(19:7–11; 119:92–104). In language evoking the foundation of the
cosmos, the psalmist speaks of God's testimonies as having been
"founded from eternity" (*lĕ'ôlām yesadtām*, Ps 119:152). In its *qal*
form, the verb *yāsad* ("found, establish") is nearly a technical term
referring to God's "establishment" of the cosmos.[19] By intentional

[17] On the identification of Torah and wisdom in Ben Sira, see Eckhard J. Schnabel,
*Law and Wisdom from Ben Sira to Paul: A Tradition Historical Enquiry into the Rela-
tion of Law, Wisdom, and Ethics* (Tübingen: J. C. B. Mohr, 1985); Blenkinsopp, *Wisdom
and Law in the Old Testament*, 138–44; Michael E. Stone, "Ideal Figures and Social
Context: Priest and Sage in the Early Second Temple Age," in *Ancient Israelite Religion:
Essays in Honor of Frank Moore Cross* (ed. P. D. Miller, Jr., et al.; Philadelphia: Fortress,
1987) 578–82; Alan W. Jenks, "Theological Presuppositions of Israel's Wisdom
Literature," *HBT* 7 (1985) 63–68.

[18] Joseph Blenkinsopp sketches out the "scribalization of the priestly office" ("The
Sage, the Scribe, and Scribalism in the Chronicler's Work," in *The Sage in Israel and
the Ancient Near East* [ed. J. G. Gammie and L. G. Perdue; Winona Lake, IN: Eisenbrauns, 1990] 307–15). David E. Orton, however, wisely cautions against the notion
that the movement from "scribe" to "*Schriftgelehrte*" was total. Orton demonstrates
that the older notion of scribe as political adviser and composer continued to affect
usage in second temple Judaism and, in fact, laid the basis for the distinction between
the *Schriftgelehrte* (Pharisees) and the "ideal scribe" in the book of Matthew (*The
Understanding Scribe: Matthew and the Apocalyptic Ideal* [Sheffield: JSOT Press, 1989]
41, 56–58, 162–75).

[19] Cf. the phrase *kĕ'ereṣ yĕsādāh lĕ'ôlām* in Ps 78:69 as well as the copious use
of the verb *yāsad* in Pss 24:2; 89:12; 102:26; 104:5, 8; Isa 48:13; 51:13, 16; Amos 9:6;
Zech 12:1; Job 38:4.

use of this language, the psalmist is drawing an obvious analogy between Torah and the very foundations of the cosmos.[20] Furthermore, the conviction that Yahweh "by wisdom founded the earth" (*YHWH běḥokmâ yāsad-'āreṣ,* Prov 3:19) led to the logical association of this preexistent wisdom with God's preexistent Torah, fully expressed by Ben Sira as noted above.

The roots of such Torah piety can be traced back further yet to the book of Deuteronomy, which recognizes that the keeping of Torah is one's "wisdom and understanding." For Deuteronomy the Torah is a witness to the nations that "Surely this great nation is a wise and understanding people" (Deut 4:6–8). Finally, it may be possible to trace the connection between Torah and wisdom to ancient Israel's clan structures, particularly if the connection between clan wisdom and apodictic pronouncements proposed by Erhard Gerstenberger can be sustained.[21]

The confluence of Israel's Torah and wisdom ethos is demonstrated also in the critique of Israel's sacrificial cult, expressed in the psalms by texts such as Pss 40:6; 50:9–13; 51:16–17; and 69:30–31. This "antisacrificial" critique has often been understood to result either from the incursion into the cult of an external prophetic polemic or as the rising up of an internal challenge by cult prophets. Studies by H.-J. Hermisson and L. Perdue, however, have suggested that such a critique is not particularly prophetic at all but represents a common ancient Near Eastern ethos that has its primary attestation in oriental wisdom traditions. Hermisson argued that the critique of sacrifice expressed in the psalms differed from a prophetic critique in that, whereas the latter called for a commitment to "justice," the former called for a commitment to "spirituality."[22] Such a divorcing

---

[20] Jon D. Levenson understands Psalm 119, in its use of the word "Torah," to stand in the Deuteronomic tradition, yet lacking Deuteronomy's "book consciousness." Its closest parallel is the book of Proverbs, where such Torah constitutes a sort of revealed natural law ("The Sources of Torah: Psalm 119 and the Modes of Revelation in Second Temple Judaism," in *Ancient Israelite Religion: Essays in Honor of Frank Moore Cross* [ed. P. D. Miller, Jr., et al.; Philadelphia: Fortress, 1987] 564–67).

[21] Erhard Gerstenberger, *Wesen und Herkunft des "apodiktischen Rechts"* (Neukirchen-Vluyn: Neukirchener Verlag, 1965).

[22] Hans-Jürgen Hermisson, *Sprache und Ritus im altisraelitischen Kult: Zur "Spiritualisierung" der Kultbegriffe im alten Testament* (Neukirchen-Vluyn: Neukirchener Verlag, 1965) 46, 50.

of the ethical and the spiritual dynamics of Israel's cult is most certainly wrong, however, as evidenced by Prov 15:8, where the divine
acceptance of prayer, a primary expression of spiritualization, is itself
subject to moral conditions ("the prayer of the upright"). But
Hermisson did point in the right direction when he suggested that
such a concern for spirituality had its roots in Israel's wisdom tradition.[23] As shown by Perdue, texts such as Prov 21:2–3 demonstrate
not a prophetic critique but rather a sapiential critique of the cult
based on a common ethos that underlay both priestly and prophetic
self-consciousness.[24] A similar critique is evidenced also in 1 Sam
15:22 (*hinnēh šĕmōaʿ mizzebaḥ ṭôb lĕhaqšîb mēḥēleb ʾêlîm*), which
has been all too quickly identified as a "prophetic critique."[25] Its formal
character as a typical *ṭôb*-saying indicates again that the proper context for such a critique of sacrifice is not an antagonistic prophetic
movement but rather a common cultural ethos as expressed in Israel's
wisdom literature. This inner-cultic self-assessment based on a common wisdom ethos again demonstrates the confluence of wisdom
and Torah in Israel's theological traditions.

The details of the relationship between Torah and wisdom are
extremely complicated and are the focus of considerable debate. We
cannot agree, however, with those who insist that the confluence
of these two great streams occurred only late in Israel's life.[26] The
association of wisdom and Torah made by Ben Sira is not to be
explained as the result of the incursion of a foreign theological expression, whether from Hellenistic or other sources. It is wholly
intelligible as the full development of the biblical notion attested
at least as early as the compilation of the Deuteronomic tradition.[27]

[23] Ibid., 146–47.

[24] Leo G. Perdue, *Wisdom and Cult: A Critical Analysis of the Views of Cult in
the Wisdom Literatures of Israel and the Ancient Near East* (Missoula, MT: Scholars
Press, 1977) 118–19, 156, 160–62.

[25] E.g., Bruce C. Birch, *The Rise of the Israelite Monarchy: The Growth and Development of 1 Samuel 7–15* (Missoula, MT: Scholars Press, 1976) 100–101.

[26] E.g., Roland Murphy, "Religious Dimensions of Israelite Wisdom," in *Ancient
Israelite Religion: Essays in Honor of Frank Moore Cross* (ed. P. D. Miller, Jr., et al.;
Philadelphia: Fortress, 1987) 452.

[27] For a study on the development that argues against the notion that Ben Sira
understood Torah in terms of the Stoic notion of a cosmic *nomos*, see Eckhard J.
Schnabel, *Law and Wisdom from Ben Sira to Paul: A Tradition Historical Enquiry
into the Relation of Law, Wisdom, and Ethics* (Tübingen: J. C. B. Mohr, 1985) 79–85.

Nor can we agree with those who insist that Ben Sira represents not so much the coalescence of Torah and wisdom as the subordination of wisdom to Torah piety.[28] As stated above, because of their common epistemological commitments, wisdom and Torah were from the beginning closely related, and their confluence (if indeed they were ever understood to be separate) was essential to their common nature. In fact, the question of whether postexilic Judaism was characterized by a legalizing of wisdom or rather by a sapentializing of Torah is flawed by presuming too great a distance between the basic epistemological commitments of the two. Although Gerald Sheppard has made a strong case for the latter—that is, the sapentializing of Israel's Torah tradition—he nevertheless admits the ambiguity of the issue.[29] If wisdom became a "hermeneutical construct" by which to interpret Israel's nonwisdom traditions in the postexilic period, it is only because of the natural affinity that Torah and wisdom had for each other, and is evidence of the central premise of this chapter: the priest's *tôrâ*, the prophet's *dābār*,[30] and the sage's

---

Schnabel argues that Ben Sira never lost the association of Torah with the revelation to Moses.

[28] Jenks, "Theological Presuppositions of Israel's Wisdom Literature," 68. Blenkinsopp argues that an earlier form of amoral secular wisdom, with its focus on the distinction between the wise and the fool, gave way in the postexilic period to a process of theologization rooted in the "fear of Yahweh" with its focus on the distinction of righteous and wicked (*Wisdom and Law in the Old Testament*, 23–24). Cf. Crenshaw, "Studies in Ancient Israelite Wisdom," 24–25. P. Kyle McCarter, Jr., sees this shift from early amoral secular to later moralistic sacral wisdom occurring already as early as Deuteronomy ("The Sage in the Deuteronomistic History," in *The Sage in Israel and the Ancient Near East* [ed. J. G. Gammie and L. G. Perdue; Winona Lake, IN: Eisenbrauns, 1990] 289–93). Most, however, reject the notion of such an evolutionary development, arguing that Israel's wisdom literature had a "theological" center from the beginning (e.g., Jenks, "Theological Presuppositions of Israel's Wisdom Literature," 43–44).

[29] Gerald T. Sheppard, *Wisdom as a Hermeneutical Construct: A Study in the Sapientializing of the Old Testament* (New York: Walter de Gruyter, 1980) 116–19.

[30] In his earlier study, *Prophecy and Canon: A Contribution to the Study of Jewish Origins* (Notre Dame, IN: University of Notre Dame Press, 1977), J. Blenkinsopp spoke of the "scribalization" of Israel's prophetic tradition, by which he meant its subsumption under Israel's developing scribal Torah. In his more recent work, *Wisdom and Law in the Old Testament*, Blenkinsopp restates the thesis, stressing that prophecy comes under the interpretive hermeneutic of the sage (p. 138). He notes that Ben Sira compares his scribal teaching explicitly with prophecy (Sir 24:33), and that the rabbinic dictum was that prophecy was taken from the prophets and given to the sages (*b. Baba Bathra* 12a); however, such a coalescence of prophet, Levite, temple

'ēṣâ are much more closely intertwined than is often assumed and are in fact reflexes of one another.

Nature, History, and the Question of Revelation _____

The answer to the epistemological question, how it is that humans gain knowledge and true insight, lies beyond the scope of this study. The focus of our study has been the various manifestations of power and authority in Israel's institutions. When discussing issues pertaining to authority, however, the issue is not simply one of "power." A narrow focus on the issue of how certain institutions convey *auctoritas* or *potestas* misses the fundamental point that the answer to the question of authority is precisely an epistemological one. The issue is not primarily concerned with how power is expressed. The more fundamental issue is how knowledge is gained, or at least how the community *perceives* that knowledge is gained.

Obviously, power and epistemology cannot be divorced. The *claim* to knowledge is itself a form of power—perhaps the *primary* form of power. The idealist claim is that ideas drive material concerns (history, economics, social values). Knowledge produces power. The materialist claim is that material concerns drive the world of ideas, that socioeconomic forces drive ideas in the shape of ideologies. Power produces knowledge. The debate is simply a reheated version of the Platonic-Aristotelian debate over the priority of the world of ideas over against the world of matter. By insisting that authority is fundamentally an epistemological issue, we are admitting the impasse of the old debate and expressing the desire to opt out of the hunt for such polarities in the search for a new way of asking the question.

Having clearly stated a dis-ease with the nature of the historic debate, however, avoiding the problem of taking sides is probably impossible. Any study that is interested in sociohistorical issues will by definition align itself more with the Aristotelian/materialist perspective, because its interest will lie less in the idealist's question of how knowledge is gained and conveyed than in the materialist's

---

singer, and scribe is already attested in the chronicler's history. See Orton, *Understanding Scribe,* 47.

question of how and why a particular society *believes* that knowledge is gained and conveyed.

Tradition, Reason, and Revelation as Sources of Knowledge

The classical symbol used to summarize the epistemological debate is that of the three-legged stool. Involved in the process of "knowing" are three interrelated dynamics: tradition, reason, and revelation. Without challenging the adequacy of this truism, two questions must be addressed before turning to the issue of Israel's theory of knowledge. The first relates to the question of where experience enters the system, and the second concerns the matter of how reason and revelation relate to each other.

The term "experience" is often invoked as one of the indices of epistemology, but often inconsistently. Crenshaw, for example, issues conflicting statements concerning the role of experience in Israel's system of knowledge. On one hand, under the influence of a contemporary concern to understand praxis in relation to theory and experience, he speaks of "two types of knowledge": systematic (philosophical reflection) and gnomic (experience).[31] On the other hand, he refers to "three ways of acquiring knowledge," in which case "experience," by which he means the observation of nature and human behavior, is contrasted with "tradition" (creeds) and "revelation" (encounter with the transcendent one).[32] In this broader sense, experience, for Crenshaw, is synonymous with and a replacement for "reason" in the three-legged stool. As with Crenshaw, Thompson too equates experience with reason when he speaks of the experience of nature or of the world as the human capacity to comprehend and control the world.[33]

On the other hand, "experience" is used by some to refer to the *personal* experience of individuals, which stands over against the *traditional authority* of the community.[34] In this sense, experience is not

[31] James L. Crenshaw, "The Acquisition of Knowledge in Israelite Wisdom Literature," *W & W* 7 (1987) 246.

[32] Ibid., 247–52.

[33] Thompson, *Form and Function of Proverbs*, 72.

[34] James G. Williams, *Those Who Ponder Proverbs: Aphoristic Thinking and Biblical Literature* (Sheffield: Almond, 1981) 35–54. Roland E. Murphy, *The Tree of Life: An Exploration of Biblical Wisdom Literature* (New York: Doubleday, 1990) 20–21.

synonymous with reason but rather with the charismatic dynamic of revelation insofar as charisma is understood in Weberian terms to refer to the inspired individual as opposed to the bureaucratized institution. The term "experience" can thus have reference both to reason, insofar as it is experience of the world and its systematization, and to revelation, in terms of the personal charismatic endowment of the inspired individual. But it can also have reference to tradition if such experience is understood as a collective and corporate accumulation of shared experiences.

To refer to experience as an index of epistemology is therefore not very helpful. It is too easily confused with tradition as corporate experience, with revelation as individual experience, or with reason as experience of the world. Experience is nothing in and of itself—it is always experience *of* something—and the term cannot bear the weight it is often given in the discussion.

The second major difficulty is the manner in which reason and revelation (or faith) are counterposed in the debate. If these are two separate legs of the stool, then are they by definition different things? Studies by Brueggemann and George Mendenhall are characteristic of a popular tendency to force apart reason and revelation. We have already alluded to Brueggemann's theory of the epistemological collision of Israel's prophetic and wisdom tradition. According to Brueggemann, prophecy is regarded as a theological divine word over against wisdom, which is regarded as an ideological social construction of reality and the sages as "ideologues for social justification."[35] An even more extreme position is articulated by Mendenhall when he launches a virulent attack against reason and the wise, whom in his own experience he has come to distrust.[36] His comment that "Luther was only half right; 'reason' alias 'wisdom' is not only a whore but also a pimp"[37] can only be regarded as a noble commitment to a Reformation hermeneutic out of control. Mendenhall's anti-

[35] Walter A. Brueggemann, "The Social Significance of Solomon as a Patron of Wisdom," in *The Sage in Israel and the Ancient Near East* (ed. J. G. Gammie and L. G. Perdue; Winona Lake, IN: Eisenbrauns, 1990) 125.

[36] George E. Mendenhall, "The Shady Side of Wisdom: The Date and Purpose of Genesis 3," in *A Light unto My Path: Old Testament Studies in Honor of Jacob M. Myers* (ed. H. N. Bream et al.; Philadelphia: Temple University Press, 1974) 319–34.

[37] Ibid., 323–24.

rationalist fury, generated evidently by his revulsion to an intellectual "Solomonic institution" managing God's wisdom,[38] is regrettable.

Such attempts to play "faith" off against "reason" and inappropriately to apply our peculiar fears to the Hebrew biblical witness do considerable damage to the integrity of biblical theology. Israel's belief structures made no fundamental distinction between "faith/revelation" and "reason." For Israel's faith, natural knowledge—knowledge gained by a reasonable assessment of nature—did not yield different information from revealed knowledge—that gained by a revelation of the divine will. For Israel, experience of the world was in some sense always experience of the divine will, and what was learned from their experience of creation was necessarily associated with what was learned from their historical traditions.[39] The point being made here is simply a reiteration of that made in the previous chapter when discussing the relationship of "nature" and "history": they are not antagonists in some eternal morality play. One cannot construe natural reason and historical revelation against each other in a manner that does not do violence to Israel's faith. Israel understood creation and redemption, nature and history, and now we would add reason and revelation, to be inextricably related.

An Old Testament Epistemology

How would the Hebrew intellectual tradition have understood the question of how it is that knowledge is gained? To apply a theory of the three-legged stool to the question of Israel's theory of knowledge poses more problems than it solves, not because of the triadic nature

[38] Ibid., 330.

[39] Roland E. Murphy, *The Tree of Life: An Exploration of Biblical Wisdom Literature* (New York: Doubleday, 1990) 114, 124–25; Nel, *Structure and Ethos of the Wisdom Admonitions,* 91, 101. See also Roland E. Murphy, "Wisdom and Creation," *JBL* 104 (1985) 3–11, who, against von Rad, insists that the "self-revelation" of creation in wisdom is not simply revelation of an abstract order but is the very voice of the Lord. See Ronald W. Duty, "Creation, History, and the Ethics of the Book of Proverbs," *W & W* 7 (1987) 261–71, who protests against Klaus Koch's notion of an autonomous act–consequence model (creation theology) opposed in some sense to a model of divine intervention (salvation history) (Koch, "Gibt es ein Vergeltungsdogma im Alten Testament?" *ZTK* 52 [1955] 1–42).

of the proposal itself but rather because terms such as tradition, reason, and revelation are so problematic given Israel's blurring of distinctions between the individual and the community as well as between creation and history. We propose organizing an Old Testament epistemology around the topics of wisdom as "divine mediator," as "divine gift," and as "innate human character or quality." Such a proposal expresses not a circular arrangement of three legs on a stool but rather a linear movement from external sources of knowledge to internal.

The clearest paradigm for wisdom as "divine mediator" is of course that of the personification of Dame Wisdom in Prov 8:22–31 and throughout the book, where wisdom is understood as an objectified entity standing perpetually outside of the realm of human experience. Wisdom mediates to us an experience of the divine that would otherwise fail us. It allows itself to be grasped by humans, but because it is preexistent and is closely identified in some way with the notion of deity itself, it is never reducible to a human quality. It stands on the street and beckons the listening ear, vying for attention with Dame Folly on the opposite side of the street. It eventually is identified with Torah, that divine principle which stands outside of our human experience, bringing to us awareness of that truth which stands over against us. Wisdom is something that lies so far outside our human condition that we must seek after its elusive truths like silver, search for it as for treasure, and store it up for life (Prov 2:1–8). It is something to be sought and found, or to be missed or even to be hated (8:35–36). At a primal level, such wisdom was ultimately unfathomable, and the mediation of such wisdom was always only partial.

Closely related to this notion, however, is that of wisdom as a "divine gift." Here the acquisition of knowledge represents a process of internalization: wisdom still remains an essentially nonhuman quality with its source in God's own identity, but it is not the elusive object of a quest. Rather, it is something that God implants as a gift in the discerning or receptive heart, and it becomes a part—though rather like an implanted prosthesis—of one's humanity. It is recognizable as a special superhuman quality which the specially endowed possess on a permanent basis. The paradigm for this epistemological metaphor is the story of Solomon's request for an "understanding mind" (*lēb šōmēaʿ*) with which to be able to "discern between good and evil" (*lĕhābîn bên-ṭôb lĕrāʿ*, 1 Kgs 3:9).

The final metaphor in this sketch of an Old Testament epistemology is that of wisdom as an innate human quality. This metaphor represents the full internalization of that which still is recognizable as divine in origin but which is now fully absorbed and integrated into the basic character of the human condition. The paradigm for this third metaphor is the story of the acquisition of knowledge by Adam and Eve in the garden. Discerning between good and evil, according to this metaphor, is no longer dependent on a special gift from God, a special Solomonic endowment. It is precisely this divine quality of "knowing good and evil" (*yōdĕʿê ṭôb wārāʿ*, Gen 3:5, 22) which Adam and Eve secured *for the human condition*, even if it was an illicit encroachment on divine prerogatives. Such divine wisdom is no longer the object of a quest nor even a gift to be implanted in the discerning heart. It is innate to the human condition. This metaphor of the illicit seizure of a divine quality has played a major role in the development of an antirationalistic perspective in Christianity, especially in its Reformation traditions. The function of the metaphor, however, was not to lament the possession of this innate human quality but rather to celebrate the fact that humans are, after all, "little less than gods" (Ps 8:5).[40]

Such a sketch of an Old Testament epistemology takes its cue not from philosophical metaphors concerning the interplay of tradition, reason, and revelation, but rather from biblical metaphors that are expressive of the dynamic of the Hebrew intellectual tradition itself. To speak of wisdom as "mediator," as "gift," and as "innate human character or quality" does not simply provide us with a different three-legged stool. More importantly, it allows us to understand wisdom in Israel without imposing on it our notions of the non-solubility of reason and revelation or of corporate tradition and individual inspiration. Some of the same dynamics are of course still at work in the new metaphorical field. The movement from external to internal still captures the dynamic of an epistemology that knew of tensions in its self-understanding. However, that which is

---

[40] Rodney R. Hutton, "God or Beast? Human Self-Understanding in Genesis 2–3," *Proceedings: Eastern Great Lakes and Midwest Biblical Societies* 6 (1986) 128–41.

external is not simply reducible to the invasion of an antirationalist charisma that blasts its way into the human condition. Nor is that which is internal reducible to a lowest common denominator of "reasonableness" cut off from the divine will. A movement from externalization to an internalization of wisdom speaks not of polarities opposing one another but rather of a sliding scale which, though recognizing complexities and ambiguities, incorporates them into a coherent system that insists on both the reasonable and the revealed nature of wisdom at the same time.

Wisdom as a Social Construction of Order

The biblical witness attests to a *human urge toward order.* The witness of the Bible, furthermore, is that this human urge is expressive of the *prior* divine urge toward order. God's wresting of an ordered cosmos from the jaws of Chaos did not come easily nor without cost—it was an urge requiring sweat, tears, and blood, language that ought not be lost on Christian ears. Israel's wisdom literature, consistent with the biblical witness as a whole, demonstrates a primary commitment to this divine/human urge toward order.[41]

I use the term "toward" in order to avoid dividing Israel's wisdom tradition into two (or more) discordant voices. As with many others, Leo Perdue has divided the tradition into two conflicting camps, one focused on a "paradigm of order" (Proverbs and Qoheleth; others would add Ben Sira) and the other on a "paradigm of conflict" (the book of Job). The former, argues Perdue, understood order to be unchallenged and indigenous to the cosmos, whereas the latter understood order to be ever under threat and achieved only by the continuing defeat of chaos.[42] In order to hold these two paradigms apart, Perdue must presume some reason for their mutual existence.

[41] Carole R. Fontaine comments that the function of proverbs was not so much to discover some preexistent world order as it was to create and consolidate order (*Traditional Sayings in the Old Testament* [Sheffield: Almond, 1982] 150–51). However, we can *only* discover by creating, and to assume otherwise again does not adequately admit to the incarnational nature of theological expression.

[42] Leo G. Perdue, "Cosmology and the Social Order in the Wisdom Tradition," in *The Sage in Israel and the Ancient Near East* (ed. J. G. Gammie and L. G. Perdue; Winona Lake, IN: Eisenbrauns, 1990) 458–60.

The difficulty is that he suggests two solutions that are contradictory, the first diachronic and the second synchronic. First, he claims that the difference was due to historical evolution: the shift from the order model to the conflict model was occasioned by the sequence of historical disasters.[43] Second, he claims that the difference was due to the variable social locations of those responsible for the different models: the "order model" was produced by traditional sages with access to political power and wealth, and the "conflict model" was produced by the "declasses," who stood outside the channels of power.[44] That both diachronic and synchronic arguments are invoked to explain a presumed dichotomy between models raises questions about the adequacy of Perdue's analysis.

A much more carefully nuanced and therefore more satisfying analysis is seen in Williams's distinction between "order" and "counter-order" models of Israel's wisdom literature. Williams connects the order model to an interest in the typical and general, and the counter-order model to a focus on the novel and the individual.[45] More importantly, Williams insists that even the order model recognizes that disorder and paradox are always a present threat. Therefore, Williams consciously resists using the terms "order" and "dis-order." He understands these models as not wholly disconnected. Further, though the counter-order model may initially seek to disorient, what it ultimately seeks is another and better kind of order.[46]

The supposed polarity between order and conflict is overcome by understanding the tension between form and reform to be expressive of the human/divine *urge toward* order. Experience of reality is never wholly one or the other. There are not firmly stationed camps anchored respectively in ideologies of "order" and "dis-order." Rather the *urge toward* order involves God and humans in a constant dynamic movement characterized at every level and in every instance by ambiguity. Even the book of Proverbs, taken by Perdue and

[43] Ibid., 468–69. Even here, however, Perdue is inconsistent, since he also says that this shift was due to the fact that the order model had grown increasingly tyrannical. But the "tyranny of order" and the historical "disconfirmation of order" are not logical corollaries.

[44] Ibid., 476–78.

[45] Williams, *Those Who Ponder Proverbs*, 35–45.

[46] Ibid., 65, 81.

Williams to be expressive of the order model, attests to such ambiguity by proposing conflicting responses to the same situation. The obvious contradiction explicit in Prov 26:4–5 recognizes that the order of reality is illusive: both "answering a fool" and "not answering him" may correctly discern the proper order. The obvious corollary is that either may, at the same time, be illustrative of life's chaos. The proper response lies in a discernment of the particular circumstances defining a situation. It is never sufficient simply to apply general rules to any given question. Proverbs express a *relative* truth whose meaning, rather than being independent of the proverb itself, is contextually specified.[47] Israel's proverbial wisdom recognized its limitation vis-à-vis the inscrutability of God, and proverbs did not put themselves forward to be interpreted in a hardened dogmatic fashion, which is precisely the error into which Job's friends fell. The book of Proverbs resists the sort of tyranny of order represented by Job's friends when they no longer take seriously the primary claim wisdom makes to the inscrutability of the divine will. Proverbs stands under the same skeptical spirit as does Qoheleth (Prov 30:1–6) and thus expresses not "order" as such but the "*urge toward* order."

The question of whether Israel's proverbial literature carried with it a specific agenda for a certain social program is directly related to the issue of its social location. What were the vested interests of those responsible for the promulgation and collection of proverbs? This question presents us with another insoluble problem—that of the existence and function of "schools" in Israel.

That proverbs in some sense are the product of a popular ethos and reflect nonliterary rather than literary forms is granted by most. Some would insist, however, that such popular folk sayings gave way to more sophisticated literary forms with the bureaucratization of the monarchy and the "Solomonic enlightenment."[48] The corollary of this evolution from popular to literary form is the thesis that the earlier popular forms were imbued with a pan-sacral spirit that was either secularized or paganized by the Solomonic enlightenment with its driving bureaucratization. Some would understand this evolution to represent a radical shift from the power of the charismatically inspired "wit of one individual" who coins proverbs "in a moment

[47] Fontaine, *Traditional Sayings in the Old Testament,* 48.
[48] Thompson, *Form and Function of Proverbs,* 20, 57–67.

of creative insight"[49] to the power of the bureaucratized institution, which coopts them for its own purposes. Others would understand the evolution as a shift from traditional forms of authority (family, clan) to the institutional (or in Weber's terms, the "legal/rational") forms of authority inherent in the bureaucratized royal schools.

As the product of schools, such wisdom is often taken to represent the vested interests of royal sages and scribes—bureaucrats in training—who will make up the elite cadre of royal advisors or who will supply the ranks of "mid-management" officials. Proverbs 1–9 is understood by Bernhard Lang, for example, to be a training manual of practice texts for such students in these court schools.[50] With this bureaucratization, it is argued, came the development of an elitist class ethos reflecting the social interests of the ruling elite or at the least of those with access to wealth and power. The morality of the book of Proverbs is taken to be expressive of such class interests: it views poverty, for example, as resulting from sloth and indolence or divine will and something to be avoided or treated with charitable kindliness.[51]

The thesis that Proverbs is the production of such elitist groups with their class ethos, or that it represents the collection and edition of originally popular proverbs now subjected to such interests, has been challenged with equal force. The book of Proverbs promotes agrarian pursuits as an "Israelitic ideal" and warns against the enticing wealth of the city and of commercial enterprises.[52] It does not presuppose direct acquaintance with the royal court, as there is only modest royal coloring in the book.[53] In fact, Proverbs often expresses

[49] Ibid., 18.

[50] Bernhard Lang, *Die weisheitliche Lehrrede* (Stuttgart: KBW, 1972). Two classic studies supporting the existence and prominent role of schools in Israel are Hans-Jürgen Hermisson, *Studien zur israelitischen Spruchweisheit* (Neukirchen-Vluyn: Neukirchener Verlag, 1968); and A. Lemaire, *Les écoles et la formation de la Bible dans l'ancien Israël* (Fribourg, Switzerland: Editions universitaires, 1981).

[51] J. David Pleins, "Poverty in the Social World of the Wise," *JSOT* 37 (1987) esp. 66–70. The earlier study by Brian W. Kovacs was much more balanced. Though insisting that Proverbs reflects a "class-ethic," he allows that this ethic was not elitist but had a broader appeal, including not only literati but also the ignorant and the young ("Is There a Class-Ethic in Proverbs?" 176–79).

[52] Joseph W. Gaspar, *Social Ideas in the Wisdom Literature of the Old Testament* (Washington, DC: Catholic University of America, 1947) 49–50.

[53] Murphy, *Tree of Life*, 5.

a naïve and even critical assessment of the monarchy and the court, portraying the king in unflattering terms as arbitrary and vain. The attitude of the book of Proverbs toward poverty and wealth can be taken to represent the interests of small landowners as well as of any supposed elitist circles.[54] Education was almost certainly not limited to court or temple schools and may have centered as much in the family where father and mother or a hired tutor were the primary "teachers."[55] That there even existed a social group known as "sages" or "the wise" who would have made up the leadership of royal schools is at least doubtful. Proverbs were likely the product not of any particular class of sages but rather of a more generally diffused and noninstitutionalized "intellectual tradition."[56] Any ethos reflected in the book of Proverbs, therefore, represents the social values and goals not of one elitist group or another but rather of the community as a whole.[57] It presents a common social ethos illustrative of the "mythic consciousness" of the larger community as it gives expression to its natural "urge toward order."

[54] Roger N. Whybray, "Poverty, Wealth, and Point of View in Proverbs," *ExpTim* 100 (1989) 333–34. Whybray's use of the term "middle class" is to be avoided, however, as an extremely anachronistic designation. Whybray reiterates his views in his more recent comprehensive study, *Wealth and Poverty in the Book of Proverbs* (Sheffield: JSOT Press, 1990) 60–61, 116–17.

[55] On the "sage functions" exercised by the father of a family, see Carole R. Fontaine, "The Sage in Family and Tribe," in *The Sage in Israel and the Ancient Near East* (ed. J. G. Gammie and L. G. Perdue; Winona Lake, IN: Eisenbrauns, 1990) 156–57. On the role of the mother in the education of the family, where she provided the "gluey-ness" bonding families together, see ibid., 160, and Claudia V. Camp, "The Female Sage in Ancient Israel and in the Biblical Wisdom Literature," in *The Sage*, 188. The classic critical assessment of the existence of schools in Israel is Friedemann W. Golka, "Die israelitische Weisheitsschule oder 'Des Kaisers neue Kleider,'" *VT* 33 (1983) 257–70; idem, "Die Königs- und Hofsprüche und der Ursprung der israelitischen Weisheit," *VT* 36 (1986) 13–36. Golka argues that education took place primarily as training of young children through a "Famulus" or "tutorial" system and, in the latter work, bases his thesis on a study of African proverbs. Crenshaw rejects the extremity of Golka's position, but himself gives the most pessimistic response: No answer can be given at all to the question of where education took place ("Education in Ancient Israel," *JBL* 104 [1985] 609, 614).

[56] Whybray, *Intellectual Tradition in the Old Testament*, 31, 54, 69–70; also idem, "The Sage in the Israelite Royal Court," in *The Sage in Israel and the Ancient Near East*, ed. Gammie and Perdue, 133–39; James L. Crenshaw, "The Sage in Proverbs," in *The Sage*, 213–14.

[57] Crenshaw, "Studies in Ancient Israelite Wisdom," 20.

The Effective Performance of Proverbs _____

What is it that endows the proverb with its effective power? Proverbs do not gain power because of the force lying behind the particular group that pens them. The effectiveness of Israel's proverbial literature is not to be ascribed simply to any presumed social location of literati, sages, or courtiers. Nor is it to be understood simply as a reflex of parental authority by means of which children are subjected to the traditions of the elders. We must take seriously Crenshaw's admonition not to be overly preoccupied with questions of the existence or nonexistence of schools in Israel, as well as Nel's insistence that the force of authority behind proverbial literature lies not in some presumed institution but rather in its own formal character.[58] The power of proverbs is generated by two indices: first, by their ability to symbolize the essence of a community's mythic consciousness, its "urge toward order," and, second, by their ability to reduce this urge to its simplest rules and premises.

Capturing the community's ethos, its mythic consciousness, its urge toward order, and demonstrating a reduction of this urge to its simplest parameters give proverbs their force of persuasion. The common assumption is that such authority is based on an appeal to nature, to tradition, or to the revealed will of God. We demonstrated above, however, that such an appeal to the three-legged stool is less than helpful when considering Israel's epistemological commitments. Proverbial literature may *indeed* appeal to natural data, to traditional values, or to the divine will. However, these are but secondary manifestations of the primary force of appeal—the reduction to simplest terms of the community's urge toward order. Proverbs attempt to predict, harmonize, and systematize human behavior, and the extent to which they achieve their goal of persuasion or their ability to tease reality into patterns is what can be spoken of as "proverb performance."[59]

---

[58] Crenshaw, "Education in Ancient Israel," 614–15; Nel, *Structure and Ethos of the Wisdom Admonitions,* 89–91.

[59] In her study of proverb performance, Fontaine argued that such performance is a measure of the proverb's ability to bring about resolution in a specific ambiguous conflict situation. She denies, therefore, that proverbs have the ability to convey a "truth" in some abstract sense divorced from a specific semantic fit (*Traditional

The Reduction to a Binary View of Reality

The prime feature of Israel's proverbial wisdom is its ability to reduce the complexity of life to its simplest possible level of conflict, to effect the coherence of Israel's mythic universe by reducing all paradox and ambiguity to a simple binary equation. The proper response in a given situation is either *this* or *that*. Language becomes a toggle switch by which all human relations are reducible to the simplest possible configuration: they are good or bad, righteous or wicked, wise or foolish. There is no middle ground in this binary system, no ambiguity, and no uncertainty.

By far the most common form of proverb in Israel's literature is the antithetical parallel construction "X but Y." "Folly is a joy to one who has no sense, but a person of understanding walks straight ahead" (Prov 15:21). Formally, it does not seem to matter whether the negative datum or its contrasting positive datum is stated in the first colon: both forms occur with relative frequency. What does seem to be characteristic, however, is that the first colon is generally longer than is the second, the most frequent meter being 4+3, with 4+4 and 3+3 meter also being well represented. Only rarely is the first colon ever shorter than the second.[60] The predominant weight placed on the first colon gives a sense of importance to it that seems to provide the basis for moving on to the second. The truth of the couplet is anchored, as it were, by the claim made in the first colon, to which the secondary claim made in the next colon is a response.

While anchoring the truth in the first colon, the power of these proverbs is also generated by what James Williams has referred to as their "stroboscopic projection." They are seen quickly side by side;

Sayings in the Old Testament, 50, 154–57). Of course, all her references are drawn from specific conflict situations, so her conclusion is predetermined by the nature of the evidence. The performance of proverbs is dependent not on their ability to resolve conflict in specific instances but rather on their ability to resolve conflict in its broadest parameters, that is, in their ability to homogenize, synthesize, and systematize the conflict and discontinuity of our life experiences.

[60] Prov 10:2–32, for example, offers the following synopsis:

4+3:   vv. 2, 3, 4, 8, 9, 10, 13, 17, 19, 20, 23, 24, 25, 27, 29, 31, 32 (total 17)
4+4 or 3+3:   vv. 5, 7, 11, 16, 18, 21, 22, 28, 30 (total 9)
3+4:   vv. 6, 12, 14, 15 (total 4)

then they are shut off as quickly.[61] The truth claim made by the first colon is flashed before the hearer and is removed before the hearer has time to withhold consent. By bombarding the hearer with such stroboscopic projection, a simple claim is being made that is not negotiable. Consent is elicited whether or not the hearer is prepared to consider granting it.

Though life is reduced to its absolute simplest binary equation in this form of proverb, it should not be assumed that reality was actually thought of in such terms. For example, Prov 10:4–5 expresses an absolutely "synthetic" view of life: industry is rewarded. It is preceded, however, by two statements that attest to some amount of ambiguity if not direct contradiction of the synthetic view. Wickedness *does* produce treasures, even if they do not ultimately profit (10:2). The righteous sometimes *do* verge on the brink of hunger, even if the Lord intervenes at the last moment to prevent it (10:3). The fact that the conflicting claims of 10:2–3 and 4–5 could be tolerated in such close proximity to one another ought to warn us against the presumption that the reduction of life to a binary system was thought of as a *final* solution to the dilemma of life's ambiguity. It is a *mythic* solution precisely because it taps into the wellspring of Israel's (and a *human*) urge toward order.

A less frequent formal expression of such a binary reduction, but one that is nonetheless significant for Israel's proverbial wisdom, is that of the "*tôb*-saying": X is better than Y. For example: "Better is a dinner of vegetables where love is than a fatted ox and hatred with it" (15:17). The authority lying behind this form is not immediately apparent. Why should I be inclined, for example, to accept the truth of the proverb in 27:10b: "Better is a neighbor who is nearby than kindred who are far away"? Or what is it about the statement in 28:6 that calls for my assent without further comment? In general, such forms appeal directly to personal experience. I know that something is true because I have already experienced it as true. Such proverbs describe something the hearer has already experienced rather than preparing the reader for some unknown experience. The proverb in 21:9—"It is better to live in a corner of the housetop than in a

---

[61] James G. Williams, "The Power of Form: A Study of Biblical Proverbs," in *Gnomic Wisdom* (ed. J. D. Crossan; Semeia 17; Chico, CA: Scholars Press, 1980) 41.

house shared with a contentious wife"–carries authority for one to the extent that it resonates with his or her experience. It will be less appreciated by someone who has not yet experienced living with a contentious person. Thus, the authority implicit in these forms is based on personal experience. Such experience, however, is always ambiguous. The *primary* power of such proverbs, and the basis for their effective "performance," is really derived from their ability to satisfy our urge toward order by capturing something of our mythic consciousness and thereby reducing the complexity of life to two alternatives: we have only *this* and *that* before us, and one is clearly a preferable slice of our corporate consciousness.

The Reduction to Urgent Social Values

A predominant form of address in Israel's proverbial literature is the so-called wisdom admonition, which makes its appeal to the hearer with its vetitive form (the negative particle *'al* plus a jussive verbal form), "Do not . . . ." For example: "Do not desire her [the neighbor's wife's] beauty in your heart and do not let her capture you with her eyelashes" (6:25). In his discussion of the wisdom admonition, Nel made a solid case for the fact that the authority of the admonition–that is, its "effective performance"–is based not in the group promulgating it but rather in its structural form, especially in its motivative clause. It depends on its intrinsic truth, made explicit in its motivation.[62]

Nel is certainly correct in his objection to the idea that the authority implicit in the wisdom admonition was fundamentally different from that explicit in the prohibition. He objects to the thesis proposed by Hermisson and Zimmerli that wisdom admonitions, in contrast to apodictic prohibitions, carried no authority other than that of human counsel. Nel correctly insists that the ethos of wisdom admonitions is not fundamentally different from that of prohibitions, since both forms–the prohibitive and the vetitive–are but types of one genre, the wisdom admonition.[63]

Where I disagree with Nel is in placing so much emphasis on the motivative clause itself as the source for the wisdom admonition's

---

[62] Nel, *Structure and Ethos of the Wisdom Admonitions,* 90–91.
[63] Ibid., 5, 14–15.

authority. First, not all wisdom admonitions have motivative clauses, in spite of Nel's claim to the contrary.[64] Second, the function of these motivative clauses differs in individual cases—sometimes simply giving a further perspective on the issue (3:31–32; 23:3, 6–7, 9; 24:1–2, 19–20) and sometimes sounding a warning about the consequences (6:25–26; 22:22–23, 24–25; 23:10–11, 20–21, 31–35). Whereas the latter group certainly provide "motivation" for prudent behavior, the former group can be spoken of as giving "motivation" only in the most general sense of the term. Third, the fact that prohibitions are unmotivated does not mean that they had an immediate commanding presence. They, too, required further clarification before the exact nature of their authority could become evident for the community. The command "You shall not murder" (*lō' tirṣaḥ*), for example, did not speak with immediate clarity, since the community had to determine which specific actions constituted murder (*rōṣēaḥ*) and which did not. The fact that honor of father and mother was commanded did not seem to preclude the development of a rather pointed motivation to discourage inappropriate behavior (Prov 30:17).

The wisdom admonition gains its performative force by the *urgency* implicit in the form of the vetitive itself rather than in the motivating force of the secondary additions. The vetitive form conveys not so much a sense of permanency of prohibition as an *urgency of obedience*. It has much the same sense of authority as the parent telling the child "Don't you *dare* get near that street!" Second, the wisdom admonition gains its performative force insofar as it explicates a small piece of the community's mythic consciousness as expressed in the moral realm. Traditional norms valued by the community are upheld, social values and mores that are clearly articulated in the legal and epic literature of the people. Offenses such as adultery and harlotry (6:24–35), corrupt business practices (20:10, 23), moving landmarks (23:10), and abuse of the vulnerable (31:9) find their authority in the fact that they are traditional values long sanctioned in the public life of the community. Wisdom admonitions represent the urgency of reducing human behavior to long-cherished values expressive of the community's mythic consciousness. Behavior is reduced to its

---

[64] Prov 23:22; 24:28a, 28b, 29; perhaps also 27:10a, 10b.

simplest level when one is told with extreme urgency, "Don't you *dare* go near that street!"

The Reduction to a Comprehensive System

A characteristic form of proverbial saying is the X, X+1 pattern, a listing of items in sequence in which one number is stated followed by an increase to the next greatest integer.

> Three things are too wonderful for me; four I do not understand: the way of an eagle in the sky, the way of a snake on a rock, the way of a ship on the high seas, and the way of a man with a girl. (Prov 30:18–19)[65]

The performative force of this form is derived in part from its "listing" character, which suggests a certain exhaustive comprehensiveness even if only four items are listed. Just as the authority of Solomon's wisdom was conveyed in the very comprehensiveness of his proverbs and onomastica (1 Kgs 4:32–33), so the X, X+1 pattern impresses by its sheer comprehensiveness, which reaches even beyond normal limits for that one additional and final fact that brings the list to perfect completion. The performative power of this style is also contained in its ability to suspend closure on a riddle format as long as possible. The hearer is trapped in suspense until that final element falls into place.

In the proverb cited above, the suspense has a considerable payoff: the riddle's wonderment is not left to dangle in the remote areas of the sky or the sea. It concludes on a surprising note that leaves the hearer as baffled as it does pleased and humored. How is it that the man with the girl is to be equated with the eagle in the sky, the snake on the rock, or the ship on the sea? Does it have to do with the question of propulsion—of what makes these things go? Such would, after all, be suggested by the use of the word *derek* ("way") throughout the proverb. The point of the riddle might be how it is that these three things—the eagle, the snake, and the ship—"tread" or "march" through their respective domains since none of them has legs or feet. They are ill-equipped to perform what they seem to be doing. In a delayed reaction, then, the reader realizes the point

---

[65] Cf. Prov 30:15–17, 21–23, 24–28, 29–31.

of the proverb—a poking fun at how ill-equipped a man is to "tread" his way through the high seas or rarified atmosphere of a relationship with a woman.

Part of the performative force of these proverbs, then, is their very open-endedness. Rather than going on to explain why it is that the man is like the eagle, the snake, or the ship, or what the fire is that "never says 'Enough'" (30:16), they allow the hearer to complete the equation as its various nuances unfold. Such proverbs gain their force of appeal by evoking a series of reflection as well as by provoking surprise.[66] In providing such a list, however, there is not only a systematization of the complexities of reality but also a guaranteed comprehensiveness which satisfies the hearer that all possible combinations, even if only four, have been considered.

The Reduction from Margin to the Center

Characteristic of Israel's proverbial literature is a concern to stay clear of the extremities of life and to keep to the center. The ambiguities and complexities of reality are held more in equilibrium when one stands at the center of the spinning disk than when one ventures out onto the risky edge. The performative force at work in these proverbs is a centripetal force that pulls one away from the precipice into the mythic consciousness located in the heart of the community ethos.

The most highly desired attributes in this context are prudence, propriety, and moderation. The prudent are encouraged to be restrained in speech (10:19) and to ponder their response (15:28). They are to refrain from criticizing others or gossiping about them (11:12, 13). They are to listen rather than talk (12:15–16; 13:3) and to be restrained in possibly risky ventures (14:15–16). The prudent person will seek to avoid extreme life-styles as well—recognizing that both poverty and wealth have their pitfalls (30:8–9). The most direct statement eliciting such prudential moderation is that of Qoh 7:16–17: "Do not be too righteous, and do not act too wise . . . ; Do not be too wicked, and do not be a fool." Wisdom's appeal is to moderation rather than to any form of radical or unbalanced commitment.

---

[66] Williams, "Power of Form," 38.

In making this appeal to the reduction to the center, life's discontinuities and anomalies are avoided or are given coherence in the mythic consciousness which is located at the nucleus of the community ethos.

Reduction from the Unknown to the Known

The reduction of the unknown to the known is accomplished by the similitude, such as Prov 25:14: "Like clouds and wind without rain is one who boasts of a gift never given." The similitude finds its performative force in the comparison made between a neutral or unformed value ("a man boasting of a gift he does not give") and an image or symbol that has a clear value already built in ("clouds and wind without rain"). The affirmation of the person responding to the proverb's performative force is induced by soliciting agreement to the part of the similitude that immediately relates to a shared consciousness. "Yes, we know what it is like to be frustrated with clouds but no rain!" Having assented to this part of the similitude's equation, which normally comes first,[67] the person has (unwittingly) yielded assent to the entire similitude, the real point of which is conveyed in the other part—the unformed value—which normally comes second.

The similitude in 10:26 functions in the same manner. First the hearer's assent is gained in recognizing what effect vinegar has on the teeth and smoke on the eyes. Once this recognition and assent are gained, the person is, in a sense, committed to going through with the equation: "so are the lazy to their employers." The real *power* of the proverb is generated by the invariably graphic image proposed from common experience, which sets the hook in the hearer's imagination. The *truth* of the proverb is generated when the second line is delivered and the hearer is reeled in.

Most of the time the interpretive frame of reference connecting the two parts of the equation is clear. The connection between the two parts of Prov 26:17 leaves no room for misinterpretation: "Like somebody who takes a passing dog by the ears is one who meddles in the quarrel of another." However, a second type of similitude is

---

[67] The only exception is 25:11.

found frequently in Proverbs which functions much differently from the first. In this type an initial similitude elicits an explanation, apparently not wanting to leave the construal of meaning to the hearer alone. Consider Prov 16:24: "Pleasant words are like a honeycomb, sweetness to the soul and health to the body." The equation of "pleasant words" and "honeycomb" is sufficiently vague that the proverb forces the interpretation by limiting the possible frame of reference. The meaning of the similitude is limited by the words "sweetness" and "health." One might have focused on "wax," "hexagonal holes," or "sticky mess," but those options would not have helped identify "pleasant words." Therefore the proverb does the reader a favor and protects its own integrity of meaning by providing guardrails for the interpretive process. Similar similitudes with limited interpretive frames of reference are found in 17:8; 20:2; 25:13; and 26:22.

Similar in function is Prov 26:2: "Like a sparrow in its flitting, like a swallow in its flying, an undeserved curse goes nowhere." The regular similitude form would have shortened the second line to "so is an undeserved curse." Evidently it was felt that the interpretive frame of reference was not adequately limited, so a rather unique formal arrangement was chosen in order to limit the range of meaning to that of the lack of distance covered by the flitting of the birds mentioned. This clear desire to *limit* the interpretive frame of reference demonstrates that, while proverbs may characteristically be open to many interpretations,[68] they are not tolerant of threatening ambiguity.

A unique similitude is found in Prov 17:14. Here the similitude proper is followed by a moral imperative: "The beginning of strife is like letting out water; so stop before the quarrel breaks out." The similitude proper would have functioned perfectly well on its own. The addition is not for point of clarification, but instead draws a moral consequence from the insight proposed by the similitude.

The Reduction to Basic Principles

The final proverbial form we will discuss is one that reduces the ambiguity of reality by drawing a second principle from a first which

---

[68] Williams, "Power of Form," 53–54.

is posited as an a priori truth. This form is not very common but occurs five times in the book of Proverbs. The basic form of this proverbial style is as follows: "Since X is the case, how much more (or how much less) is Y the case." For example: "If the righteous are repaid on earth, how much more the wicked and the sinner!" (11:31).

The force of this performance derives from the fact that the hearer is never solicited about an opinion regarding the first element in the equation. It is simply stated as beyond dispute: Sheol and Abaddon lie open before the Lord (15:11); fine speech is not becoming a fool (17:7); it is not fitting for a fool to live in luxury (19:10); the sacrifice of the wicked is an abomination (21:27). There is no opportunity for dissent, and there probably needs to be none since these statements are a priori precisely because they express the common social ethos and mythic consciousness. They provide the basic power for this form. The power is channeled, however, by the tension set up in the second part of the equation. Here the hearer is engaged in the interpretive process in a way similar to that of the similitude. The tension between the two parts of this form keep sufficient pressure on the interpretive process to hold the hearer's imagination.

In all these various forms we have seen how it is that proverbs seek to express a primary urge toward order. While not succumbing to the naïve notion that reality is simple, the book of Proverbs witnesses to the attempt, sometimes carried out more optimistically than the situation might warrant, to reduce the ambiguities of life to their simplest possible forms and to cut through the tangles of paradox. Here is a world in which, if even for a fleeting moment, the hearer can imagine that there are heroes and villains, that life's solutions are manageable, and that most things in this world operate the way they are supposed to operate. The very act of synthesizing and simplifying conveys authority as it helps to make sense out of life. So the book of Proverbs continually focuses on the polarization of good and bad, wicked and righteous, wise and foolish, industrious and sluggard. All persons are reduced to one or the other. There is no middle ground in the proverbs. This process of simplifying and synthesizing conveys authority because it reduces the complex to the manageable and minimizes ambiguity.

The Charismatic Attribution of Wisdom _____

If one locates the "performative force" of the book of Proverbs in circles of institutionalized literati and court sages, it is natural to assume that the book represents the ideology and vested interests of an elite class and therefore stands on the institutionalized fringe of authentic Yahwistic faith. The purpose of this book has been to challenge at every step the notion that one can easily divorce institution from charisma. Creation and redemption, nature and history, and reason and revelation cannot be wrenched apart in assigning discrete areas of Israel's faith to charisma and others to institution.

The "charismatic attribution" that Israel's proverbial literature elicits is granted to it not on the basis of its being produced by an inspired individual but rather in its revealing the mind of God. This power of wisdom, even viewed as a divine charism, is a social phenomenon whose effective performance is governed by social conventions relating to literary form and appropriateness of context. We are prepared by our particular social conventions, by our immediate context, and by our common participation in the mythic consciousness of Israel's conceptual world, to grant or withhold the power which proverbs seek.

Such charismatic attribution, whether solicited on behalf of the king, prophet, temple cult, or a proverb, is always made in degrees. It is never a matter of full attribution or none at all. Whenever we are solicited to grant endorsement to claims of charisma made upon us, we always apportion our bestowal relative to the extent to which the claim is expressive of our mythic consciousness. The proverb "A penny saved is a penny earned" claims "charismatic endowment," and we will attribute charisma to it to a certain extent—not because Ben Franklin penned it, but rather because it in part reflects a deeply seated truth that our corporate mythic consciousness impresses upon us.

In many studies today it is perceived to be an anomaly to speak of the "Charisma of Order." I purposefully chose that title, however, to insist not only that charisma is a social function but also that it is anchored deeply in that mythos which lies at the order-conferring center of a community's soul. The reason we are so willing to assent to the claims proverbs make on us and to attribute charisma to them is because of the extent to which they satisfy our burning urge toward order.

Conclusion:
Charisma and Leadership

THE PHENOMENON of charismatic empowerment has long been the object of romantic fascination. Weber's understanding of charisma romanticized the "epileptic prophet" as a messianic hero in whom lay the only salvation from the increasingly rationalized and bureaucratized bleak future that he envisioned would be characterized by its oppressive technology. Weber, however, held out little hope for the survival of charisma, suspecting that its fading light of passion would not be able to survive the crushing inertia of rational bureaucracy and technology. Durkheim, on the other hand, romanticized the "collective effervescence" of the group, of which the charismatic figure was a symbolic expression and mirror image. Like Weber, however, Durkheim too was pessimistic about the survivability of charisma, but for different reasons. Durkheim feared the demise of charisma because he feared the demise of the group. For Durkheim, the disintegration of social cohesion and the movement toward individualism undermined the experience of essential group unity which was necessary for the stimulation of collective effervescence.

Both Weber and Durkheim romanticized charisma, seeing in it the generating power for society. Such romanticism, however, led them to long for what they believed to be in danger of extinction— whether the superhero of antirational passion or the coherent group bonded by a nearly mystical sense of primitive suprapersonal transcendence. One can only suspect that Weber and Durkheim were attempting to capture the romantic spirit of their respective contexts, a spirit they felt to be in jeopardy and for which they longed:

for Weber, the romance of German Protestantism with its focus on the heroic individual; and for Durkheim, the romance of French Catholicism and the French Revolution, both of which focused on the heroic community in fraternity.

The question of charismatic empowerment today is not its survivability but rather the shape it will take and the value it will be given. The intent of this study has been to suggest some lines for the continuing discussion, with regard both to where charisma is located and to the value we apply to it. Throughout this book there has been a concerted effort to avoid the traps inherent in extreme positions. If one presses the Weberian solution to its logical conclusion, charisma becomes the bizarre and irrational behavior of the possessed individual whom rational society has no option but to declare insane. It is precisely this conclusion to which psychology has been driven in its analysis of charismatic behavior, understanding it in terms of pathology: charisma reflects the psychosis of the individual and the neurosis of the group. Forced to this extreme, charisma is not a generative force that sustains society; it is a pathological condition that needs to be healed. If one presses the Durkheimian solution to its logical conclusion, charisma is reduced to the tamed and domesticated feeling of a bubbly group effervescence. In this case, if charisma is generative of anything at all, it is generative of a warm cozy feeling of belonging. Given these extreme solutions, charismatic involvement is either regarded with suspicion as though it were diseased, or it is "eviscerated so that the corpse may be safely embraced."[1]

Our primary concern has been to question the first trap—the pitting of charisma over against the traditional or rational institution as though they were implacable foes. It may be argued, however, that, in running in fear from the Weberian epileptic wild-man, we have fallen headlong into the Durkheimian morass of cozy communal sentimentality. What has been *attempted* here, at least, is the breaking down of such polarities so that one no longer feels constrained by the need to position Weber's charismatic individual against Durkheim's charismatic community. The symbolic figure of Moses served as the "intimate outsider" who reflected both the commu-

---

[1] Charles Lindholm, *Charisma* (Cambridge, MA: Basil Blackwell, 1990) 73.

nity's "effervescence" and its sense of being confronted by that which was determinative of its shape. The judges were expressive both of the community's own nurtured leadership and of the fiery hand of divine appointment. The charismatic appointment of the kings was similarly anchored both in community endorsement and in divine designation. The prophetic experience was moored in traditional patterns of divine intermediation that were learned through socialization and were recognized by groups who would grant such charismatic attribution to the extent it met their expectations. Even limited social deviance was itself part of the expected patterning of such prophetic behavior. The charismatic endowment of the priest and of Israel's aphoristic wisdom, though tending toward a more regularized charisma of "the book" or of "order," was not understood to be antithetical to the charismatic empowerment of the prophets. We have resisted the Weberian temptation to reduce the empowerment of priest and wisdom to the rationalized inertia of bureaucracy and technology.

Therefore, how is charismatic endowment to be evaluated? Charles Lindholm has attempted to rescue the reputation of charisma from its recent demise at the hands of a negative psychological assessment. He correctly notes that modern psychological theories of charisma have been traumatized by the direction which mass movements have taken in recent history, so that charisma has become synonymous with evil.[2] Lindholm's own treatment, however, is barely able to salvage much apart from the scraps of charisma's character. First, he too focuses precisely on three movements that can only serve to endorse the contemporary negative assessment: Hitler and the Nazi party, Charles Manson and his "family," and Jim Jones and the People's Temple. Such treatments could now add to their list the tragic events concerning the Branch Davidian cult in Waco, Texas. It is small wonder that Lindholm too can only conclude that the psychoanalytical assessment is correct: unleashing savage charismatic power appears to be unremittingly destructive.[3] Second, the best that Lindholm can say is that charisma in its primitive shamanistic form had a positive intent with benefit for the entire community.[4]

[2] Ibid., 89.
[3] Ibid., 156–57.
[4] Ibid., 157–66.

Lindholm himself finally succumbs to the Weberian view, which he attempts to modify. He suggests that only in less complex societies is charismatic involvement regarded positively. As society becomes highly centralized, impersonal, and rationalized, charisma acquires a negative value. Rather than atrophying at the hands of increased rationality, as Weber suggested it would, Lindholm suggests that charisma is transmuted into increasingly distorted and fanatical forms.[5] Short of recapturing a primitive shamanistic communal spirit, then, Lindholm succumbs to the same negative psychological evaluation he seeks to reject. For him, the only good charisma is primitive charisma. Contemporary charisma is by definition a deformed mutation.

By considering Israel's primary institutions as bearers of charismatic attribution and empowerment, this study attempts to propose a more favorable basis for discussing charisma in relationship to institutional forms of leadership. Two observations are important. First, Israel's institutions cannot be ransacked in order to find examples of charismatic and institutional forms of leadership. The common temptation is to isolate the prophet as a charismatic prototype of community leadership who replicates Weber's superheroic epileptic magician, or to ascribe institutional authority to the priestly dispenser of grace, who as the "manager" of Israel's creation traditions replicates Weber's rationalized and bureaucratized technocrat. Whether it is prophet, priest, king, or sage which serves as a metaphorical model for leadership, and particularly for leadership within the church, none lends itself to a crass distinction between institutional and charismatic empowerment.

Second, each of the metaphors has found its way into the characterization of leadership as portrayed in the New Testament and in the early church, some more plainly than others. As judge, the leader is one who is raised up from among the people to deliver them from sin and death. As king, the leader is the community's symbolic presence of universal justice and righteousness who, on behalf of the community, embodies its commitment and passion toward the vulnerable members of society. As prophet, the leader is the community's primary intercessor, one who intuits how God is speaking

[5] Ibid., 167–71.

to the present situation and who risks treading on the fringes of appropriateness in order to signify God's volatile word. As priest, the leader is charged with the integrity of the community's holiness, with making proper distinctions between what is foundational for its identity and what will infect it and will diminish the proclamation of the gospel. As such, the leader has the task of filtering potential "words" of God through the screen of received canons so as to make the diffused and potent word both concentrated and usable. As sage, the leader is charged with the integrity of the community's epistemology, to lead in reflection upon how God's will is incarnate in human history and upon how the community discerns the divine will in its own context. As such, the leader is one who helps focus the community's attention on its core ethos, reduces it to its binary levels, and then extrapolates this ethos back out to encompass the entirety of daily life.

These are different functions, but each of them is charged with charismatic empowerment in its own way. Furthermore, the attribution of such charismatic power is effected because of the need and desire of the social group to give expression to its own mythic consciousness, its own vision of justice and holiness, its own urge toward order. This study has resisted the evolutionistic notion that there is such a thing as pure charisma which, when subjected to the acid effect of institutionalized forces of law and reason, is eventually routinized and transmuted into office charisma, or atrophies and dies. Such a diachronic view of power does not take seriously the dialectical struggle within each human heart in which the desire for the free and even violent expression of one's most cherished hopes and visions clashes with the equally passionate craving for structure and orderliness.

Finally, as our communities continue to reflect upon their public forms of leadership, they would do well to foster the sense of charismatic empowerment implicit in each metaphorical model and to resist the temptation to dichotomize too strongly between inward and outward aspects of designation. Charismatic attribution is essentially a social phenomenon. Just as the boundaries between nature and history, creation and redemption, and reason and revelation are artificial, so too is the presumed boundary between what is inward and outward. To suggest otherwise would be to misunderstand the full implication of a God who becomes wholly incarnate in human existence.

Bibliography

Abramski, Shmuel. "The Beginning of the Israelite Monarchy and Its Impact upon Leadership in Israel." *Immanuel* 19 (Winter 1984–85) 7–21.

Ahlström, Gösta W. "Solomon, the Chosen One." *HR* 8 (1968–69) 93–110.

Alt, Albrecht. "Das Königtum in den Reichen Israel und Juda." In *Kleine Schriften zur Geschichte des Volkes Israel*, 2:116–34. Munich: C. H. Beck, 1959.

———. "Die Staatenbildung der Israeliten in Palästina." In *Kleine Schriften zur Geschichte des Volkes Israel*, 2:1–65. Munich: C. H. Beck, 1959.

Anderson, Bernhard W. *Creation Versus Chaos: The Reinterpretation of Mythical Symbolism in the Bible*. Philadelphia: Fortress, 1987.

Anderson, Gary A. *Sacrifices and Offerings in Ancient Israel: Studies in their Social and Political Importance.* Atlanta: Scholars Press, 1987.

Auerbach, Elias. *Moses*. Detroit: Wayne State University, 1975.

Austin, J. L. *How To Do Things with Words*. Oxford: Clarendon, 1955.

Beattie, J. H. M. "On Understanding Sacrifice." In *Sacrifice*, ed. M. F. C. Bourdillon and Meyer Fortes, 29–44. London: Academic, 1980.

Beidelman, T. O. "Nuer Priests and Prophets: Charisma, Authority, and Power among the Nuer." In *The Translation of Culture: Essays to E. E. Evans-Pritchard*, ed. T. O. Beidelman, 375–415. London: Tavistock, 1971.

Berger, Peter L. "Charisma and Religious Innovation: The Social Location of Israelite Prophecy." *ASR* 28 (1963) 940–50.

Bernhardt, Karl-Heinz. *Das Problem der altorientalischen Königsideologie im Alten Testament*. Leiden: E. J. Brill, 1961.

Beyerlin, Walter. "Das Königscharisma bei Saul." *ZAW* 73 (1961) 186–201.

Birch, Bruce C. *The Rise of the Israelite Monarchy: The Growth and Development of 1 Samuel 7–15.* Missoula, MT: Scholars Press, 1976.

Blenkinsopp, Joseph. *Wisdom and Law in the Old Testament: The Ordering of Life in Israel and Early Judaism.* New York: Oxford, 1983.

Boecker, Hans Jochen. *Die Beurteilung der Anfänge des Königtums in den deuteronomistischen Abschnitten des I. Samuelbuches: Ein Beitrag zum Problem des "deuteronomistischen Geschichtswerks."* Neukirchen-Vluyn: Neukirchener, 1969.

Buss, Martin J. "The Social Psychology of Prophecy." In *Prophecy: Essays Presented to Georg Fohrer,* ed. J. A. Emerton, 1–11. New York: Walter de Gruyter, 1980.

Carroll, Robert P. *When Prophecy Failed: Reactions and Responses to Failure in the Old Testament Prophetic Traditions.* London: SCM, 1979.

Chaney, Marvin L. "Systemic Study of the Israelite Monarchy." *Semeia* 37 (1986) 53–76.

Clegg, Stewart. *Power, Rule and Domination: A Critical and Empirical Understanding of Power in Sociological Theory and Organizational Life.* Boston: Routledge & Kegan Paul, 1975.

Clifford, Richard J. "The Hebrew Scriptures and the Theology of Creation." *TS* 46 (1985) 507–23.

Coats, George. *Moses: Heroic Man, Man of God.* JSOTSup 57. Sheffield: JSOT Press, 1988.

——. *Rebellion in the Wilderness: The Murmuring Motif in the Wilderness Traditions of the Old Testament.* Nashville: Abingdon, 1968.

Coote, Robert B., and Keith W. Whitelam. *The Emergence of Early Israel in Historical Perspective.* Sheffield: Almond, 1987.

——. "The Emergence of Israel: Social Transformation and State Formation following the Decline in Late Bronze Age Trade." *Semeia* 37 (1986) 107–47.

Crenshaw, James L. "The Acquisition of Knowledge in Israelite Wisdom Literature." *W & W* 7 (1987) 245–52.

——. "Education in Ancient Israel." *JBL* 104 (1985) 601–15.

——. *Prophetic Conflict: Its Effect upon Israelite Religion.* New York: Walter de Gruyter, 1971.

——, ed. *Studies in Ancient Israelite Wisdom.* New York: Ktav, 1976.

Crüsemann, Frank. *Der Widerstand gegen das Königtum: Die antiköniglichen Texte des Alten Testamentes und der Kampf um den frühen israelitischen Staat.* Neukirchen-Vluyn: Neukirchener Verlag, 1978.

Day, John. *God's Conflict with the Dragon and the Sea: Echoes of a Canaanite Myth in the Old Testament.* Cambridge: Cambridge University Press, 1985.

De Vries, Simon J. *Prophet Against Prophet: The Role of the Micaiah Narrative (I Kings 22) in the Development of Early Prophetic Tradition.* Grand Rapids: William B. Eerdmans, 1978.

Dietrich, Walter. *David, Saul und die Propheten: Das Verhältnis von Religion und Politik nach den prophetischen Überlieferungen vom frühesten Königtum in Israel.* Stuttgart: W. Kohlhammer, 1987.

Douglas, Mary. *Purity and Danger: An Analysis of Concepts of Pollution and Taboo.* New York: Frederick A. Praeger, 1966.

Eisenstadt, S. N., ed. *Max Weber on Charisma and Institution Building: Selected Papers.* Chicago: University of Chicago Press, 1968.

Eliade, Mircea. *The Myth of the Eternal Return.* New York: Pantheon, 1954.

Engnell, Ivan. *Studies in Divine Kingship in the Ancient Near East.* Oxford: Basil Blackwell, 1967.

Fiensy, David. "Using the Nuer Culture of Africa in Understanding the Old Testament: An Evaluation." *JSOT* 38 (1987) 73–83.

Finkelstein, Israel. "The Emergence of the Monarchy in Israel: The Environmental and Socio-Economic Aspects." *JSOT* 44 (1989) 43–74.

Fohrer, Georg. *Die symbolischen Handlungen der Propheten.* 2nd ed. Zurich: Zwingli, 1968.

Fontaine, Carole R. *Traditional Sayings in the Old Testament.* Sheffield: Almond, 1982.

Frick, Frank S. *The Formation of the State in Ancient Israel: A Survey of Models and Theories.* Sheffield: Almond, 1985.

———. "Social Scientific Methods and Theories of Significance for the Study of the Israelite Monarchy: A Critical Review Essay." *Semeia* 37 (1986) 9–52.

Friedland, William H. "For a Sociological Concept of Charisma." *Social Forces* 43 (1964) 18–26.

Gammie, J. G., et al., eds. *Israelite Wisdom: Theological and Literary Essays in Honor of Samuel Terrien.* New York: Union Theological Seminary, 1978.

———, and Leo G. Perdue, eds. *The Sage in Israel and the Ancient Near East.* Winona Lake, IN: Eisenbrauns, 1990.

Gaspar, Joseph W. *Social Ideas in the Wisdom Literature of the Old Testament.* Washington, DC: Catholic University of America, 1947.

Girard, René. *Violence and the Sacred.* Baltimore: Johns Hopkins University Press, 1977.

Glassman, Ronald M., and W. H. Swatos, eds. *Charisma, History, and Social Structure.* New York: Greenwood, 1986.

Golka, Friedemann W. "Die Königs- und Hofsprüche und der Ursprung der israelitischen Weisheit." *VT* 36 (1986) 13–36.

Gottwald, Norman K. "The Participation of Free Agrarians in the Introduction of Monarchy to Ancient Israel: An Application of H. A. Landsberger's Framework for the Analysis of Peasant Movements." *Semeia* 37 (1986) 77–106.

Gressmann, Hugo. *Mose und seine Zeit: Ein Kommentar zu den Mose-Sagen.* Göttingen: Vandenhoeck & Ruprecht, 1913.

Gunneweg, Antonius H. J. *Leviten und Priester: Hauptlinien der Traditionsbildung und Geschichte des israelitisch-jüdischen Kultpersonals.* Göttingen: Vandenhoeck & Ruprecht, 1965.

——, and Walther Schmithals. *Authority.* Nashville: Abingdon, 1982.

Hahn, Ferdinand. "Charisma und Amt: Die Diskussion über das kirchliche Amt im Lichte der neutestamentlichen Charismenlehre." *ZTK* 76 (1979) 419–49.

Halpern, Baruch. *The Constitution of the Monarchy in Israel.* Chico, CA: Scholars Press, 1981.

Haran, Menahem. *Temples and Temple-Service in Ancient Israel: An Inquiry into the Character of Cult Phenomena and the Historical Setting of the Priestly School.* Oxford: Clarendon, 1978.

Hengel, Martin. *The Charismatic Leader and His Followers.* Edinburgh: T. & T. Clark, 1981.

Herion, Gary A. "The Impact of Modern and Social Science Assumptions on the Reconstruction of Israelite History." *JSOT* 34 (1986) 3–33.

Hermisson, Hans-Jürgen. *Studien zur israelitischen Spruchweisheit.* Neukirchen-Vluyn: Neukirchener Verlag, 1968.

Herrmann, Siegfried. *Ursprung und Funktion der Prophetie im alten Israel.* Opladen: Westdeutscher, 1976.

Holstein, Jay. "Max Weber and Biblical Scholarship." *HUCA* 46 (1975) 159–79.

Hubert, Henri, and Marcel Mauss. *Sacrifice: Its Nature and Function.* London: Cohen & West, 1964.

Ishida, Tomoo. *The Royal Dynasties in Ancient Israel: A Study on the Formation and Development of Royal-Dynastic Ideology.* New York: Walter de Gruyter, 1977.

Janowski, Bernd. *Sühne als Heilsgeschehen: Studien zur Sühnetheologie der Priesterschrift und zur Wurzel KPR im Alten Orient und im Alten Testament.* Neukirchen-Vluyn: Neukirchener Verlag, 1982.

Jenks, Alan W. "Theological Presuppositions of Israel's Wisdom Literature." *HBT* 7 (1985) 43–75.

Kimbrough, S. T., Jr. *Israelite Religion in Sociological Perspective: The Work of Antonin Causse.* Wiesbaden: Otto Harrassowiz, 1978.

Kiuchi, N. *The Purification Offering in the Priestly Literature: Its Meaning and Function.* Sheffield: JSOT Press, 1987.

Knierim, Rolf. "Cosmos and History in Israel's Theology." *HBT* 3 (1981) 59–123.

———. "Exodus 18 und die Neuordnung der mosäischen Gerichtsbarkeit." *ZAW* 73 (1962) 146–71.

Knight, Douglas A. "Cosmogony and Order in the Hebrew Tradition." In *Cosmogony and Ethical Order: New Studies in Comparative Ethics,* ed. R. W. Lovin and F. E. Reynolds, 133–57. Chicago: University of Chicago Press, 1985.

Kovacs, Brian W. "Is There a Class-Ethic in Proverbs?" In *Essays in Old Testament Ethics,* ed. J. L. Crenshaw and J. T. Willis, 173–89. New York: Ktav, 1974.

Kraus, Hans-Joachim. "Schöpfung und Weltvollendung." *EvT* 24 (1964) 462–85.

Lang, Bernhard. "Israels Propheten im Licht von Sundéns Rollenpsychologie." *ArRel* 14 (1980) 19–27.

———. "Max Weber und Israels Propheten: Eine kritische Stellungnahme." *ZRG* 36 (1984) 156–65.

Lemche, Niels Peter. *Early Israel: Anthropological and Historical Studies on the Israelite Society Before the Monarchy.* Leiden: E. J. Brill, 1985.

Levenson, Jon D. *Creation and the Persistence of Evil: The Jewish Drama of Divine Omnipotence.* San Francisco: Harper & Row, 1988.

———. *Sinai and Zion: An Entry into the Jewish Bible.* Chicago: Winston, 1985.

Levine, Baruch A. *In the Presence of the Lord: A Study of Cult and Some Cultic Terms in Ancient Israel.* Leiden: E. J. Brill, 1974.

Lindholm, Charles. *Charisma.* Cambridge, MA: Basil Blackwell, 1990.

Long, Burke O. "Social Dimensions of Prophetic Conflict." In *Anthropological Perspectives on Old Testament Prophecy,* ed. R. C. Culley and T. W. Overhold, 31–53. Chico, CA: Scholars Press, 1982.

———. "The Social World of Ancient Israel." *Int* 36 (1982) 243–55.

Lyonnet, Stanislas, S.J., and Leopold Sabourin, S.J. *Sin, Redemption, and Sacrifice: A Biblical and Patristic Study.* Rome: Biblical Institute, 1970.

Malamat, Abraham. "Charismatic Leadership in the Book of Judges." In *Magnalia Dei: The Mighty Acts of God. Essays on the Bible and Archaeology in Memory of G. Ernest Wright,* ed. F. M. Cross et al., 152–68. Garden City, NY: Doubleday, 1976.

————. "The Period of the Judges." In *The World History of the Jewish People*, vol. III, ed. Benjamin Mazar, 129–63. Tel-Aviv: Massada, 1971.

Mayes, A. D. H. *Israel in the Period of the Judges*. London: SCM, 1974.

————. "The Rise of the Israelite Monarchy." *ZAW* 90 (1978) 1–19.

Meeks, Wayne A. *The Prophet-King: Moses Traditions and the Johannine Christology*. Leiden: E. J. Brill, 1967.

Mettinger, Tryggve N. D. *King and Messiah: The Civil and Sacral Legitimation of the Israelite King*. Lund: Gleerup, 1976.

Mikasa, T., ed. *Monarchies and Socio-Religious Traditions in the Ancient Near East*. Wiesbaden: Otto Harrassowitz, 1984.

Milgrom, Jacob. *Cult and Conscience: The ASHAM and the Priestly Doctrine of Repentance*. Leiden: E. J. Brill, 1976.

————. *Studies in Cultic Theology and Terminology*. Leiden: E. J. Brill, 1983.

Miller, J. Maxwell. "Saul's Rise to Power: Some Observations Concerning 1 Sam 9:1–10:16; 10:26–11:15 and 13:2–14:46." *CBQ* 36 (1974) 157–74.

Miller, Patrick D. "Cosmology and World Order in the Old Testament: The Divine Council as Cosmic-Political Symbol." *HBT* 9 (1987) 53–78.

Morgan, Donn F. *Wisdom in the Old Testament Traditions*. Atlanta: John Knox, 1981.

Muilenburg, James. "The 'Office' of the Prophet in Ancient Israel." In *The Bible in Modern Scholarship*, ed. J. P. Hyatt, 74–97. London: Carey Kingsgate, 1966.

Murphy, Roland E. *The Tree of Life: An Exploration of Biblical Wisdom Literature*. New York: Doubleday, 1990.

Nel, Philip J. *The Structure and Ethos of the Wisdom Admonitions in Proverbs*. New York: Walter de Gruyter, 1982.

Neusner, Jacob. *The Idea of Purity in Ancient Judaism*. Leiden: E. J. Brill, 1973.

Noth, Martin. "Das Amt des 'Richters Israels.'" In *Festschrift Alfred Bertholet zum 80. Geburtstag*, ed. W. Baumgartner et al., 404–17. Tübingen: J. C. B. Mohr, 1950.

Osswald, Eva. *Das Bild des Mose in der kritischen alttestamentlichen Wissenschaft seit Julius Wellhausen*. Berlin: Evangelische Verlagsanstalt, 1962.

————. *Falsche Prophetie im Alten Testament*. Tübingen: J. C. B. Mohr, 1962.

Overholt, Thomas W. *Channels of Prophecy: The Social Dynamics of Prophetic Activity.* Minneapolis: Fortress, 1989.

——. *Prophecy in Cross-Cultural Perspective: A Sourcebook for Biblical Researchers.* Atlanta: Scholars Press, 1986.

——. "Prophecy: The Problem of Cross-Cultural Comparison." In *Anthropological Perspectives on Old Testament Prophecy,* ed. R. C. Culley and T. W. Overholt, 55–78. Chico, CA: Scholars Press, 1982.

——. "Seeing is Believing: The Social Setting of Prophetic Acts of Power." *JSOT* 23 (1982) 3–31.

——. "Thoughts on the Use of 'Charisma' in Old Testament Studies." In *In the Shelter of Elyon,* ed. W. B. Barrick and J. R. Spencer, 187–303. Sheffield: JSOT Press, 1984.

Parsons, Talcott. *Politics and Social Structure.* New York: Free Press, 1969.

Perlitt, Lothar. "Mose als Prophet." *EvT* 31 (1971) 588–608.

Petersen, David L. *The Roles of Israel's Prophets.* Sheffield: JSOT Press, 1981.

Porter, J. R. *Moses and Monarchy: A Study in the Biblical Tradition of Moses.* Oxford: Blackwell, 1963.

——. "The Origins of Prophecy in Israel." In *Israel's Prophetic Tradition: Essays in Honour of Peter R. Ackroyd,* ed. R. Coggins et al., 12–31. Cambridge: Cambridge University Press, 1982.

Rendtorff, Rolf. "Mose als Religionsstifter? Ein Beitrag zur Diskussion über die Anfänge der israelitischen Religion." In *Gesammelte Studien zum Alten Testament,* 152–71. Munich: Kaiser, 1975.

——. *Studien zur Geschichte des Opfers im alten Israel.* Neukirchen-Vluyn: Neukirchener Verlag, 1967.

Rendtorff, Trutz, ed. *Charisma und Institution.* Gütersloh: Gerd Mohn, 1985.

Reviv, Hanoch. *The Elders in Ancient Israel: A Study of a Biblical Institution.* Jerusalem: Magnes, 1989.

Richter, Wolfgang. "Zu den 'Richtern Israels.'" *ZAW* 77 (1965) 40–72.

Rigby, Paul. "A Structural Analysis of Israelite Sacrifice and Its Other Institutions." *EgT* 11 (1980) 299–351.

Rodd, Cyril S. "Max Weber and Ancient Judaism." *SJT* 32 (1979) 457–69.

Rösel, Hartmut N. "Die 'Richter Israels': Rückblick und neuer Ansatz." *BZ* 25 (1981) 180–203.

Rustow, Dankwart A. *A World of Nations: Problems of Political Modernization.* Washington, DC: The Brookings Institution, 1967.

Sabourin, Leopold, S.J. *Priesthood: A Comparative Study.* Leiden: E. J. Brill, 1973.

Sanders, James A. "Hermeneutics in True and False Prophecy." In *Canon and Authority: Essays in Old Testament Religion and Theology,* ed. G. W. Coats and B. O. Long, 21–41. Philadelphia: Fortress, 1977.

Schmid, H. H. "Creation, Righteousness, and Salvation." In *Creation in the Old Testament,* ed. B. W. Anderson, 102–17. Philadelphia: Fortress, 1984.

Schmid, Herbert. *Die Gestalt des Mose: Probleme alttestamentlicher Forschung unter Berücksichtigung der Pentateuchkrise.* Darmstadt: Wissenschaftliche Buchgesellschaft, 1986.

———. *Mose: Überlieferung und Geschichte.* Berlin: Alfred Töpelmann, 1968.

Schmidt, Ludwig. "König und Charisma im Alten Testament: Beobachtungen zur Struktur des Königtums im alten Israel." *KD* 23 (1982) 73–87.

Schnabel, Eckhard J. *Law and Wisdom from Ben Sira to Paul: A Tradition Historical Enquiry into the Relation of Law, Wisdom, and Ethics.* Tübingen: J. C. B. Mohr, 1985.

Schulz, Hermann. *Leviten im vorstaatlichen Israel und im Mittleren Osten.* Munich: Kaiser, 1987.

Seebass, Horst. *Mose und Aaron, Sinai und Gottesberg.* Bonn: H. Bouvier, 1962.

Sheppard, Gerald T. "True and False Prophecy within Scripture." In *Canon, Theology and Old Testament Interpretation: Essays in Honor of Brevard S. Childs,* ed. G. M. Tucker et al., 262–82. Philadelphia: Fortress, 1988.

———. *Wisdom as a Hermeneutical Construct: A Study in the Sapientializing of the Old Testament.* New York: Walter de Gruyter, 1980.

Shils, E. "Charisma, Order, and Status." *ASR* 30 (1965) 199–213.

Smend, Rudolf. *Das Mosebild von Heinrich Ewald bis Martin Noth.* Tübingen: J. C. B. Mohr, 1959.

Soggin, J. Alberto. "Charisma und Institution im Königtum Sauls." *ZAW* 75 (1963) 54–65.

Steck, Odil Hannes. *World and Environment.* Nashville: Abingdon, 1980.

Thiel, Winfried. *Die soziale Entwicklung Israels in vorstaatlicher Zeit.* Neukirchen-Vluyn: Neukirchener Verlag, 1980.

Thompson, John Mark. *The Form and Function of Proverbs in Ancient Israel.* Paris: Mouton, 1974.

Thompson, R. J. *Penitence and Sacrifice in Early Israel Outside the Levitical Law: An Examination of the Fellowship Theory of Early Israelite Sacrifice.* Leiden: E. J. Brill, 1963.

Thornton, Russell, and Peter M. Nardi. "The Dynamics of Role Acquisition." *AJS* 80 (1974–75) 870–85.

Thornton, T. C. G. "Charismatic Kingship." *JTS* 14 (1963) 1–11.

Veijola, Timo. *Das Königtum in der Beurteilung der Deuteronomistischen Historiographie: Eine redaktionsgeschichtliche Untersuchung.* Helsinki: Suomalainen Tiedeakatemia, 1977.

Webb, Barry G. *The Book of the Judges: An Integrated Reading.* Sheffield: JSOT Press, 1987.

Weber, Max. *Ancient Judaism.* Glencoe, IL: Free Press, 1952.

———. *Economy and Society: An Outline of Interpretive Sociology.* New York: Bedminster, 1968.

Weisman, Ze'ev. "Charismatic Leaders in the Era of the Judges." *ZAW* 89 (1977) 399–411.

Westermann, Claus. *Creation.* Philadelphia: Fortress, 1974.

Whitelam, Keith W. *The Just King: Monarchical Judicial Authority in Ancient Israel.* Sheffield: JSOT Press, 1979.

Whybray, Roger N. *The Intellectual Tradition in the Old Testament.* New York: Walter de Gruyter, 1974.

———. "Poverty, Wealth, and Point of View in Proverbs." *ExpTim* 100 (1989) 332–36.

———. *Wealth and Poverty in the Book and Proverbs.* Sheffield: JSOT Press, 1990.

Williams, James G. "The Power of Form: A Study of Biblical Proverbs." In *Gnomic Wisdom,* ed. J. D. Crossan, 35–58. Semeia 17. Chico, CA: Scholars Press, 1980.

———. "The Social Location of Israelite Prophecy." *JAAR* 37 (1969) 153–65.

———. *Those Who Ponder Proverbs: Aphoristic Thinking and Biblical Literature.* Sheffield: Almond, 1981.

Willner, Ann Ruth, and Dorothy Willner. "The Rise and Role of Charismatic Leaders." *The Annals of the American Academy of Political and Social Science* 358 (March 1965) 77–88.

Wilson, Bryan R. *The Noble Savages: The Primitive Origins of Charisma and Its Contemporary Survival.* Berkeley: University of Calfornia Press, 1975.

Wilson, Robert R. "Prophecy and Ecstasy: A Reexamination." *JBL* 98 (1979) 321–37.

———. *Prophecy and Society in Ancient Israel.* Philadelphia: Fortress, 1980.

Wrong, Dennis H. *Power: Its Forms, Bases and Uses.* Oxford: Basil Blackwell, 1979.

Index

Authors

Abba, R., 141, 143, 156
Abramski, S., 74
Ahlström, G., 80, 104
Albright, W., 19, 75
Allen, L., 23
Alt, A., 51, 52, 54, 55, 71–75, 79, 80, 82, 83, 99
Anderson, B., 164, 165, 168
Anderson, G., 160
Auerbach, E., 19, 35, 36
Auld, A. G., 117

Balentine, S., 122
Barr, J., 167
Baumgärtel, F., 21
Beattie, J., 156
Beegle, D., 19, 20
Begrich, J., 139, 154
Beidelmann, T., 112
Bendix, R., 135
Bensman, J., 131
Bentzen, A., 21
Berger, P., 8, 105
Bernhardt, K.-H., 74, 83
Beyerlin, W., 74, 75, 91
Birch, B., 85, 87, 91, 182

Blenkinsopp, J., 18, 176, 179, 180, 183
Boecker, H. J., 92, 94
Boff, L., 2
Boling, R., 48, 57–59, 61
Boman, T., 166, 167
Bright, J., 72, 79
Brueggemann, W., 108, 123, 145, 168, 170, 173, 176, 179, 186
Buccellati, G., 74
Budd, P., 26, 34, 35, 154
Budde, K., 19
Burney, C. F., 61
Buss, M., 109, 119, 134
Butler, T., 32

Camp, C., 194
Campbell, E., 19, 20
von Campenhausen, H., 3
Carroll, R., 117, 119, 128, 132
Causse, A., 10
Chaney, M., 77
Childs, B., 133
Clegg, S., 63
Clifford, R., 168
Coats, G., 20, 22, 32, 35, 40

Cody, A., 140, 144, 150
Cohen, M., 117
Cooke, B., 2
Coote, R., 70, 76–78
Crenshaw, J., 108, 132, 176, 177, 183, 185, 194, 195
Cross, F. M., 33, 108, 143
Crüsemann, F., 75, 77, 84, 85, 92

Davies, D., 156
De Vries, S., 36, 132
Dietrich, W., 85, 93
Douglas, M., 155
Dozeman, T., 132
Duhm, B., 162
Durkheim, E., 9–11, 75, 206, 207
Dus, J., 53
Duty, R. W., 187

Eakins, K., 22
Edelman, D., 84, 86, 94, 95, 99
Eichrodt, W., 19, 20
Eissfeldt, O., 91
Eliade, M., 164, 166, 167
Evans-Pritchard, E., 75
Ewald, H., 19

Fensham, F. C., 19, 53
Fiensy, D., 77
Finkelstein, I., 78
Flanagan, J., 76, 77, 80
Fohrer, G., 33, 98, 99, 128, 135
Fontaine, C., 190, 192, 194, 195
Fortes, M., 75
Fretheim, T., 167
Frick, F., 70, 75, 78
Friedland, W., 63, 65, 68
Fritz, V., 84, 85, 87
Fuerst, W., 128

Gamberoni, J., 26
Gaspar, J., 193
Gerstenberger, E., 181

Giddens, A., 15
Girard, R., 156
Givant, M., 131
Glassman, R., 131, 136
Golka, F., 194
Good, R. M., 149
Gottwald, N., 13–16, 22, 70, 72, 73, 75, 76
Gressmann, H., 19, 32, 33, 35
Grether, O., 44, 51, 52, 54, 55
Grønbeck, J., 99
Gross, H., 38
Gunkel, H., 163
Gunneweg, A. H. J., 5, 142

Habel, N., 134
Hahn, F., 2
Haldar, A., 105, 106
Halpern, B., 76, 85, 99
Hanson, P., 168
Haran, M., 143, 144, 149
von Harnack, A., 2
Hauer, C., 78, 143, 149
Hauerwas, S., 137, 138
Hauser, A., 57, 61
Hengel, M., 2
Hennen, M., 7
Herion, G., 5, 11, 13–15
Hermisson, H.-J., 163, 181, 182, 193, 198
Herrmann, S., 19, 108, 135
Hertzberg, H. W., 52, 54, 61
Hobbs, T. R., 101, 116
Hölscher, G., 162
Høgenhaven, J., 117
Holladay, J., 116
Holladay, W., 155
Holmberg, B., 6
Holstein, J., 5
Hubert, H., 156
Hutton, R., 41, 189

Ishida, T., 53, 54, 74, 75, 81, 85, 87, 91, 94

Janowski, B., 157, 158
Jenks, A., 180, 183
Jepsen, A., 141
Jeremias, J., 106
Jobling, D., 10
Johnson, A. R., 105, 106

Kimbrough, S., 10
Kiuchi, N., 159
Klein, L., 58, 59, 67, 69
Knierim, R., 20, 21, 167–170
Koch, K., 21, 187
Kovacs, B., 176, 193
Kraus, H. J., 20, 52, 141, 146, 169, 170
Kselman, J., 106

Lang, B., 106, 114, 127, 134, 135, 193
Lemaire, A., 193
Lemche, N., 50, 70, 77
Levine, B., 157–159
Levenson, J., 165, 169, 170, 181
Levy-Bruhl, L., 9, 10
Lindars, B., 75
Lindholm, C., 207–209
Lods, A., 10, 19
Lohse, E., 31
Long, B. O., 6, 133, 134
Lovin, R., 169

McCarter, P. K., 183
McKenzie, D., 54
Malamat, A., 49–51, 54, 55, 57, 60, 67, 68
Malina, B., 11–13
Mann, T., 23, 41
Mauss, M., 156
Mayes, A. D. H., 15, 55, 84, 85, 87, 92

Meeks, W., 21, 40
Mendenhall, G., 13, 72, 186
Mettinger, T. N. D., 84, 85, 87–89, 91, 92, 94, 99, 149
Metzger, M., 104
Milgrom, J., 147, 149, 157–159
Miller, J. M., 83, 85, 87
Miller, P., 22, 41
Morgan, D., 176–178
Mosala, I., 5, 11, 12
Mottu, H., 133
Mowinckel, S., 105, 106, 115, 135, 162
Muilenburg, J., 21, 37
Mullen, E., 58, 59
Muntingh, L., 99
Murphy, R., 182, 185, 187, 193

Nel, P. J., 176, 187, 195, 198
Neusner, J., 159
Nohrnberg, J., 41
Noth, M., 19, 20, 37, 51–55, 72, 79, 85

Olyan, S., 143
Orton, D., 180, 184
Osswald, E., 19, 20, 133
Östborn, G., 154
Overholt, T., 6, 111, 112, 122, 123, 125, 131, 134, 135

Pannenberg, W., 164, 165, 167
Parker, S., 115, 135
Parsons, T., 65
Pedersen, J., 10, 21
Perdue, L., 23, 26, 27, 35
Perlitt, L., 23, 26, 27, 35
Petersen, D., 115, 119, 123, 135, 136
Phillips, A., 136
Pleins, J. D., 193
Polzin, R., 17
Porter, J. R., 21, 110, 116, 134

Prigge, W.-U., 7

Quell, G., 132

von Rad, G., 20, 164, 165, 167, 175, 187

Rendtorff, R., 21, 156, 158

Reviv, H., 174

Reynolds, F., 169

Richter, W., 53, 67

Rigby, P., 156

Rimbach, J., 132

Ringgren, H., 107, 116

Roberts, J. J. M., 153

Robinson, H. W., 33

Rodd, C., 10, 11

Rösel, H., 51, 56

Rogerson, J., 77, 156

Ross, J. F., 115

Rowley, H. H., 143, 144, 158

Rozenberg, M., 57, 66

Rudolph, W., 48

Russell, L., 2

Rustow, D., 63, 68

Sabourin, L., 140, 142, 144, 148, 151

Sanders, J., 133

Schmid, H., 22, 26, 28, 31, 33, 167

Schmid, H. H., 167

Schmidt, L., 74, 79–81

Schmidt, W. H., 167

Schmithals, W., 5

Schmitt, G., 142

Schnabel, E., 180, 182

Schunck, K.-D., 53, 54, 61

Schulz, H., 142

Schweizer, E., 3

Scott, R. B. Y., 178

Seebass, H., 33

Seitz, C., 37

van Selms, A., 53

Sheppard, G., 109, 133, 183

Shils, E., 64, 65, 130

Sigrist, C., 75

Smend, R., 19, 22

Smith, W. R., 9

Söderblom, N., 19

Soggin, J. A., 56, 57, 60, 74, 85, 93, 94

Sohm, R., 2

Spencer, J., 142

Stade, B., 19

Starr, I., 111

Steck, O. H., 167

Stone, M., 180

Stuart, D., 131

Terrien, S., 168, 177

Thiel, W., 43, 75, 77

Thompson, J., 178, 185, 192

Thompson, R. J., 146

Tönnies, F., 4, 7

Thornton, T., 80, 81

Turner, V., 156

Van Leeuwen, R., 177, 178

de Vaux, R., 10, 44, 55

Vawter, B., 115, 118

Veijola, T., 84, 92

Vogels, W., 29

Vollborn, W., 52, 54, 67

Vriezen, T., 19

Watts, J. D. W., 48

Webb, B. G., 58, 59, 61, 67

Weber, M., 3, 4, 5, 9, 50, 51, 55, 56, 60, 63–65, 105–107, 151, 172, 173, 193, 206, 207, 209

Weiser, A., 48

Weisman, Z., 26, 27, 31, 55, 56, 98

Wellhausen, J., 19, 85, 107, 138, 162, 164

Westermann, C., 134, 168

Whedbee, J. W., 177

Whitelam, K., 11, 70, 76–79, 104

Whybray, R. N., 177, 194

Widengren, G., 20, 23, 24

Wilckens, U., 2

Williams, J., 105, 185, 191, 192, 195, 197, 201, 203

Willner, A. R., and D., 130

Wilson, B., 63, 65

Wilson, R., 116, 117, 123, 125, 134–136

Wolff, H. W., 48, 114, 118, 177

Wrong, D., 64, 65

Wyatt, N., 104

Yoder, J., 137, 138

Zimmerli, W., 175, 198

Scripture

Genesis		29:1-9	146	Numbers	
1–2	165	29:22-25	146	1:47-49	148
3:5, 22	189	29:26-28	146	3:11-13	148
12:3	127	30:11-16	148	3:44-45	148
14:18	150	32:1-24	145	5:6-7	158
20:7	109, 122	34:19-23	148	5:8	148, 158
39:4	34	35:20-29	148	5:11-31	154
41:40	34	Leviticus		6:22-27	139
44:1, 4	34	1–7	139	8:14-19	148
45:27	30	2:1-10	146	10:35-36	139
46:13	47, 60, 61	5:1-4	158	11:1-15	25
46:14	60, 61	5:13	146	11:2	123
Exodus		5:16	148	11:16-30	24, 25
2:17	62	6:14-16	145	11:17	27, 30
7:1	109	6:24-30	146	11:25	26, 27, 30, 31, 90
15:20	33, 109	7:1-7	146	11:26-29	26, 27
18	20, 30	10:10-11	155	11:31-35	25
18:13-27	24, 25	10:12-15	146	12:1-16	32, 34
19:9	37	12–15	155	12:5	33
20:19-22	37, 38	16:21	158	12:6-8	34
21:17	125	19:14	125, 126	16:1-40	32, 35
22:7-13	139	21:1–22:9	145	18:21-32	148
22:8-11	152, 154	22:10-16	146	21:7	123
22:18	153	23:36	161	22–24	125
22:28	125	23:37-38	148	22:27	62
23:19	148	26:40	158	26:23	47, 60
28:38	148	27:1-34	148		

26:23-26	61	31:9-13	155	10:1-5	51, 54,
26:26	47, 60	31:14-15, 23	24, 28		56, 60
27:12-23	24, 28,	31:24-26	154	11:1-3	69
	29	33:5	20	11:6	56
27:18	30, 31	33:8-10	152	11:8	56
27:20	30, 31	34:9	24, 28, 29,	11:9	69
29:35	161		30, 31	11:11	69
31:28-30	148	34:10	31, 39, 40	11:29	69
31:54	148	40:21	129	12:7-15	51, 54, 56,
32:41	47, 60, 61	42:9	129		59, 60
		43:18-19	129	12:8-9	61
Deuteronomy		51:9-11	129	12:11-19	45
3:14	45, 60, 61			12:13-14	61
4:7-8	154, 181	*Joshua*		13:5	69
5	39	2:11	30	13:25	69
5:24-31	38	5:1	30	14:19	69
6:6	129	10:6	62	15:14	69
6:7-9	129	13:30	47	15:19	30
9:20, 26	123	15:17	47, 67	17	143
11:18-21	129			18:30	23
13:1-5	132	*Judges*		20:18-28	139
14:28-29	148	1:13	67		
16:8	161	3–16	46, 49	*Ruth*	
16:10-17	148	3:10	66, 67	1:1	44
17:8-13	52, 139,	3:15	67		
	154	3:30	48	*1 Samuel*	
18	20	3:31	67	2:12-36	145
18:1-8	143, 148	4:1	67	4:4-9	139
18:3-4	146	4:4, 5	68, 109	7:15	49
18:9-14	38	5:6	67	8:1-22	85, 91
18:10	153	6:11-16	87	9:1	91
18:15-22	32, 36,	6:12	68, 69	9:1—10:16	83, 85,
	38, 39	6:15	68		86, 88, 93,
18:18	39	6:27	68		94, 96, 97
18:16-18	37	6:34	69, 87	9:1—11:15	83, 84,
18:22	126, 132	6:35	87		95, 96, 97
19:16-17	139	8:18	68	9:2	68
22:9	148	8:22	87	9:6	120
23:21	148	8:23	87	9:9	109, 115
28:13, 44	119	9:37	153	9:15	120
30:14	129	9:56-57	61	9:16	62
31:6, 7, 14, 23	28	10:1	61, 62	9:20	120

9:21	68	17:19-58	98	20:23-26	142
10:1-13	88, 89,	19:5	87	20:26	149
	90, 120	20:15-16	82	21:7, 8	82
10:5-10	109	20:31	74, 81	24:11-18	109
10:8	86	22:5	109	28:7	153
10:11	95	22:17	121		
10:16	95	23:1-12	139, 152	*1 Kings*	
10:17-21	84, 85,	23:2, 5	62, 87	1:7-10	101
	86, 91, 92	23:11-12	121	1:32-39a	101
10:17-27	94, 95,	24:6, 10	81	1:39b-40	101
	96, 97	26:9	81	2:15	101
10:17–11:15	85	28:6	111	2:26-27	150
10:20-24	86, 91	28:13	111	3:9	189
10:24	94, 95	30:12	30	4:2	149
10:26-27	85, 87,			4:5	149
	95, 97	*2 Samuel*		4:6	34
10:26–11:15	83	1:14-16	81	4:13	47, 60
10:27	62	2:4	100	4:19	142
11:1	100	2:8-9	81	4:32-33	200
11:1-15	84–88, 90,	2:10	81	5:1–8:66	150
	91, 94, 96, 97	3:7	82	9:25	24
11:2-3	86	3:18	87	10:5	30
11:3	62, 87	4:1-12	81	11:4-8	150
11:4-5	86	5:3	99	11:29-39	109, 115
11:9	97	7:2-17	109, 115	12:1-6	100
11:12-13	85, 87, 97	7:7	47	12:26-33	150
11:14-15	86, 87, 95	7:11	47, 49	13	132
12:1-25	86	8:6, 14	97	14:1-18	121
12:11	49	8:17	149	15:27	100
13:2-15	88, 89, 90	9:1-8	81	16:9-10	34, 100
13:2–14:46	83	9:1-13	82	16:16	100
13:3	86	10:11	62	17:17-24	121
13:7	86	10:19	62	17:24	121
13:13-14	74	12:1-15	109	18:3	34
14:36-37	120, 139	12:7-13	127	19:14	105
14:41-42	120	14:4	62, 87	21:1-16	148
14:50	82	16:3	81	21:19-22, 23	126
15:22	163, 182	16:5-13	127	22	114, 120
16:1-13	98	16:12	126	22:28	132
16:7, 12, 18	93	16:23	176		
16:14-23	98	19:14-43	102	*2 Kings*	
		19:26-30	81	1:2-4	121

2:24 126
4:18-37 121
5:1-14 121
6:18 126
6:26 87
6:27 62
8:7-10 121
9:1-10:31 100
10:5 34
10:15-16 100
10:18-27 145
11:2-12 101
11:12 100
11:14, 18-20 101
11:17 100
12:4-8 24
12:4-16 150
12:16 141, 146, 158
13:5 62
13:20-21 121
14:21 102
14:27 87
15:5 34
15:10 101
15:14-16 101
15:25 100
15:30 101
16:7 62
16:8 150
16:10-16 151
17:7-18 45
17:17 153
18:1-4 151
18:4 23
18:15-16 150
19:14-28 115
20:1-6 127
20:7 121
21:3-9 151
21:6 153

21:24 102
22:11 155
22:8-10 154
23:4 149
23:4-25 151
23:5 145
23:20 145
23:22 47, 49
23:30 102
25:18 149

1 Chronicles
2:22 47
7:1-2 47, 60, 61
7:17 49
17:6 47
17:10 47
22:6-10 36
23–28 36

2 Chronicles
8:13 24
19:8-11 139
24:6, 9 24
33:6 153
35:18 49

Ezra
7:6 180

Nehemiah
8:1-8 155
9:26-30 45, 46

Job
12:17 47
38:4 180

Psalms
8:5 189
18:50 87
19 180
20:7, 10 97
24 165, 180

29 165
33 165
36:8 [36:9] 165
40:6 162, 181
44:1 [44:2] 165
47 165
50:8-15 162, 181
51:16-17 162, 181
66:5 165
69:30-31 162, 181
74 165
77:11-20 166
77:21 23
78:1-72 166
78:54-72 45
78:69 165, 180
80:8-11 166
81:10 166
89 165, 180
90 23, 123
93–100 165
99:6 23
102:26 180
103 23
103:7 23
104 165, 180
105 46
105:5-45 166
105:26 23
106:7-46 166
106:16 23
106:23 23
106:32 23
106:34-46 46
110:4 39, 150
119 180, 181
124:8 166
134:3 166
135:8-12 46, 166
136:23-24 46
144:10 87, 97
146:6 166

Proverbs

1–9	193
2:1-8	188
3:19	181
3:31-32	199
6:24-35	199
6:25-26	198, 199
8:22-31	188
8:35-36	188
10:2-5	197
10:2-32	196
10:19	201
10:26	202
11:12, 13	201
11:31	204
12:15-16	201
13:3	201
14:15-16	201
15:8	163, 182
15:11	204
15:17	197
15:21	196
15:28	201
16:24	203
17:7	204
17:8	203
17:14	203
18:14	30
19:10	204
20:2	203
20:10, 23	199
21:2-3	163, 181
21:9	197
21:27	181, 204
22:22-23, 24-25	199
23:3, 6-7, 9, 10-11, 20-21, 22, 31-35	199
24:1-2, 19-20, 28-29	199
25:11	202

25:13	203
25:14	202
26:2	203
26:4-5	192
26:17	202
26:22	203
27:10	197, 199
28:6	197
30:1-6	192
30:8-9	201
30:15-17	200
30:16	201
30:17	199
30:18-19	200
30:21-23, 24-28, 29-31	200
31:9	199

Qoheleth

7:16-17	201

Isaiah

1:11-17	161
1:21-26	48
1:26	47
2:3	145
2:6	153
3:1-3	47, 142, 153
5:21	178
6:1-8	115
6:7	141
6:10	123
9:15	119
19:11-12	178
19:20	62
29:14	178
33:5-6	179
36:3	34
44:25	178
47:9, 12	153
47:10	178

48:13	180
51:3	165
51:4	145, 155
51:9-10	166
51:13-16	180
58:1-9	162
61:6	147
63:9-14	45, 46
66:3	161

Jeremiah

2:6-7	45
2:8	145, 154, 171
5:31	154
6:19-20	161
7:1-2	115
7:8-11	161
7:16	123
7:21-26	45, 161
8:7	175
8:8	154, 174, 178
8:10	175
9:12	178
9:22-23	176, 178
10:6-10	178
10:12	179
11	23
11:2-10	45
14:9	62
14:11	123
14:14	112, 153
15:1-2	23, 123
18:18	138, 145, 174, 175
19:1	150
19:14	115
20:1-2	113, 150
20:6	153
21–23	161
21:1-2	115
22:1-2	115
23:14	132

23:28   132
26:16-19   118, 128
27:9   111, 142, 152
28:8, 9   123, 128, 132
29:8   153
29:26-27   113, 150
31:31-34   45, 129
32:20-23   45
33:18, 21-22   142
36:20-26   127
37:3   123
42:2, 4   123
51:15   179

Ezekiel
7:26   125, 174, 175
13:6, 9   153
13:20-23   153
16:1-34   45
20:27, 28   45
20:46   118
21:2   118
21:21-22   152
22:26   145, 154, 155
22:28   153
23:1-4   45
28:1-10   178
28:13-16   165
36:35   165
43:19   142
44:10-16   142, 144
44:23-24   145, 154
45:5   142
46:24   147
48:11   144
48:11-13   142

Hosea
2:14-23   129
4:1-6   145, 154, 155

4:5   118
4:8   140
4:8-10   147
6:5   118
6:6   161
6:7   45
8:4   80
8:11   141, 147
8:11-13   145
8:12-13   140, 154, 161
9:7-8   118
9:10   45
9:15   45
10:9   45
11:2-4   45
12:10, 13   118
12:13   23, 109, 123
13:4-6   45
13:10   62, 87

Joel
2:3   165

Amos
2:9-12   45
4:4-5   161
5:21-25   161
7:2-3, 5-6   123
7:10-13   113, 150
7:10-17   116
7:11   126
7:14-15   118
7:16   118
9:6   180

Obadiah
17, 19-20   48
21   48

Jonah
3:4   128

4:2   128

Micah
2:6-11   118
2:11   136
3:5-7   118
3:6, 11   112, 145, 153, 154
3:12   128
5:1   52
5:12   153
6:4   23
6:6-8   161

Zephaniah
1:4-6   145
3:3-4   142, 145, 154

Haggai
2:10-13   155

Zechariah
9:2   178
10:2   153
12:1   180

Malachi
2:4-9   142
2:6-7   145, 154
3:3   142
3:5   153

Sirach
24:23   180
24:33   183

Matthew
21:23   1

John
9   122
20:27   171

Acts
3:22-26   40